MARKET PLANNING FOR NEW INDUSTRIAL PRODUCTS

RONALD SERIES ON MARKETING MANAGEMENT

Series Editor: FREDERICK E. WEBSTER, Jr.

*The Amos Tuck School
of Business Administration
Darmouth College*

GEORGE S. DOMINGUEZ, *Marketing in a Regulated Environment*
ROBERT D. ROSS, *The Management of Public Relations: Analysis and
Planning External Relations*
VICTOR WADEMAN, *Risk-Free Advertising: How to Come Close to It*
FRANK H. MOSSMAN, W. J. E. CRISSY, and PAUL M. FISCHER,
Financial Dimensions in Marketing Management
JACOB JACOBY and ROBERT W. CHESTNUT, *Brand Loyalty:
Measurement and Management*
WILLIAM E. COX, JR., *Industrial Marketing Research*
FREDERICK E. WEBSTER, JR., *Industrial Marketing Strategy*
CLARK LAMBERT, *Field Sales Performance Appraisal*
JEAN-MARIE CHOFFRAY and GARY L. LILIEN, *Market Planning for
New Industrial Products*

Market Planning for New Industrial Products

JEAN-MARIE CHOFFRAY

Ecole Supérieure des Sciences Economiques et Commerciales

GARY L. LILIEN

Massachusetts Institute of Technology

A RONALD PRESS PUBLICATION

JOHN WILEY & SONS, New York · Chichester · Brisbane · Toronto

For our children:
Alexandre, Jean-Christophe and Amy Jo

Library of Congress Cataloging in Publication Data

Choffray, Jean Marie.
  Market planning for new industrial products.

  (Ronald series on marketing management)
  "A Ronald Press publication."
  Bibliography: p.
  Includes indexes.
    1. Product management. 2. Product management—
Case studies. 3. New products. I. Lilien, Gary L.,
1946- joint author. II. Title.

HF5415.15.C47   658.8'3   80-11347
ISBN 0-471-04918-2

Printed in the United States of America

10 9 8 7 6 5 4 3 2 1

Series Editor's Foreword

Marketing management is among the most dynamic of the business functions. On the one hand it reflects the everchanging marketplace and the constant evolution of customer preferences and buying habits, and of competition. On the other hand, it grows continually in sophistication and complexity as developments in management science are applied to the work of the marketing manager. If he or she is to be a true management professional, the marketing person must stay informed about these developments.

The Wiley Series on Marketing Management has been developed to serve this need. The books in the series have been written for managers. They combine a concern for management application with an appreciation for the relevance of developments in such areas of management science as behavioral science, financial analysis, and mathematical modeling, as well as the insights gained from analyzing successful experience in the market-place. The Wiley Series on Marketing Management is thus intended to communicate the state-of-the-art in marketing to managers.

Virtually all areas of marketing management will be explored in the series. Books now available or being planned cover advertising management, industrial marketing research, brand loyalty, sales management, product policy and planning, public relations, overall marketing strategy, and financial aspects of marketing management. It is hoped that the series will have some effect in raising the standards of applied marketing management.

Hanover, New Hampshire　　　　　　　　　　　　　　FREDERICK E. WEBSTER, JR.
March 1980

Preface

The days are past when a good product was thought to sell itself. As markets become more competitive, the need increases for careful analysis in the marketing decision-making process. The last twenty years have seen major advances in the science of marketing data-gathering along with advances in the models used to analyze those data.

Although consumer marketing analysis has led the way in scientific applications, industrial marketing is beginning to come of age. There is an evident, increased desire among industrial marketing managers to discard traditional rules of thumb and adopt a more systematic approach.

This book presents a complete approach to measure, analyze, and model response to industrial marketing strategy. It is written for professional managers, market researchers, and graduate students in marketing science. We have aimed at the nontechnical reader, but have included complete technical details in extended appendices.

The reader may be curious to learn how this book evolved. We faced the problem of communicating to both a managerial and a technical audience. There were no examples of how to do this. After some thought, we realized that this was precisely what we face when writing an internal company report: executive summary, followed by a complete review of the study and its managerial implications, followed by appendices. Although we've never seen this structure used in a book, it is so commonly used in practice that we chose to risk using it.

A possible scenario for using the book might be as follows: a division manager in an industrial company faces market assessment problems. He gets the book, reads the first two chapters and decides it is relevant. He passes it on (maybe he orders another copy) to the appropriate product manager whose problem is, say, market segmentation. He reads chapters 1, 2, 4 and 9 (at least) and decides that the approach is applicable. He then involves his market researcher (a third copy), who covers the same material, but reads the appendices as well to determine how to do it.

We have used the book in courses at MIT and ESSEC. It is appropriate for a senior or graduate level course in industrial market analysis for students with quantitative or technical backgrounds. In fact, the idea for the book grew from our desire to teach this material at MIT. Its development was accelerated after a managerial audience at MIT's three-day 1978 Industrial Marketing Science Symposium expressed great interest in seeing this material presented in a form appropriate for them. Thus, our emphasis is on managerial relevance and rigorous treatment of industrial marketing problems.

We illustrate our approach to assessing industrial market response by introducing a case-example and following it throughout the text. This example involves assessing market potential for a new industrial cooling system. We include many graphs and diagrams to facilitate understanding. We also refer extensively to published sources for those who wish to dig deeper.

The first Chapter presents the problems associated with developing new products and assessing industrial markets. It demonstrates the need for a careful analysis of market response before product introduction.

Chapter Two reviews important issues in understanding and modeling. The chapter leads to the overall structure of our methodology for assessing response to industrial marketing strategy. It also presents a map for finding out where to find what in the book.

Chapter Three deals with macrosegmentation: the definition of the target market for a product and the assessment of overall potential for the product class. Input-output analysis and forecasting methods are reviewed there and their use is illustrated.

Chapter Four shows how to segment markets into subsets of firms with similar buying patterns. We call this microsegmentation. It provides a better understanding of differences in organizational purchasing, useful for targeting communication programs and selling strategies.

In Chapter Five we address product design questions. What should the product look like? What features should it have? What options should it offer? We show how the market potential for the product is affected by these decisions. The approach, combined with production cost information, allows effective product design.

Chapter Six deals with how decision participants view and evaluate products in the product class. Methods to extract evaluation criteria from perceptions are reviewed. We then assess how product evaluations affect individual preferences in different ways for different groups of decision participants.

Chapter Seven addresses the question of group decision making. Four structures are developed to model the way individuals pool their separate judgments in making a group choice.

Chapter Eight concentrates on how the market for the product will develop over time. It provides a conceptual and analytical framework to help plan the evolution of the product from the time it is introduced to the time it meets its potential.

Chapter Nine feeds the system with data. It describes how an industrial market research control system should appear. The integration of data gathering and analysis in the decision-process is described. Measurement issues associated with gathering the data needed to run the models are reviewed.

Finally Chapter Ten sums up and reviews issues of implementation. We describe how such procedures integrate into a firm's planning process and what conditions and environment will accelerate acceptance of the research.

Thus the book describes the approach in a brief overview, redescribes it in non-technical terms, and gives complete details for the technical implementor. This structure builds in redundancy. Our experience in management communications is that redundancy is less of a sin than omission.

The major problem with this material is that it is new. Although it is not inherently difficult, the material will be unfamiliar to most readers. We face the problem associated with introducing an entire product line rather than just a line extension — market resistance. We hope our packaging, and the associated marketing communications will help, but we do recognize that, like all new concepts, traditional ways of thinking have to be disturbed before the new ideas can settle. That is sometimes a jarring (although worthwhile) experience.

JEAN-MARIE CHOFFRAY
GARY L. LILIEN

Cergy-Pontoise, France
Cambridge, Mass.
January 1980

Acknowledgments

This book would not be if it had not been for the help of a number of people. First, our thanks go to Frederick E. Webster, Jr., of Dartmouth, who encouraged us to begin the project and who suggested the current structure for the book. Without Fred's help an obscure monograph would have emerged.

John Hauser of Northwestern, Bernard Pras of ESSEC, and Jagdish Sheth of the University of Illinois all reviewed earlier drafts and made many helpful comments and suggestions. Our colleagues at MIT and at ESSEC provided important stimulation and critical evaluation.

The Sloan School of Management at MIT and ESSEC provided important support during the writing and final development of this book. The typing and production was ably handled by Dianne Carpenter Smith, Odile Firette, and Debbie Reynolds, who now, as promised, get to see their names in print. Frank Fuller and Dorothy Lilien provided proofreading support in exchange for acknowledgments.

Finally we should like to thank our wives and children for putting up with the inconveniences that writing a book demands. Their suffering, if not silent, at least was not too noisy.

Contents

MARKET PLANNING FOR NEW INDUSTRIAL PRODUCTS

CHAPTER ONE

Science, Industrial Marketing and New Products

... if the weight of invention or discovery is one, the weight to bring it to actual development should be ten and the weight to produce and market it should be one hundred.

> Masaru Ibuka,
> President of Sony

The aim of Marketing is to know and understand the customer so well that the product or service fits him and sells itself.

> Drucker

The factors which emerge as being most important to success [of a technological innovation] are those related to the importance of *need satisfaction.*

> Rothwell et al.

... But always, regardless of the amount, R&D money has gone to the development of instruments for which there was a *real need* ...

> Hewlett-Packard

Industrial marketing, as a science, is coming of age. Our business publications as well as our scholarly journals are publishing increasing numbers of articles about industrial marketing problems. Models have been developed, (and are being used), to determine marketing spending levels, to allocate salesmen's efforts among clients, to evaluate distribution channels, and to help understand organizational buying patterns.

These efforts, although individually profound, have not had the impact that they might have had, were they integrated and organized. In this volume we try to perform that integration for a pervasive and important problem: the market assessment for new industrial products. We are concerned with communication as well as implementation. We describe methods for assessing markets, while emphasizing the steps needed to translate the concepts into action.

The importance of new product assessment in industrial markets is apparent both to marketers and to academics. One trend we see that has characterized the latter half of the twentieth century has been a shortening of product life cycles. It is becoming increasingly common, in such industries as electronics and computers, to find a life cycle from introduction to growth, maturity and decline, taking less than three to four years (Servan-Schriber, 1969). To survive in such markets, industrial marketers must develop a continuous stream of successful new products. Cultivating new markets has become a necessary condition to industrial firms' survival (Murray, 1979).

The human element in the product development process is central: a manager or management team must make decisions about target market definition, product design features, positioning, and communication strategies. These decisions must be made to assure customer satisfaction consistent with the achievement of the firm's financial objectives. This articulation of business objectives has been called the marketing concept (Kotler, 1980).

Ideally, these decisions are based on accurate information on customers' buying behavior and total market size. Here is where management science and marketing research enter the picture. Properly used, they help the manager make new product decisions by providing information and guidelines for action.

The purpose of this book is to describe a comprehensive, model-based approach to support new product introduction in industrial markets. We investigate and structure the organizational buying process to determine the key variables that affect industrial market response. In the final analysis, the reader, by either using or not using the methods presented here, will determine if our new product is a success.

Before proceeding with the main subject — the market assessment procedure — we set the stage and introduce the actors. The backdrop is industrial marketing, and the stars are new industrial products.

1.1. INDUSTRIAL MARKETING

Industrial marketing is the marketing of goods and services to industrial and institutional customers for their use, in turn, in their own production of goods and services. One important characteristic of the industrial goods market is that its demand is derived from the demand for final consumer goods and services. This implies that demand for most important goods is fairly inelastic. A major increase in the price of steel cord in radial tires, for example, will not reduce the demand for tires by auto manufacturers (although it may cause manufacturers to look for substitute materials). Rather, the price increase will (eventually) be passed on to the consumer. If consumer demand goes down as a result, then auto manufacturers will reduce purchases.

This characteristic of industrial demand does not imply that it is steady over time. Rather, derived demand may vary quite a bit due to the multiplier effect of inventories that build up when consumer sales rise and deflate when sales are falling. Industrial marketers then face highly fluctuating levels of aggregate demand for their products.

Independent of the relative inelasticity of aggregate demand for most industrial goods, individual manufacturers often face very competitive situations. Many industrial markets see significant price competition among suppliers even with inelastic industry demand. This can result from industrial customers seeking multiple sources of supply both to ensure regularity of deliveries and to encourage price competition. In addition, many industrial products are bought according to specification. Here, the buyer encourages uniformity and, hence, purer competition. Suppliers, in a further competitive response, try to differentiate their offerings by improving the design and features of the products and services they offer.

What makes industrial marketing so different from consumer goods marketing, however, is not so much the derived nature of industrial demand as the complexity of organizational buying. The process is characterized by the involvement of several individuals (whom we will call decision participants) who interact with each other (in what we call a Buying Center or Decision-Making Unit) within the framework of an organizational structure, and whose product choices are affected by environmental as well as organizational constraints.

We have to take explicit account of this purchasing complexity in any procedure to assess the market for a new industrial product. To do this we must address the following questions:

- What are the dimensions of purchasing needs? (We call these Need Specification Dimensions – warranty period, performance specifications, etc.)
- Who is most likely to be involved in and influence the purchasing process in a customer organization? (What is the composition of the Buying Center?)
- How do individuals differ in the way they think about and value product alternatives? (Are managers performance conscious, and controllers concerned only about price?)
- How do these individuals interact with one another in making a purchase choice? (Is the purchasing agent as important as he thinks?)

There is no simple answer to any of these very complex questions. If there were, canny managers would be using them now to their competitive advantage. It is this very complexity and richness of industrial marketing situations, however, that makes analytical solutions to industrial marketing problems both appropriate and potentially valuable.

1.2. NEW PRODUCTS IN INDUSTRIAL MARKETS

The future of many companies is closely tied to their ability to develop and successfully market new products. Few industrial firms dare risk standing by current product lines without contemplating changes in response to a turbulent environment. Highly sophisticated industrial products are most prone to technological obsolescence. The best way for an industrial company to stay competitive is through active participation in the development of the latest technologies and through the continual use of those technologies in the form of new products to satisfy changing customers' needs.

1.2.1 A Source of Industrial Growth

New products are a substantial source of growth in industrial markets. And they are perceived to be increasing in importance.

In the scientific instruments area, the Office of Economic and Cultural Development (1977) reports many American firms having 60–80% of their sales from products that were not in existence a half a decade earlier. Generally, such figures are not available for non-U.S. firms; however, one Swedish instrument firm in 1966 noted that 60% of its sales were generated by a half a dozen products with an average age of 14 months, and no product was older than 5 years.

Pegram and Bailey (1967) report that for the majority of industrial companies, more than a quarter of current sales volume is attributable to products introduced in the last five years. For some industrial companies, these products generate more than half of current sales volume. One Japanese pharmaceutical company stated recently that 90% of its sales were associated with products that were less than 6 years old.

Hopkins (1979) reports on industrial goods manufacturers' dependence on new products. Over 25% of the companies responding report that more than 30% of their current sales were attributable to major new products first marketed by the company within the preceeding 5 years (Exhibit 1.1).

Terleckyj (1963) investigates the relationship between rate of growth and of new products and R&D intensity. His resulting relationship is positive – no surprise – but as Exhibit 1.2 shows, its strength is striking: those industries spending more on R&D as a percent of sales are almost uniformly those for which new product contribution is highest.

Exhibit 1.3 gives the annual growth of some technologically innovative companies in the period 1945–65. Companies such as Polaroid, 3M, IBM, Xerox and Texas Instruments that relied heavily on new products during the period 1945–65 experienced growth rates substantially higher than the GNP (DeSimone, 1967).

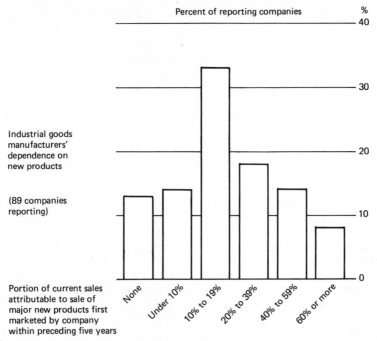

Exhibit 1.1. Industrial goods manufacturers' dependence on new products (89 companies reporting). Source: Hopkins, The Conference Board, private communication.

Booz Allen & Hamilton (1965) and McDonald and Eastlack (1971) show the importance that management places on new products as a source of sales and company growth. Exhibit 1.4, from the Booz Allen study, gives management estimates of the expected contribution of new products to sales volume growth in different sectors.

A study by McDonald and Eastlack (1971) based on an attitude survey of board chairmen of United States corporations, showed that new products will play a relatively more important role than existing products in the near future than they did in the recent past. Exhibit 1.5 summarizes some of their findings.

And, finally, this emphasis on growth for new industrial products is not unfounded. In a United Nations seminar conducted in 1976, each of the 10 product areas projected to experience the greatest world-wide growth in demand in the period 1970–1985 were industrial products (United Nations Commission for Europe, 1978).

1.2.2. A Source of Troubles

New industrial products are not a panacea; there are risks. For industry as a whole, about two-thirds of technically successful products that emerge from R&D departments fail to become commercial successes. From a cost standpoint, more than 70%

Exhibit 1.2 Rate of growth of new products related to intensity of research and development

Industry	Total R&D spending as percent of industry net sales, 1958[a]	Sales of products not in existence in 1956 as percent of 1960 net sales
Aircraft, ships, and railroad equipment	18.7[b]	35
Electrical machinery	12.9[c]	12
Machinery	4.4	14
Chemicals	4.3	16
Motor vehicles and parts	4.2[d]	10
Fabricated metals and instruments	3.5	17
Rubber	2.0	2
Petroleum and coal products	0.9[e]	2
Nonferrous metals	0.9	8
Paper	0.7	9
Iron and steel	0.6	5
Food and beverages	0.3	6
Textiles	0.2	9
All manufacturing	4.0	10

Source: Nestor E. Terleckyj, assisted by Harriet J. Halper, *Reserach and Development: Its Growth and Composition* (New York: National Industrial Conference Board, 1963), p. 56.

[a]For companies performing R&D.

[b]Aircraft and missiles.

[c]Includes communication.

[d]Transportation equipment except aircraft.

[e]Petroleum refining and extraction.

Exhibit 1.3 Average annual growth (compounded) of some technologically innovative companies for the period 1945-65

Company	Net sales	Jobs
	%	%
Polaroid	13.4	7.5
3M	14.9	7.8
IBM	17.5	12.5
Xerox (Haloid Co.)	22.5	17.8
Texas Instruments (1947–65 only)	28.9	10.0

Average annual growth in GNP over the same period = 2.5 percent.

Source: DeSimone, (1967).

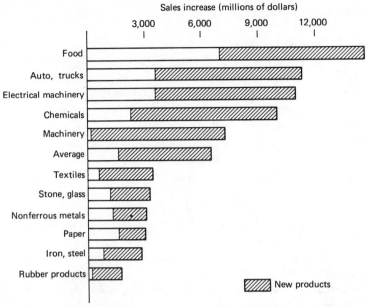

Exhibit 1.4. Contribution of new products to expected sales growth. Source: Booz Allen & Hamilton (1965).

Exhibit 1.5 Top management perception of growth sources. Past 5 years versus next 5 years. Highly important as source of profit

Source of growth	Percentage of respondents	
	Past 5 years	Next 5 years
Existing products	68	48
Product modifications	45	43
New products — present markets	34	50
New products — new markets	19	34
Acquisitions — present markets	11	23
Acquisitions — new markets	16	34

Source: McDonald and Eastlack, (1971)

of all money spent on new product activities is spent on products that are never commercial successes (Booz Allen & Hamilton, 1965). Nau (1976) reports over $20 billion in 1973 was spent in R&D; combining this with the failure rates suggests that over $15 billion is being spent annually on products that will be failures.

We illustrate how some problems come about with the following cases.

Case 1: British Plastics Company Case:

A plastics company decided to enter the market for plastic chairs in Britain to achieve greater market diversity. It aimed its initial efforts at public buildings and hospitals, although it had no experience marketing products to this market. After a few months, the sales achieved were very low: the product was found to be too weak and unsuitable for temporary stacking. In addition, U.S. dimensions were used on the chairs although the requirements in the U.S. differed.

The company attempted to reformulate the product and marketing approach. They redesigned the chair and brought out a new line of colors. During this time rival manufacturers, with powerful marketing experience and acceptance in this area, entered the market, profiting from the company's mistakes. Competitive products succeeded, and the company was forced to withdraw from the market.

The Lesson: The point of this story is that the company *appeared* to have a potential winner. The product failed because of an insufficient understanding of the market: product design did not meet user needs and potential users were reluctant to purchase from an unknown supplier (the company's previous experience was with automobile and appliance manufacturers). The new product assessment process must include a measure of customer needs and product-company-customer fit.

A number of researchers have studied industrial product successes and failures. Mansfield and Wagner (1975) have investigated the success probabilities of new industrial products in different stages of their development cycle. They reported:

• 57% rate of technical completion, the development of a working product prototype;
• 65% rate of commercialization, bringing the product to market, following successful technical completion;
• 74% probability of economic success after commercialization.

Exhibit 1.6   Rates of commercial success for new industrial product projects

	Rate of commercial success for product development projects	Rate of commercial success for new products introduced
Chemical	.18	.59
Electrical machinery	.13	.63
Metal fabricators	.11	.71
Nonelectrical machinery	.21	.59
Raw material processors	.14	.59
Average	.15	.62

Source: Booz Allen & Hamilton (1965).

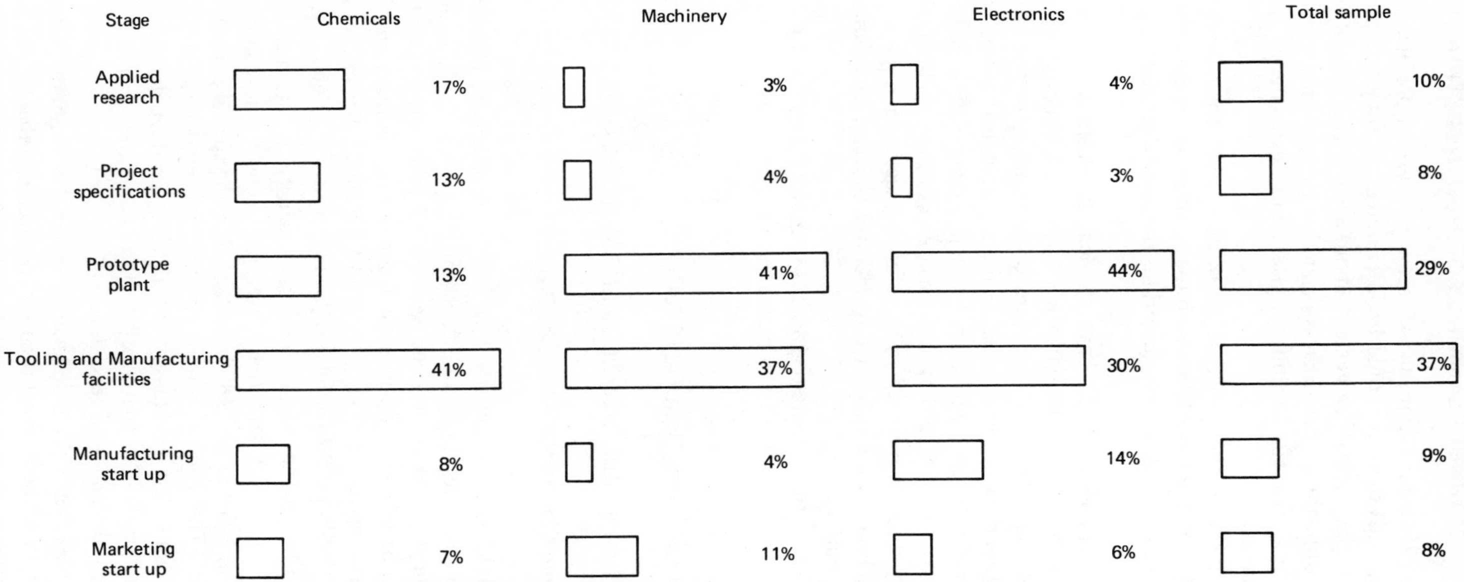

Stage	Chemicals	Machinery	Electronics	Total sample
Applied research	17%	3%	4%	10%
Project specifications	13%	4%	3%	8%
Prototype plant	13%	41%	44%	29%
Tooling and Manufacturing facilities	41%	37%	30%	37%
Manufacturing start up	8%	4%	14%	9%
Marketing start up	7%	11%	6%	8%

Exhibit 1.7. Structure of costs associated with the development of new industrial products. Source: Mansfield and Rapoport (1975).

This leads to a 27% commercial success rate for industrial product development projects. Although this number should be interpreted carefully because of sample size considerations and lack of agreement about what a commercial success is, it provides a gross estimate of the risks associated with new product development activities in industrial markets. Exhibit 1.6 gives similar estimates by Booz Allen & Hamilton across industries.

New industrial products, however, are more than risky. Their development and production usually require large financial outlays, often in the multimillion dollar range. Risks of losses of this scale underline the need for careful prior market evaluation.

Mansfield and Rapoport (1975) have studied the costs associated with new product development in different industries, including chemicals, machinery, and electronics. Surprisingly, the cost structure corresponding to the phases of the development process does not vary substantially across industries (see Exhibit 1.7). The major expenditures are encountered when contemplating development of tooling and manufacturing facilities, after market assessment, but before market entry. This clearly suggests the need for careful engineering and market studies of the product's potential before this stage to identify and correct product problems before major cost outlays.

Thus, it is important for corporate growth to innovate, yet it is risky and costly. But what should a manager look for to reduce the likelihood of market failure?

1.3. WHY DO INDUSTRIAL PRODUCTS FAIL?

Here are two cases of industrial product failure with some lessons.

Case 2: The Gould Corporation/Graphics Division:

In 1967, Gould Inc. was investigating ways to broaden the company base through new product development. Their objectives were to maintain a 15% growth in earnings per share over the next 10–15 years. To do that they felt (a) they had to be willing to invest at that rate in new products, and (b) they had to be in growing markets. They looked to the electronics market for that growth. They introduced the Gould 4800, an electrostatic printer.

The printer, a by-product of the company's activity in data display instruments, evolved from the fact that "everyone knows that computer line printers are slow." The Gould 4800 was fast, but the special paper it needed was very costly. The company tried to enter the market without market research and found that key (easily identifiable) product deficiencies precluded a strong position in that market. Two years after introduction, no main line printer sales had been recorded.

The product was eventually redesigned to enter the computer-plotter market. A later version of the product is currently successful there.

The Lesson: Time and money would have been saved here with some basic market analysis. What "everyone knew" about the market turned out to be not quite true.

Case 3: Philco:

Before World War II, Philco was the second biggest manufacturer of radio sets (behind RCA) and one of the leading firms in the consumer electronics area. In 1951 it took part in the Bell Symposium to acquire knowledge of transistors. The company subsequently explored semiconductor fields not covered by the basic Bell patents. They developed an entirely new electrochemical process for surface barrier transistors. They used this technology to develop a faster transistor, called the MADT and used it to help enter the computer market.

Together with this and other product and process innovations, Philco had over 70 % of the U.S. high frequency alloy transistor market to itself. By 1955 it was second only to Bell Telephone in semiconductor technology.

In the following years Philco became enamored of its own technology and lost sight of the market and competitive trends. Philco was unable to respond to silicon technology and the mesa transistor. Because of these and other troubles, the company's profits dropped by 90% between 1953 and 1956.

The Lesson: Myopia and excessive emphasis on internal developments can blind a company to changing market and environmental needs. Successful, innovative companies constantly seek to make their own products obsolete.

There are over a score of studies that have appeared during recent years about the determinants of new industrial product failures. These studies are mainly of three types:

Case analyses of some new industrial products that emerged successfully from R&D programs only to become market failures (Briscoe, 1973).

Cross-sectional studies of new industrial product failures (Cooper, 1975, Calantone and Cooper, 1977, Hopkins and Bailey, 1971, von Hippel, 1978).

Experimental or quasi-experimental studies that focus either on differences between successful and unsuccessful innovations competing in the same market (Rothwell et al., 1974) or on factors influencing new product success probabilities (Mansfield and Wagner, 1975).

By and large the results reported by these studies are consistent. They stress, as major causes of failure:

- the lack of appreciation for the way customers perceive and evaluate the new product;
- the misassessment of the firm's existing stock of resources, especially its marketing skills;

• the lack of specific objectives for the new product in terms of its target market and place in the company's product mix.

Some of these studies deserve further discussion. Mansfield and Wagner (1975) systematically analyze organizational and strategic factors associated with probabilities of success in industrial R&D. They relate the probability of technical completion, commercialization, and economic success to three key variables:

• speed of market analysis;
• percent of money spent on demand pull (as opposed to technology-push) projects;
• percentage of projects originating in R&D.

Their results show that early market analysis improves all three success rates. The percent of demand pull projects is positively related to probabilities of technical completion and commercialization but not, interestingly, to the likelihood of economic success. And, the probability of technical completion is negatively related to the percent of projects stemming from R&D departments. This could suggest that R&D departments tend to support projects that are more ambitious and, thus, less likely to reach technical completion. However, economic success is greater, given technical completion, with the more ambitious R&D-originated products.

The message of this analysis is clear: perform market analysis early and consider a portfolio of market-based and R&D-based products to maximize both success and company growth. Exhibit 1.8 summarizes these results.

Cooper (1975) reports on the causes of failure of 114 new industrial products. Exhibit 1.9 shows the extent to which resource deficiencies contributed to product failure; note here the dominance of the lack of market research skills and people. Another related result indicates that a detailed market study rated as most deficient among activities performed during the development process for the product failures.

Mansfield and Wagner (1975) also investigated the effect of the degree of integration of R&D and marketing activities and the degree of formalization of the project selection system on success probabilities. Their results suggest that a closer integration of R&D and marketing increases all three probabilities of success, but that a formal product selection system, although increasing the likelihood of commercialization, reduces the likelihood of economic success.

Exhibit 1.8 Summary of key relationships associated with product success

	Early analysis	Percent demand pull	R&D source
Probability of technical completion	+	+	−
Probability of commercialization	+	+	
Probability of economic success	+		+

Source: Mansfield and Wagner (1975).

Exhibit 1.9 Extent to which resource deficiencies contributed to product failure (N = 114)

	Percent of product failures		
Resource deficiency	Very much	Somewhat	Very much plus somewhat
Lack of financial resources	5.5	17.3	22.5
Lack of engineering skills or people	8.2	32.7 (3)	40.9
Lack of R&D skills or people	7.3	30.0	37.3
Lack of marketing research skills or people	21.6 (1)[a]	43.2 (1)	64.8 (1)
Lack of general management skills	9.0 (3)	42.1 (2)	51.1 (2)
Lack of production resources or skills	4.5	15.3	19.8
Lack of selling resources or skills	13.5 (2)	32.4	45.9 (3)

[a]Numbers in parentheses indicate rank in each column.
Source: Cooper (1975).

It may be that the use of careful controls limits the review of risky projects with potentially high payoffs. This underscores the necessity for a new product assessment procedure to be flexible enough to foster creativity. This requirement should be designed into the new product development and assessment process.

Calentone and Cooper (1977) provide an empirically based description of new industrial product failures, along with a profile of the major causes of these failures. They distinguish:

• sales and competitive environment misassessment;

• deficient prior market research;

• deficient engineering and marketing skills;

• lack of integration of the new product/technology into the company's experience base.

Exhibit 1.10 gives their "typology" of new product failure – the kinds of situations most closely associated with new product failures. For example, the most frequent category of failure – "The Better Mousetrap Nobody Wanted" – comes about when the market for the product fails to materialize.

Von Hippel (1978) has studied the sources of several successful industrial product and process innovations. His results point out that in industrial markets, innovative users are frequently the source of successful new industrial products (see Exhibit 1.11).

These innovations come about as follows:

IBM designed and built the first printed circuit card component insertion machine of the X-Y Table type to be used in commercial production. IBM needed the machine to insert components into printed circuit cards which were, in turn, in-

Exhibit 1.10   A typology of new product failures

Cluster I: "The Better Moustrap Nobody Wanted"
(28% of failures)

Product failures in this group were unique products rejected by the market. The number of potential customers who might buy and use the product was over-estimated. There simply wasn't a widespread need for the product.

Cluster II: "The Me-Too Product Meeting a Competitive Brick Wall"
(24% of the failures)

These products were similar to those already on the market. The market was correctly assessed, but the ease of dislodging competition was underestimated.

Cluster III: "Competitive One-Upmanship"
(13% of failures)

These are me-too products hurt by concurrent competitive entry. Thorough market studies and market testing was difficult – the product was not prepared to withstand competitive pressure.

Cluster IV: "Environmental Ignorance"
(7% of the failures)

Products here were not matched with customer needs. There was a complete misreading of the environment: customers, competitors and government.

Cluster V: "Technical 'Dog' Products"
(15% of the failures)

These were bad products – they didn't do what they were supposed to do. Poor R&D and engineering were blamed.

Cluster VI: "The Price Crunch"
(13% of the failures)

The product was being offered at prices higher than customers were willing to pay. When the product was introduced, competition cut prices. Inadequate market research was performed to understand customer needs: "the company offered a Cadillac when the market wanted a Ford."

Source: Calentone and Cooper (1977)

corporated into computers. After building and testing the design in-house, IBM, in 1959, sent engineering drawings of their design to a local machine builder along with an order for 8 units. The machine builder completed this and subsequent orders satisfactorily and later (1962) applied to IBM for permission to build essentially the same machine for sale on the open market. IBM agreed and the machine builder became the first commercial manufacturer of X-Y Table component

Exhibit 1.11   Frequency with which manufacturers initiated work on an industrial innovation in response to a customer request

Study	Nature of innovations and sample selection criteria	N	Data available regarding presence of customer requests
A. Studies of Industrial Products			
Meadows[a]	All projects initiated during a two-year period in "Chem Lab B"–Labratory of a chemical company with $100–300 million in annual sales in "industrial intermediates."	29	9 of 17 (53%) commercially successful product ideas were from customers.
Peplow[b]	All creative projects carried out during a six-year period by an R&D group concerned with plant process, equipment and technique innovations.	94	30 of 48 (62%) successfully implemented projects were initiated in response to direct customer request.
Von Hippel[c]	Semiconductor and electronic subassembly manufacturing equipment; first of type used in commercial production (n = 7); major improvements (n = 22); minor improvements (n = 20).	49	Source of initiative for manufacture of equipment developed by users (n = 29) examined. Source clearly identified as customer request in 21% of cases. In 46% of cases frequent customer-manufacturer interaction made source of initiative unclear.
Berger[d]	All engineering polymers developed in U.S. after 1955 with > 10 million pounds produced in 1975.	5	No project-initiating request from customers found.
Boyden[e]	Chemical additives for plastics; all plasticizers and UV stabilizers developed post-W.W. II for use with four major polymers.	16	No project-initiating request from customers found.
Utterback[f]	All scientific instrument innovations manufactured by Mass. firms which won IR-100 Awards, 1963–1968 (n = 15); sample of other instruments produced by same firms (n = 17).	32	75% initiated in response to need input. When need input originated outside product manufacturer (57%), source was most often customer.
Robinson et al[g]	Sample of standard and non-standard industrial products purchased by three firms.	NA	Customers recognize need, define functional requirements and specific goods and services needed *before contacting suppliers.*

15

Exhibit 1.11 (*Continued*)

B. Studies of Research-Engineering Interaction

Isenson (*Project Hindsight*)[h]	710	85% initiated in response to description of problem by application-engineering group.
Materials Advisory Board[i]	10	In almost all cases the individual with a well-defined need initiated the communications with the basic researchers.

[a]Dennis Meadows, "Estimate Accuracy and Project Selection Models in Industrial Research," *Industrial Management Review*, Spring 1969. Also, "Data Appendix: Accuracy of Technical Estimates in Industrial Research Planning," M.I.T. Sloan School of Management, Working Paper #301–67.

[b]M. E. Peplow, "Design Acceptance," in *The Design Method*, S. A. Gregory, ed. (London: Butterworth, 1960).

[c]E. Von Hippel, "Transferring Process Equipment Innovations from User-Innovators to Equipment Manufacturing Firms," *R&D Management*, October 1977; see also M.I.T. Sloan School of Management, Working Paper #857–76, May 1976 (revised January 1977).

[d]A. Berger, *Factors Influencing the Locus of Innovation Activity Leading to Scientific Instrument and Plastics Innovations* (unpublished S.M. thesis, M.I.T. Sloan School of Management, June 1975).

[e]J. Boyden, *A Study of the Innovation Process in the Plastics Additives Industry* (unpublished S.M. thesis, M.I.T. Sloan School of Management, January 1976).

[f]J. Utterback, "The Process of Innovation: A Study of the Origination and Development of Ideas for New Scientific Instruments," *IEEE Transactions on Engineering Management*, November, 1971.

[g]Robinson, Farris and Wind, *Industrial Buying and Creative Marketing* (Boston: Allyn and Bacon, 1967).

[h]R. Isenson, "Project Hindsight: An Empirical Study of the Sources of Ideas Utilized in Operational Weapon Systems," in W. Gruber and D. Marquis, eds., *Factors in the Transfer of Technology* (Cambridge, MA: M.I.T. Press, 1969), p. 157.

[i]Materials Advisory Board, Division of Engineering, National Research Council, *Report of the Ad Hoc Committee on Principles of Research-Engineering Interaction*, Publication MAB-222-M (Washington, D.C.: National Academy of Sciences–National Research Council, July, 1966), pp. 15, 16.

Source: Von Hippel (1978)

insertion machines extant. This episode marked that firm's entry into the component insertion equipment business. They are a major factor in the business today.

Von Hippel (1977a)

Or, as another example:

"Solderless Wrapped Connection" is a means of making a reliable, gas-tight electrical connection by wrapping a wire tightly around a special terminal whose edges press into the wire. The system is much faster than soldering and allows much closer spacing of terminals.

The entire system, including a novel hand tool needed to properly wrap the wire around the terminal was invented and developed at Bell Labs for use in the Bell System in 1947–48. After several years of testing by the Labs, it was given to Western Electric for implementation. Western Electric decided to have the hand tool portion of the system built by an outside supplier and Keller Tool (now part of the Gardner-Denver Company) bid for and won the job in 1952–53.

Keller had other customers who did electronic assembly work and realized that some of these would also find the solderless wrapped connection system useful. It therefore requested and obtained a license to sell the hand tool on the open market. Currently, the system is a major wire connection technique and Gardner-Denver (Keller) is the major supplier of solderless wrapped connection equipment.

Von Hippel (1978)

On the basis of his observations, von Hippel proposes three paradigms for industrial product development. These are reproduced in Exhibit 1.12.

Exhibit 1.12   Three proposed paradigms for industrial product generation

Paradigm	Sequence of activities							Universe of standard industrial products
1. Customer-Active	product request from customer	→	"custom" industrial product	→	adoption by others	→		
2. Manufacturer-Active	needs research by mfr.	→	idea generation	→	idea testing	→		
3. Unfilled "Known Need"	"generally known" user need	→	advance in technology	→	development of responsive product	→		

Source: Von Hippel (1978)

Paradigm 1, Customer-Active, reflects a situation in which customer surveillance is most likely to yield an efficient stream of potentially successful new product ideas. Paradigm 2 reflects a situation where inferred needs through careful conventional market research is most likely to yield a new product success. Paradigm 3 reflects a situation awaiting an R&D breakthrough such as advances in computer memory speed or superior plastic resiliency.

Evidence about ways to reduce new industrial product failure therefore points strongly to the need for a better understanding of customers' requirements and the market structure as well as a closer integration of market research and engineering activities. High failure rates in industrial markets are undoubtably related to attempts to sell R&D output instead of satisfying users' needs.

1.4 WHAT IS THE VALUE OF ASSESSING MARKETS?

So far we have established that new products are important — most companies need them for growth — but they are both risky and costly. Adequate market analysis is a key missing element in new industrial product failures. So what should the marketing manager do? Market analysis? How much, and of what type? Can he justify it to his management?

If the foregoing argument is valid, market analysis should be an investment and not an expense. The following case suggests the opportunities that may be lost by an inadequate market research job:

Case 4: High Fructose Corn Syrup.

The case of the development of high fructose corn syrup, or isomerized corn syrup is interesting: the syrup provides an alternative and (currently) cheaper source of sweetener to replace the sucrose derived from sugar cane or beet. Annual consumption of sugar (sucrose) was about 25 billion pounds in 1976 — about 40% of this is used directly, and 60% is consumed in soft drinks and other prepared food.

The high fructose syrup was first introduced in 1967, primarily in Japan. Although it was commercially feasible to produce the product in large quantities, poor market research led to a less than enthusiastic view of the product. One reason — a very low world price for sugar. A second reason was the (closely related) low corn syrup selling price.

The ten fold jump in world sugar prices in 1972 turned this situation around. The top management of one U.S. company took the initiative in 1967 to license the Japanese process. The company was rewarded with a major share of the current fructose market, projected to account for 30–40% of industrial sugar consumption in the next several years.

The Lesson: The lesson here is that early market entry may be rewarding even in the absence of proprietary technology. The willingness to accept risk can bring with it tremendous financial rewards. A more careful forecast of sugar price futures (the rise in prices was certainly a major possibility, given the economics of world sugar production) might have encouraged more U.S. companies to enter the market earlier.

If a manager has a new product he is considering marketing, he really has three options: introduce it, don't introduce it, or do market research. Following market research, he again has the introduce/don't introduce option. Exhibit 1.13 shows these options. How can this decision be analyzed? Several companies have used decision analysis to reduce risk in problems of this type (Balthasar, Boschi and Menke, 1978).

To illustrate the approach, take the case of John Newprod, manager in charge of new products for Innovation, Inc. He has a new, turbocharged widget that (he thinks) is going to turn the market upside down. But he is not sure how big the market is. Through in-house discussions and a review of published literature, he has decided that the market could be one thousand, two thousand or three thousand units/year. And his initial guess is that each of these market sizes is equally likely (i.e., each has one chance in three of occurring).

His cost accountant, Harvey Eyeshade, has informed him that the company will lose $1.5 million if the market is only a thousand units per year, will just break even at two thousand, and will make $2.1 million at three thousand units per year.

What should he do? Well, he has one chance in three of losing $1.5 million, one chance in three of breaking even, and one chance in three of making $2.1 million. This gives an *expected* return of 1/3 X $2.1 million + 1/3 X $0 + 1/3 X ($1.5 million) = $700 thousand – $500 thousand = $200 thousand. (Here, as on balance sheets, we use the convention ( ) to refer to a loss.)

Mr. Newprod faces another problem, however. He may lose his job if the product fails. He has one chance in three of this happening. How can marketing analysis reduce *his* risk?

Market Assessment Associates (MAA) offers $150 thousand worth of market research and will reduce Mr. Newprod's uncertainty by reporting that the market is either "Big" or "Little." They translate "Big" into a one chance in three of 2000 sales and two chances in three of sales of 3000. A "Little" MAA market report

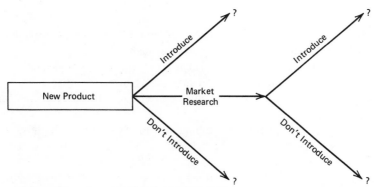

Exhibit 1.13. The options faced by the new product manager.

Exhibit 1.14   Innovation Inc., turbocharged widget data

Sales potential	Gain (loss) if product is introduced	Manager's guess at market likelihood	Likelihood w/ "Big" report	Likelihood w/ "Little" report
1000	($1.5 million)	1 in 3	0	2 in 3
2000	0	1 in 3	1 in 3	1 in 3
3000	$2.1 million	1 in 3	2 in 3	0

assessment translates into one chance in three of 2000 sales potential and two chances in three of 1000 potential. Exhibit 1.14 summarizes this information.

Suppose also that MAA has a 50–50 chance of reporting "Big" or "Little." This chance-value will not change the overall expectation about market potential, but, as we will see, will reduce uncertainty.

With a "Big" market, we get two chances in three of $2.1 million and one chance in three of $0. Thus, our expected return is $2/3 \times 2.1 + 1/3 \times 0 = \$1.4$ million. Thus, if Mr. Newprod gets a "Big" report from MAA, he is in a good position to recommend market entry for his product.

With MAA reporting "Little," we get two chances in three of a $1.5 million loss and one chance in three of a breaking even. Thus, we would expect to see $2/3 \times (\$1.5$ million$) + 1/3 \times 0 = $ a one million dollar loss. Here, Newprod should clearly not introduce the product.

But we had a 50–50 chance of seeing "Big" or "Little." If we follow the actions above (introduce if MAA reports "Big," don't if MAA reports "Little") then we would expect to see a 50% chance of a $1.4 million gain plus a 50% chance of not losing anything. This gives us a $700 thousand expected gain.

This compares with the $200 thousand expected gain from Mr. Newprod's intuition, a $700–200 thousand or $500 thousand expected improvement from $150 thousand of market research. The market research is clearly a justifiable investment (and Newprod's job is relatively secure).

So far we have seen one thing market research should do: reduce uncertainty. We can attach a monetary value to that uncertainty reduction: it would be worth up to $500 thousand to reduce our uncertainty by the amount promised by MAA, so their $150 thousand bill is really a good investment.

A second characteristic of good market research is that it should elicit creativity. Suppose Market Segmentation Associates (MSA) offers another study, costing $200 thousand. That study not only reduces uncertainty but suggests segmentation strategies as well.

It seems that there are really two submarkets for turbocharged widgets: OEM's, accounting for 47% of the market, and end users, accounting for the remainder. OEM's want low price; end users want high reliability and service.

MSA's study investigated two additional, different strategies with different product designs. Call our initial, unsegmented strategy (the one reflected in Exhibit

1.14) Strategy A. The second strategy they investigated was a low-price strategy (Strategy B) aimed primarily at OEM's. The third strategy was a high quality/service strategy (Strategy C) aimed at end users.

MSA analysis follows the pattern suggested in Chapters 4-7 here and comes out with the results in Exhibit 1.15. Our initial strategy, A, was expected to give a $700 thousand gain if the market is big. This comes from the two segments in proportion to their size.

Strategy B, low price, draws most of its $760 thousand expected gain from OEM's, and Strategy C, high quality/service, draws most of its $400 thousand gain from end users.

Given these results, Strategy B would be the one to take. It would yield $760-700 thousand or $60 thousand in added benefit over Strategy A. This more than covers the $50 thousand incremental cost of the MSA study over the MAA study ($200 thousand–$150 thousand).

In addition, these results suggest that the company might wish to consider marketing two lines of products — one to OEM's and one to end users. If that were possible, Innovation, Inc. would get just the positive returns in lines B and C in Exhibit 1.15. (The losses would be eliminated because the respective product/strategy would not apply to the inappropriate segment.)

In this dual strategy situation, Innovation, Inc., would see $860 thousand + $600 thousand or $1.46 million in expected returns. This return could justify up to $1.46 million–$760 thousand (from Strategy B, the best, single product/strategy) or $700 thousand in incremental product development and marketing.

Exhibit 1.16 summarizes the decision problem without referring to the

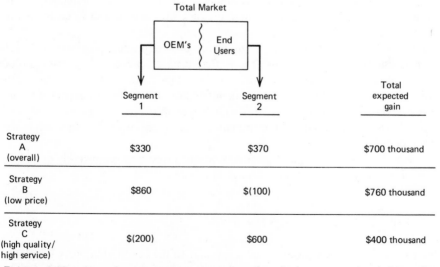

	Segment 1	Segment 2	Total expected gain
Strategy A (overall)	$330	$370	$700 thousand
Strategy B (low price)	$860	$(100)	$760 thousand
Strategy C (high quality/ high service)	$(200)	$600	$400 thousand

Exhibit 1.15. A market assessment procedure that gives segmentation information (assuming market is "Big"). Note: ( ) represents a loss.

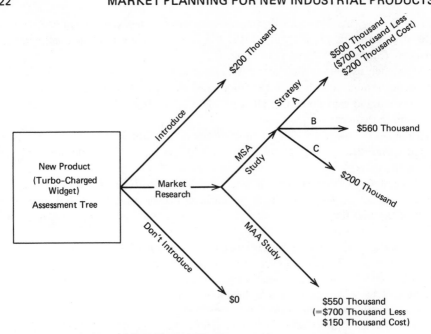

Exhibit 1.16. Decision paths, with associated benefit.

possible dual product/strategy. Here we can see one way of determing the value of market assessment in the new product development process.

This illustration is, of course, simplistic. Real world problems have many more dimensions and alternatives. But the same concepts and analyses apply. Reducing the risk of new product failure saves money. The value of that reduction can be measured. Increasing creativity in new product situations is also valuable, and its value can also be measured.

Little and Cooper (1977) report on a study of new product projects in over 150 Canadian industrial goods firms. There, they report, on average, for every $1000 of annual profits expected from a project, 6.6 manhours of market assessment were conducted; half the projects had less than two hours per $1000 of expected annual profits. They also found that firms with higher new product success rates were more likely to use first-hand information than those with less successful new product records.

It would, thus, appear that market assessment investment is currently quite low; many firms may not be spending enough in this area.

1.5 PURPOSE AND SCOPE OF THE BOOK

We have seen that new products are important to the health of industrial organizations. They are, however, risky and costly. But these risks and costs can often be reduced by careful market analysis before product introduction. This book develops a step-by-step procedure, to support the systematic analysis of industrial product-markets before product introduction.

Three main criteria have guided our efforts in developing this structure:

1. *Managerial Relevance:* The book and the sequence of models it presents have been developed to support new industrial product decisions. Our flow derives from many discussions with industrial marketing practitioners as well as from a scientific investigation of the problem area. Throughout, we aim at reducing the uncertainty surrounding new industrial product introduction. We develop concepts in a nontechnical way in the main part of each chapter and treat details in technical appendices.

2. *Fostering Creativity:* Mansfield and Wagner (1975) indicate that formal R&D project selection systems are associated with a lower likelihood of economic success. By conservatively evaluating what is, we often cut off a potential winner before it has a chance to develop. Our procedure must avoid this trap. Our methodology reports not only what the market is likely to be, but also what it would be with this segmentation, with that product modification. We develop tools aimed at being synergistic with the creative effort by pointing to those areas of product or market development where modifications can be most fruitful.

3. *Modularity of Structure:* There are many types of industrial goods evaluated and purchased in different ways. McCarthy (1975) distinguishes major capital items, accessory equipment, raw materials, component parts, supplies and services. Purchases of these products often lead to different styles of decision making. In any given situation, only pieces of our methodology may be needed or may apply. Our procedure is designed to permit custom-model construction from the general, modular structure.

Following these criteria, we develop a model of response to industrial marketing strategy and an associated measurement methodology.

The model draws upon state-of-the-art knowledge of organizational buying behavior and the theory of diffusion of innovation. It treats issues of determining the size of industrial product markets and carefully reviews segmentation procedures appropriate in industrial marketing situations. The processes of organizations' gaining awareness of and of setting purchase requirements for new products are explicitly considered. In addition, model elements deal with differences in the decision-makers' product perceptions and preferences, group decision formation, and the rate of sales growth of the new product from its introduction to its ultimate potential.

Sources of market information and methods for collecting the required data are developed in detail. Information about the product and its market, the purchasing organizations and their buying structures and the individual involved in the decision process need to be collected. Secondary sources and primary (personal, telephone and mail) data collection procedures are suggested. These sources provide the data the models need to work.

Our next chapter, Chapter Two, takes us to the beginning and builds the structure. It introduces the concept of a model and reviews what we know about organizational buying. It then develops and gives an overview of the structure we suggest for market assessment.

This book has been developed to address the important problem of assessing markets for new industrial products. It is designed to let the reader custom design a model or set of models and apply them to his situation. Pick what you need here, and perhaps product life will be a bit less risky and costly.

1.6 SUMMARY

This chapter provides an introduction to and overview of the problems and analysis associated with new industrial product marketing.

New products are important contributors to the success and growth of industrial organizations. But they are risky and costly. These risks can be measured and reduced through a better understanding of user needs and evaluation of industrial market response.

Some sucesssful innovations emerge from customer organizations. Others result from more standard market procedures. Still others come from R&D laboratories. Whatever the source of an industrial product, the increasingly competitive nature of most industrial markets requires more efficient product development and more effective marketing strategies.

The remainder of the volume is devoted to describing a modular procedure to assess markets for a wide range of industrial products. Each chapter details a different step in the analysis. For those who are planning on having the whole menu: *bon appetit!*

CHAPTER TWO

Assessing Response to Industrial Marketing Strategy: Issues, Models and Solutions

All marketing strategy decisions involve the prediction of buying behavior.

> Webster and Wind

Shortcuts to specific knowledge are delusions.

> E. O. Martin

We recently bought — or was it rented? or leased? — a desk-top copier for our office. It is a good illustration of an organizational buy. The names of the actors and competing manufacturers are camouflaged, but the main points should come through.

For as long as anyone could remember, there was a Copyking 700 in our office. It was reasonably fast, but required that an original be fed into a small slot and then be given a roller-coaster tour of the machine's inner works before returning with the copy. Copying from bound documents was impossible and had to be done in that office of sin, Central Reproduction. But we had adjusted.

One day, an eager, energetic salesman from the Samurai copier company stopped by. He looked at what we had and told us our Copyking was obsolete. And he happened to have a Samurai 6000 in his truck that he would let us have, free!, for a month, if only we would use it. It was an offer Ethel, our administrative assistant, could not refuse and there was the Samurai the next day when we got in.

After a few days of use, we called an emergency meeting of faculty and (the real powers) secretaries. We agreed that we could not go back to the Copyking 700: the Samurai salesman had uncovered a latent need.

What to do next? Ethel was put in charge of a team of information gatherers. She gathered literature and contacted salesmen from Copyking, 4H, and Nippon. A week later the Nippon salesman showed up. Although he was energetic and convincing, he did not offer a model appropriate for our needs. The 4H salesman, another two days later, arrived with his demonstration van. He was a half hour late and disheveled. He told of the virtues of his machine, the 4H VCC (called by the Samurai salesmen the "Very Crummy Copier"). He proudly copied one of our documents, and his copy showed a two-inch streak across the center. He apologized, saying that the machine probably hadn't been cleaned recently. No doubt.

A real selling feature of the 4H VCC was its ability to produce transparencies directly. He made a barely visible transparency for us and said, "Now, isn't that the best transparency you ever saw?" He seemed surprised when we said no. 4H was eliminated from consideration.

Ethel and another administrative assistant, Irma, eliminated several other manufacturers because of poor references, possible delivery problems, and insufficient service records. (One company went out of business during our consideration process. Their terms were great . . .). Two weeks later, a Copyking salesman showed up with his new model, the Copyking 2000. It met all our needs well with some different but equally good selling points compared with the Samurai.

Ethel and Irma prepared a list of credits and debits, comparing the Samurai with the Copyking. They recommended the Samurai, preferring some of its features to those of the Copyking. We were indifferent. Dr. Grand, our faculty chairman, chose the Copyking because ". . . the difference was not great enough to justify a change in manufacturer." The process took nearly two months.

Postscript: The Copyking 2000 could not be delivered until our Copyking 700 was removed by the Disposal Department, an independent department of the Copyking Company. We could not reach this department and were told that the salesman could not help us. Ethel called the salesman, and told him that unless the Copyking 700 was out and the 2000 was in by the next day, we would cancel the order. We now have a Copyking 2000. It serves our copying needs somewhat more efficiently than the older machine.

What do we see here? We follow a need, externally generated, through the formation of a buying team. A set of selection criteria was constructed and a search procedure was initiated. After a time, search terminated and the remaining candidates were evaluated. A recommendation to management was made, and a selection decision taken.

Here was a buying decision that didn't just happen. The process involved two direct users, four indirect users, a manager and several outside references. It followed an intricate set of activities, seemingly unique to the organization and resulted in a purchase commitment. A key aspect of that set of activities was that each individual in the process arrived at an individual conclusion and shared it with the other members of the team. It seems to be a difficult process to model — yet it is a process whose phases, and even whose outcome, could well have been predicted in advance.

A purchasing problem results when someone in an organization recognizes that a problem exists that can be solved by purchasing some goods or services. But there are many types of problems and a purchase may be only one of a set of solutions. A department of a large company we know was facing large costs because of delays from the slow operation of a computer scheduling procedure. Their programming staff wanted to reprogram the system, promising a 50% reduction in running time. A computer salesman suggested the purchase of a faster machine. Because of a historical inconsistency of programmer-staff results, a computer purchase was recommended as a solution to a slow operation problem.

Hence, organizational buying is a complex process. It varies from organization to organization, from purchase to purchase. It requires different kinds of people, over a period of time, to resolve differences and make choices.

This chapter reviews what we know about industrial buying behavior and provides a conceptual framework to analyze it. Next we introduce a general model of industrial market response that satisfies the criteria of relevance, modularity, and creativity introduced in Chapter One. This model is operational. It is designed to be implemented and used as a tool for industrial marketing decision support.

To be sure we mean the same thing when we use the same words, we take a short digression into the arcane world of models.

2.1 MODELS

Cheryl Tiegs — now that's a model! Our male readers will perhaps be disappointed to learn that the types of models we will be discussing do not include the Cheryl Tiegs category, although we are doing some independent investigation into the characteristics of this type.

Webster's is not much help, defining a model as "a small copy or imitation of a thing." When we in the management sciences speak of models, we may mean several different things. We distinguish three major kinds of models; Pedagogic,

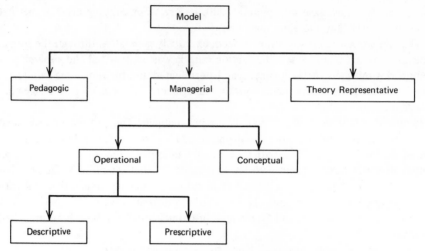

Exhibit 2.1.   A taxonomy of models.

Managerial, and Theory Representative (Exhibit 2.1 gives a taxonomy). (For a more detailed discussion, see Lilien, 1975.)

A *Pedagogic* model is designed mainly for use in teaching and explanation. A picture of the firm as a black box with raw materials going in and finished products going out is an example. These models are usually simple, unencumbered by details and only suggestive of real applications. Pedagogic models are designed to help structure thought at the expense of detail.

A *Managerial* model is the best model-representation of a situation that is still acceptable and understandable to the user. Here detail may be eliminated not because it is irrelevant but because the user mistrusts the extra complexity.

A *Theory-Representative* model is the best possible state of knowledge representative of the key aspects of a situation. It may be too complex for regular use, however.

Let's take the managerial model and consider its possible uses:

Conceptual Model.

A conceptual model (often represented as a flow chart or box-and-arrow diagram) helps one think about problems. Conceptual models generally give a qualitative representation of the structure of a system. They are most useful in isolating the variables important in a relationship and in suggesting how they interact.

Many variables in conceptual models may be difficult, if not impossible, to observe, and the actual relationships are only hinted at. Hence, output is an understanding of the process and a checklist of items to be considered.

As an example, consider Exhibit 2.2, suggesting how organizations decide on the purchase of a new piece of machinery. The Exhibit suggests that characteristics of the product (price, speed, reliability) affect demand – sales – of the product.

The model provides a checklist of factors important in influencing sales and usu-

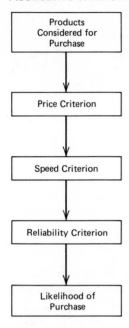

Exhibit 2.2. A conceptual model of product demand development.

ally suggests the direction of relationships, as well. But the exact nature of the relationship is not specified here.

We next consider *operational* models. There are two types — prescriptive and descriptive.

Descriptive Model.

A descriptive model (still of the managerial type) is used to describe how a system operates. Descriptive models assume that the variables in the model structure are not under the control of the manager. Descriptive models are usually operational, in the sense that quantitative relationships are specified. For example, consider a simplification of our problem, where sales (S) has been found to have the follow relationship only with equipment speed (V):

$$S = KV^{\alpha} \quad 1 > \alpha > 0$$

Exhibit 2.3 sketches this relationship.

Here we have a relationship between one of the features of the product and product sales. The proportionality factor, K, as well as the exponent, α, can be estimated by regression analysis. After determining K and α, we know not only that product speed affects demand, but in what way and by how much.

To be of most use, that is, to have true managerial value, though, we need the next form of model.

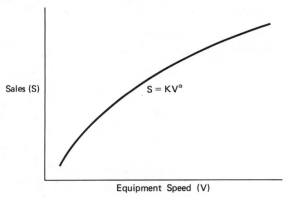

Exhibit 2.3.   Descriptive model example.

Prescriptive Model.

A prescriptive model is designed to recommend action in given situations. Thus, it prescribes. Prescriptive models contain controllable variables and can generally be manipulated to obtain good or optimum levels of those variables.

Let us modify our descriptive model in the following way. Suppose we wish to consider choosing a best speed for the machine.

Suppose also that product costs are approximately linear with changes in product speed, so cost = cV. If we take product price as given (P), then unit margin equals $P - cV$.

Let us write a profit equation:

$$\text{Profit} = \text{sales} \times \text{unit margin}$$

$$= KV^{\alpha}(P - cV)$$

Differential calculus allows us to find the value of V (call it V^*) that gives us the most profit: $V^* = \left(\dfrac{\alpha}{\alpha + 1}\right)(P/c).$

To sum up, we get more from operational models — either descriptive or prescriptive — than we get from conceptual models, but we must put in more. These models demand clear specifications of relationships and definitions of variables. The measurement of these variables and the application of statistical methods to evaluate parameters are important steps in the development of operational models.

It should be noted here also that the order in which we discussed these models — conceptual, descriptive, prescriptive — is frequently the order in which the models evolve. First, a researcher and a manager may put together a conceptual model of a situation. Thereafter, the researcher may attempt to make the model operational by specifying the form of the relationships and the measurements needed. After several cycles of model building and testing (see Urban, 1974), a prescriptive extension of the model is frequently produced, so the manager may use the model as a guideline for his actions.

The models that we develop here followed this form of evaluation.

2.2 ORGANIZATIONAL BUYING BEHAVIOR: THE STATE OF THE ART

The study of all that is known first came under the head of philosophy. Natural philosophy was soon studied separately from metaphysics, and then natural philosophy was further split into the physical and social sciences. Leonardo is said to have been the last man who truly comprehended all that was known in his time.

In our era of increasing knowledge, we each take a more and more narrow view of our subjects. So it has been with organizational buying. Researchers from several disciplines — including economics, sociology and marketing — have looked at organizational buying in their own, special ways. Webster (1979), Sheth (1976), Choffray (1977), Bonoma, Zaltman and Johnson (1977) provide comprehensive reviews of that literature.

Here, we distinguish two types of research about new-product purchasing in industrial markets: we call these Adoption Research and Behavior Research.

Adoption Research has mainly been performed by economists. It deals with an organization's final choice — the adoption or rejection of a new product or technology — and relates that choice to characteristics of the product and the market.

Behavior Research is concerned with understanding the whole purchasing process, both at the individual and organizational level, that leads to choice. Exhibit 2.4 suggests how these areas of study differ.

Adoption Research

Research on the adoption and diffusion of innovations began in sociology and anthropology at the turn of the century. Since the revolutionary study of the diffusion of hybrid corn among Iowa farmers in the early 1940's, the number of studies has mushroomed, and reaches over 2700 today (Rogers, 1976).

The object of research in this area is to relate the rate of adoption and diffusion of new products to their characteristics as perceived by different groups. To date it has focused mainly on the diffusion of technical innovations with short payoff and for which individuals, not groups, are the most likely units of adoption.

Exhibit 2.4   New product research

Type	Focus	Subject of analysis
Adoption research	Product choice	Influence on choice of: • Product factors • Environmental factors • Organizational characteristics • Individual characteristics
Behavior research	Decision process	Organizational decision process analysis at • organizational level • individual level

For example:

- Mansfield (1968) investigated the speed of adoption of fourteen innovations in four industries as a function of a potential customer firm's characteristics. He also investigated the diffusion of new industrial products (e.g. diesel locomotives) within industry and within specific firms.
- In a similar vein, Ozanne and Churchill (1971) look at the adoption of a new automatic machine tool by midwestern industrial firms. Peters and Vankatesan (1973) analyze the diffusion process for a new, small computer. O'Neal et al. (1973) study the adoption of industrial innovations through a business game. Czepiel (1976) studies the diffusion of continuous casting in the American steel industry.

For our purposes, Adoption Research is generally inconclusive. Many results obtained to date have come under criticism (Kennedy and Thiswall, 1972, Gold et al., 1970). Available studies cover a wide range of new products, whose adoption processes could differ considerably. They use generally different designs and methods of analysis. Finally they often study innovations that finally succeeded and do not address the different characteristics of failures.

Behavior Research

Marketers have been poking into the industrial purchasing process for a number of years. Previous work on industrial buying behavior has been essentially concerned with (a) the development of integrated conceptual models, and (b) the empirical verification of hypotheses pertaining to specific aspects of this behavior. For example:

- Robinson and Faris (1968) have developed a descriptive model of industrial buying behavior that categorizes this process according to purchase situations.
- Webster and Wind (1972a) have proposed a descriptive model of organizational buying, incorporating the concept of a buying center, including those involved in a purchase decision. Response of the buying center is analyzed as a function of four classes of variables: individual, interpersonal, organizational and environmental.
- Sheth (1973) has developed a model that tries to encompass all industrial buying decisions. The Sheth model distinguishes three main elements of industrial buying: (a) the psychological characteristics of the individual involved; (b) the conditions that precipitate joint decision making; and (c) the conflict resolution procedures affecting joint decision making.
- Hillier (1975) proposes a model that concentrates on (a) individual involvement in organizational buying, (b) buyer-supplier functional inter-relationships, and (c) industrial buying as a corporate process.

In addition, a number of empirical studies have dealt with certain aspects of industrial buying behavior. These studies are mainly:

- observations of actual purchase decisions (Cyert et al., 1956; Brand, 1972).
- Analyses of the involvement of various organizational functions in industrial purchasing (Harding, 1966; Scientific American, 1970; Buckner, 1967).
- Studies of the behavior and decision styles of individual decision participants (Lehman and O'Shaughnessy, 1974; Cardozo and Cagley, 1971; Hakansson and Wootz, 1975; Wilson, 1971; Sweeney et al., 1973; Scott and Bennett, 1971; Wildt and Bruno, 1974; Scott and Wright, 1976).

The most important consideration ignored in the published literature is managerial use. Although available models provide a detailed conceptual structure for the study of industrial buying behavior, they are not operational, and many of their elements have only been empirically validated in a limited way. Most important, these models give little attention to the role played by controllable marketing variables on industrial market response.

Empirical studies, on the other hand, involve a broad range of products and buying situations. Methodological problems compromise the integrity of many of the results, as the studies have often been undertaken in isolation, on the basis of small samples often limited to purchasing agents. Empirical analyses of industrial buying behavior have so far contributed little to the development of a theory of organizational buying.

2.3 AN OPERATIONAL MODEL OF
ORGANIZATIONAL BUYING BEHAVIOR

An important limitation of current models of organizational buying for an operational model-builder is their lack of parsimony. Typically, these models provide exhaustive lists of variables that might affect organizational buying. They do not, however, distinguish those variables that have a consistently major influence across product classes from those whose influence is of lesser import, dependent on specific purchase situations.

Recognizing these limitations, we propose in Exhibit 2.5 a framework to model organizational buying that is more concise than the models developed in the literature. It focuses on the links between the characteristics of an organization's buying center and the three major stages in the industrial purchasing decision process through:

1. elimination of evoked product alternatives that do not meet organizational requirements;
2. formation of decision participants' preferences;
3. formation of organizational preferences.

Although simple, this conceptualization of the industrial purchasing decision process is consistent with the current state of knowledge in the field. It reflects our concern about putting to work the concept of the buying center and explicitly deals with the issues of product feasibility, individual preferences, and organizational choice. This structure also links important characteristics of the buying center to the various stages of the industrial purchasing process.

2.4 GENERAL STRUCTURE OF AN INDUSTRIAL MARKET RESPONSE MODEL: PURPOSE OF THE BOOK

Exhibit 2.5 is still a conceptual model. To make it operational requires that customer heterogeneity be explicitly handled. Our model addresses the following issues:

1. *Need specification heterogeneity:* Potential customer organizations may differ in their need specification dimensions, that is, in the criteria they use to specify their requirements. Company A may use payback period as a criterion, but Company B uses initial cost only. They also differ in their specific requirements. Company A may require a 3-year payback; Company C may find 4 years satisfactory.

2. *Buying center heterogeneity:* Potential customers may differ in the composition of their buying center. Who is involved? What are their responsibilities? Company A has a purchasing agent and an engineer involved in the buying process for industrial cooling equipment. The engineer screens alternatives. The purchasing agent buys. In Company B, top management is also involved.

3. *Evaluation criteria heterogenity:* Decision participants may differ in their sources of information as well as in the number and nature of the criteria they use to assess alternatives. Engineers are concerned about reliability. Purchasing agents are concerned about price.

The consideration of these sources of heterogeneity in a model of industrial response requires that members of the buying center be grouped into meaningful populations. We use decision category to refer to a group of individuals whose background and responsibilities in their respective organizations are essentially similar. Examples of such participant categories are production and maintenance engineers, purchasing officers, plant managers.

In a similar way, organizations have to be grouped into microsegments homogeneous in terms of the composition of their buying centers.

Our objective here is to gain leverage by analyzing similar situations together. Hence, we focus on areas where individuals or organizational homogeneity allows meaningful aggregation. To this end, we make two assumptions:

1. Within potential customer organizations, the composition of the buying center can be characterized by the categories of participants involved in the purchasing process.

2. Decision participants who belong to the same category share the same set of product evaluation criteria and the same information sources.

These two assumptions will be developed in later chapters.

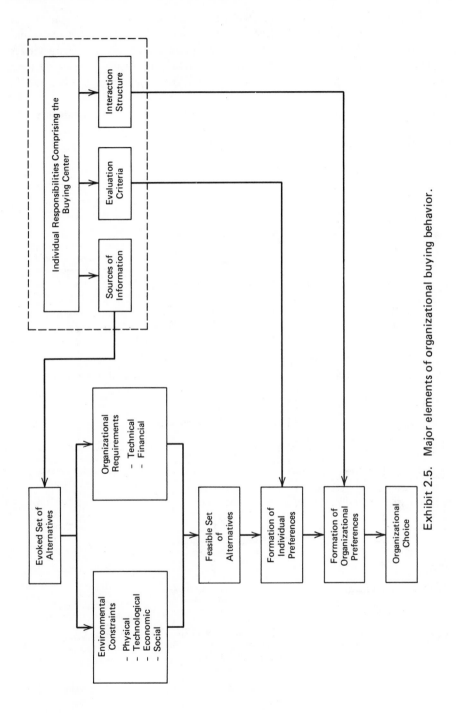

Exhibit 2.5. Major elements of organizational buying behavior.

35

Exhibit 2.6 transforms our conceptual structure into an operational sequence of measurements and models. The first two stages define the market technically and perform a first-level segmentation called macrosegmentation. This characterizes organizations likely to react to the product offering differently because of their industry or other observable characteristics. Macrosegmentation is discussed in Chapter Three.

The next step is called microsegmentation. Here we divide macrosegments into smaller groups with similar decision process structures. We propose a survey-tool,

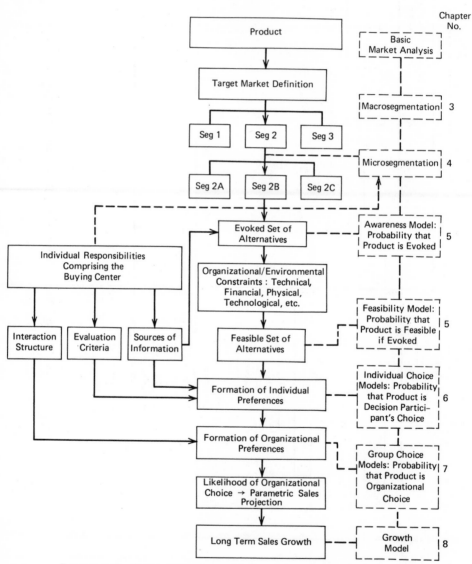

Exhibit 2.6. General structure of industrial market analysis procedure.

called a decision-matrix, to measure the involvement of different categories of individuals in a particular organization in each stage of the purchasing procedure. Organizations with similar structures across individuals and across decision-process phases are clustered together. Procedures for performing these tasks are discussed in Chapter Four.

How can we determine the likely purchase behavior of our target customers? Our first tool is an Awareness model. It relates the level of marketing support for a product (measured in terms of advertising and personal selling spending rates) to the likelihood that a potential buyer will be aware of the product. The form of those functions and methods for calibrating them are treated in Chapter Five.

The next model is the Acceptance model. It is designed to account for the process by which organizations eliminate products that are outside their range of acceptability. They do this by setting bounds on price, criteria for reliability, specifications on the number of prior successful installations, minimum values of payback period, and so forth. Our procedure is designed to measure organizational differences on those acceptance criteria and to provide managerial feedback leading to (a) insight into product design trade-offs and (b) accurate assessment of the market (or microsegment) acceptance rate for a product with a given design. Chapter Five also treats this procedure in detail.

Next we come to Individual Evaluation models. Decision participants (purchasing agents, engineers, controllers, etc.) do not always share the same criteria about product selection and usually view product alternatives quite differently. These models are decision-participant-group specific. They allow a sensitivity analysis of likely industrial market response to changes in product positioning and elicit communications trade-offs. Chapter Six reviews the measurement and use of these models.

Then we reach a difficult problem: purchasing interaction or Group Choice models. When there is disagreement between decision participants about the product to be purchased, what is the firm likely to do? Group choice models are based on a set of hypotheses about the most likely mode of interaction in potential buying organizations. The selection of the one or combination to be used is based on the marketing manager's characterization of how he feels customers in a particular microsegment buy. Chapter Seven proposes several types of models of group decision making.

Does a single estimate of market share or market potential for a new industrial product provide a sufficient basis for long-term marketing strategy formulation? Probably not: the timing of those likely sales is central. Marketers, then, need knowledge of the future growth for their product as market dynamics take effect. We introduce timing and growth in new industrial product marketing in Chapter Eight.

This market assessment model requires an associated set of measurements and controls for application. Chapter Nine addresses issues of gathering, maintaining and using the data needed to apply this procedure in particular and to support broader industrial marketing research problems in general.

The structure we presented here is modular. Only relevant models need be used.

If a single decision maker is the rule in a given application, then the group choice model becomes irrelevant. In a similar way, if decision participants are found to share a common set of product evaluation criteria, individual perceptions and choice models can be considerably simplified.

The modularity of the procedure gives considerable flexibility in terms of the buying processes and product classes that can be investigated with it. In Chapter Ten we review issues of implementation and discuss several applications.

2.5 WHAT INFORMATION SHOULD BE PROVIDED

Define the product development questions that need to be answered. These questions are generally of three kinds:

1. Does the project warrant further investment? This is the GO/NO GO evaluation that is made at the beginning and at intervals throughout the development process.
2. What product performance requirements are required by buyers? This is the product design question that positions the product in specific market segments.
3. What are the buying processes in each market segment? This is the problem of judging new product adoption patterns among buyers for purposes of planning the market introduction.

Little and Cooper (1977)

The procedure we suggest here answers all these questions. But let us compare it to more standard market research to determine what leverage we get from the additional analysis.

The analysis we propose can (and will be) used for two purposes, suggested in Exhibit 2.7. At the end of the normal market assessment studies (the type described mainly in Chapter Three) new product dogs can be identified.

The procedure developed here is most useful later; however, it helps make a potentially good product most successful in the following way:

Improving Product Design.

An important problem in the development of a new industrial product is determining the features that the product should incorporate. The product acceptance analysis provides key support for such decisions. Thus:

• The analysis forces management to identify and evaluate dimensions of organizational need.
• The acceptance model assesses design trade-offs in terms of market potential.
• The acceptance model forces industrial marketing managers to analyze product design and pricing decisions explicitly. Moreover, given data about R&D, production, and distribution costs, one can improve industrial product design within the constraints of the firm.

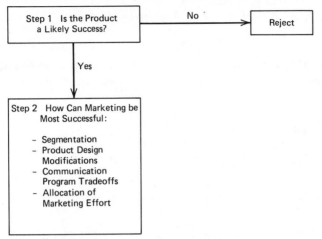

Exhibit 2.7.   The two uses of new product analysis (our procedures are directed at Step 2).

Developing and Testing Communication Programs.

Industrial communication programs, including advertising and sales presentations, affect response through the awareness model and the individual evaluation models.

The analysis of individual preferences, for each category of decision participant, allows analysis of product positioning. Results of the evaluation and preference analysis can be used in three different ways:

- Identification of those attributes of a product that are not perceived by certain categories of decision participants in ways desired by management. Then corrective action can be taken in a communication strategy for the firm.
- Development of a communication program that addresses the needs specific to each group of decision participants.
- Simulation of the impact of changes in communication content on the preferences of each category of individuals.

Segmenting Markets and Targeting
Communication Programs.

The microsegmentation procedure identifies those categories of decision participants most likely to become involved in the purchase decision. By isolating homogeneous microsegments of organizations, the procedure provides descriptions of the structure of the purchasing decision process. For example, our past studies showed substantial differences in:

- The number of decision phases in which each category of participants is involved.
- The number of participants' categories involved in each stage of the process.

• The frequency of involvement of each category of participant in each decision phase.

In addition, the segmentation analysis allows the organization to test if differentiated product-offerings, targeted at separate market segments, are cost justified.

2.6 HOW TO USE THE BOOK

The book is written for two audiences:

• The industrial marketing manager, faced with new industrial product introduction problems, and
• The industrial marketing analyst, charged with performing the assessment procedure.

The book is structured to be useful for these two diverse groups. Each Chapter deals with a particular portion of the market assessment procedure. Included in the Chapter is a complete nontechnical description of the procedure along with examples. The technical details — the how-to-do-it portion — are developed in extended working appendices, later on.

To give the book relevance and for ease of exposition throughout we introduce a running case-example: the assessment of market potential for a new industrial cooling system. The addendum to this Chapter presents the project in more detail. Abstract concepts can then be made immediately concrete through this illustration.

The book can be used in several ways. Each Chapter, in conjunction with the first two overview chapters, is designed to be used by itself. This introduces some redundancy but is, we feel, a small price to pay for modularity. A manager faced with an industrial market segmentation problem does not have to learn as much about the assessment of product perceptions.

As a whole, the book provides a menu for the industrial marketing manager. Here are analyses that can be performed for him, in support of his decision problems. This is what the analysis consists of, and this is the information he will get.

The book can also be used as a text for the analysis portion of a graduate level course in industrial marketing. Our experience has been that the material here can be covered in six to eight lectures, depending on the level and background of the students.

2.7 SUMMARY

Organizational buying is a complex process. It varies from organization to organization, from purchase to purchase. It requires different kinds of people, over a period of time, to resolve differences and make choices.

A number of comprehensive models of organizational buying have been proposed in the literature. They all fall into the category of conceptual models: useful for structuring thought and providing a checklist, but not for providing directly usable results. Some of the key characteristics of organizational buying relate to the complexity of this process: many people, different criteria, complex interaction.

We introduce a new, operational model of organizational buying. That model is the basis of this volume. It specifically addresses the issues of individual differences in choice formation and inter-organizational differences in buying behavior. It is designed to be used as a tool for industrial marketing decision support. The book is built around the structure of that model.

Addendum: Introduction to the Case Example: Industrial Adoption of Solar Cooling. Currently, over 25% of the energy used in the United States is consumed by heating and cooling of buildings and by providing hot water (Westinghouse Phase 0 Report, 1974). At a conversion efficiency of 10%, 11,000 square miles of solar collectors (or 0.3% of America's land area) could have satisfied the 1970 water, space heating and cooling needs of this country (Williams, 1974).

Space cooling is the fastest growing energy need, projected to account for over 5% of U.S. energy demand by 1980 (Westinghouse Phase 0 Report, 1974). A substantial portion of this demand is for use in industrial buildings. Thus, a considerable amount of fossil fuel could be saved by wide scale adoption of solar powered cooling systems.

There are two major classes of cooling systems in wide use today – compression systems and absorption systems comprising about 90-95% of the market and 5-10% of the market, respectively.

Compression cooling, the most familiar system used in cars, room air conditioners, most refrigerators, and the like, uses a single refrigerant in conjunction with an evaporator, a compressor and a condenser. In the evaporator, the refrigerant, under pressure, passes through an expansion valve and vaporizes. As it evaporates, the refrigerant absorbs heat from the vehicle (water or air) that it is cooling. The refrigerant vapor is then compressed and sent to the condenser where it rejects heat to the environment. Finally the refrigerant returns to the evaporator to start the cycle again. The initial cost of compression cooling systems is the lowest available, and it is also the most efficient converter of thermal or electric energy into cooling.

An absorption chiller uses a refrigerant (e.g. water) and an absorbent (e.g. lithium bromide) in conjunction with an evaporator, absorber, generator and condenser. In the evaporator, the refrigerant, in a vacuum, is vaporized by a sprayer. As it evaporates, the refrigerant absorbs heat from the water that is used to cool the building. The refrigerant vapor is then absorbed by the solution in the absorber. The resulting solution is heated in the generator to drive off the refrigerant. At the condenser, the refrigerant vapor condenses and rejects heat to the environment. The refrigerant then returns to the evaporator to start the cycle again.

Initial costs for absorption systems tend to be significantly higher than for compression systems. They are particularly inefficient at sizes under 100 tons, making single family residential applications (around five tons) inappropriate. These systems are generally used by firms (such as pharmaceutical companies) that use steam for other industrial processes and who wish to make additional use of that steam.

Recognizing the potential for substantial energy savings, the U.S. Energy Research and Development Administration, together with the U.S. Economic Development Administration, sponsored a multiyear study to (a) demonstrate the technical feasibility of solar powered absorption cooling in a commercial/industrial setting and (b) to evaluate the potential of such a system.

This application of the model, fully described in Lilien (1976), is used here not because the product is a clear winner. (It surely is not!) The application does represent one of the most complete applications of the methodology currently available in the public domain.

CHAPTER THREE

Evaluating

Market Potential

Marketing mix decisions begin with an understanding of demand.

> Hughes

Get your facts first, and then you can distort them as much as you want.

> Mark Twain

So your lab ace, Dr. New, has just come up with a process that will clean clogged drains fast, with laser beams. Or your market research department suggests that desk top 3D copiers is the field for you. Or maybe your situation is similar to that of the August Manufacturing Co., as reported in *Purchasing:*

"ROLLER ROLLS UP BIG SAVINGS"

Value Improvement: The tag for replacement rollers was slashed from $23 to $5.60 (for Rheem Mfg. Co.), for a total savings of $17,400.

Capsule View: The rollers were used to guide a conveyer chain through a coating oven. Purchasing had always gone back to the original oven manufacturer to buy replacement rollers. About 25 rollers had to be replaced each year — not unusual, since the oven temperature is $550°F$, and the rollers support fairly heavy loads as they guide the chain and parts to be coated through a 300-foot-long oven.

The $23 tag that the OEM supplier was charging for each roller was deemed acceptable by purchasing in view of how critical the coating operation is to production. But when a decision was made to completely rebuild the oven and 1000 new rollers purchased, the $23 price tag was no longer viewed so favorably . . .

The VA (Value Analysis) team worked closely with several suppliers. One (August Mfg.) helped determine the type of material and hardness required. . . . . Total cost of the new roller: $5.60. It also has proven to be superior in performance to the OEM-supplied rollers. (*Purchasing,* 1978).

August Mfg. seems to have a good product on its hands here. There must be a wider market for this product: perhaps everyone who uses coating ovens. Perhaps OEM's. How many coating ovens are there out there? Where are they? What products might this product replace?

However the new product comes about, a first task is to assess the uses and, thus, the potential for the product. First, some definitions, illustrated in Exhibit 3.1.

Market Demand: By market demand, we mean total volume that would be sold under a specified set of conditions (customer group, geographic area, time period) with a given marketing program. It may be expressed as a function of marketing effort, environmental factors, and the like.

Market Potential is the greatest amount that could be sold, (under current environmental conditions) if industry marketing effort were made arbitrarily large.

Demand Forecast refers to a specific value of market demand (sometimes outside the scope of past observations) that we expect to reach with a given marketing effort.

Exhibit 3.1 illustrates these concepts.

We start with market demand first, as opposed to company demand. This approach separates the two components of sales: industry total volume and company share of that volume. Here we focus on market demand exclusively, but much of the rest of this volume focuses on market share.

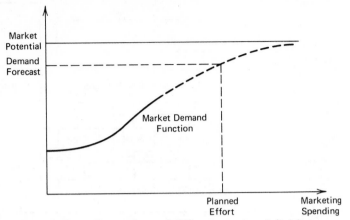

Exhibit 3.1.   Illustrations of different market definitions.

In symbols, if we let:

D_i = Company i's demand in the product class,

S_i = Company i's share of the market

D = Total market volume

then we get that

$$D_i = S_i \times D.$$

We focus here on variable D. This first step of industrial market analysis is called *macrosegmentation* in the terms outlined in Chapter Two and elaborated on in the next chapter. See Exhibit 3.2. It is concerned with target market identification and analysis. It comprises three main tasks:

- The search for markets.
- The assessment of market potential, and
- The identificiation of would-be customer firms.

Note that the level of "how-to-do-it" detail present in this chapter is lower than in the others. This is by design. The methods we describe in this chapter are the best known and most well established of those covered in the book. For example, we present a brief description of forecasting methods, illustrate and compare their use on one stream of data and provide some further technical details in Appendices 3.1 and 3.2. The interested manager should get a flavor for the trade-offs involved in selecting procedures. However, the analyst will want to look at further references to gather a complete understanding of the techniques. Our alternative was to duplicate existing texts on forecasting and input-output analysis, a poor investment of our time and yours.

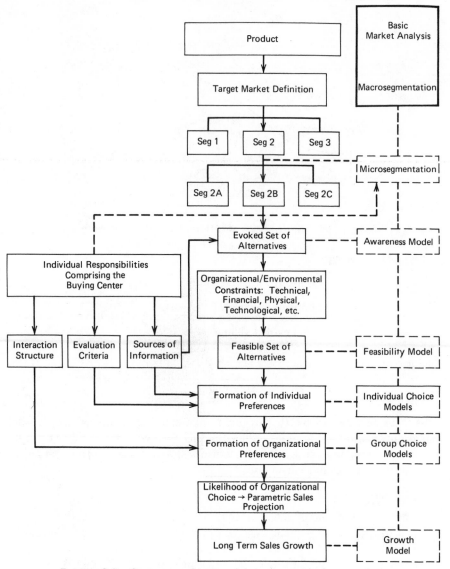

Exhibit 3.2.   Structure of industrial market analysis procedure.

3.1 THE SEARCH FOR MARKETS

Most methods described here rely on the Standard Industrial Classification System (S.I.C.). This system, developed by the Statistical Policy Division of the Office of Management and Budget, originated because of the need for statistical comparability throughout the economy. The system provides a definitional base for data collection both for the government and for marketers.

In the SIC code, economic activity is divided as follows:

General Classes. These general classes are:

A. Agriculture, Forestry and Fishing
B. Mining
C. Construction
D. Manufacturing
E. Transportation, Communications, Electric, Gas and Sanitary Services
F. Wholesale Trade
G. Retail Trade
H. Finance, Insurance and Real Estate
 I. Services.

Each of these general classes is divided into major groups or two digit SIC codes. For Class B, Mining, the major groups are:

10. Metal Mining
11. Anthracite Mining
12. Bituminous Coal and Lignite Mining
13. Oil and Gas Extraction
14. Mining and Quarrying of Nonmetallic Minerals, Except Fuels.

Each major group is divided into subgroups or three digit SIC codes. For example, Major Group 38 — Instruments and Related Products — in General Class D is divided into:

381 Engineering and Scientific Instruments
382 Measuring and Controlling Devices
383 Optical Instruments and Lenses
384 Medical Instruments and Supplies
385 Ophthalmic Goods
386 Photographic Equipment and Supplies
387 Watches, Clocks and Watch Cases

Each subgroup is further divided into detailed industry categories. For example, Subgroup 382, Measuring and Controlling Instruments, is divided into:

3822 Automatic Controls for Regulating Residential and Commercial Environments and Appliances
3823 Industrial Instruments for Measurement, Display and Control of Process Variables and Related Products
3824 Totalized Fluid Meters and Counting Devices
3825 Instruments for Measuring and Testing of Electricity and Electrical Signs
3827 Measuring and Controlling Devices, Not Elsewhere Classified

The detailed definition for SIC 3824 Totalized Fluid Meters and Counting Devices is:

Establishments primarily engaged in manufacturing totalizing (registering) meters monitoring fluid flows, such as water meters and gas meters; and producers of mechanical and electromechanical counters and associated metering devices. Establishments primarily engaged in manufacturing electricity integrating meters and electronic frequency counters are classified in Industry 3825; and industrial process instruments in Industry 3823:

Controls, revolution and timing instruments

Counter type registers

Counters: mechanical, electrical, electronic totalizing

Counters, revolution

Electromechanical counters

Electronic totalizing counters

Gasmeters: domestic, large capacity, industrial

Gasoline dispensing meters (except pumps)

Gauges for computing pressure-temperature corrections

Impeller and counter driven flow meters

Integrating meters, nonelectric

Linear counters

Magnet counters

Measuring wheels

Meters: gas, liquid, tallying, and mechanical measuring — except electrical

Odometers

Parking meters

Pedometers

Positive displacement meters

Predetermining counters

Propeller type meters with registers

Registers, linear tallying

Rotary type meters, consumption registering

Speed indicators and recorders, vehicle

Speedometers

Tachometer, centrifugal

Tally counters

Tallying meters: except electrical instruments, watches, clocks

Tank truck meters

Taximeters

Totalizing meters, consumption registering, except aircraft

Turbine meters, consumption registering

Vehicle tank meters

Watermeters, consumption registering

All of these classifications are based primarily on the product manufactured or handled or on the service performed.

In addition, the Bureau of the Census has developed the Product Classification System. This is primarily designed for industry categories (machine tools, for example) that contain a variety of different products.

A product class is a group of relatively similar products within an industry category. They are assigned a seven-digit code. The first four digits are the same as those in the four-digit SIC code. Digit five represents the product class and digits six and seven represent the individual product. For example, detailed industry category 3533, Oil Field Machinery, has four Product Classes:

3533 1 Rotary Oilfield and Gasfield Drilling Machinery and Equipment

3533 2 Other Oilfield and Gasfield Drilling Machinery and Equipment

3533 3 Oilfield and Gasfield Production Machinery and Equipment (except Pumps)

3533 4 Other Oilfield and Gasfield Machinery and Tools (except Pumps), Including Water Well

Category 3533 1 is further divided into 12 products.

35331 11 Christmas tree assemblies

13 Casing and tubing heads and supports

15 Chokes, manifolds and other accessories

19 Rodless pit lifting machinery and equipment (except pumps)

53 Pumping units and accessories, including back crank equipment

55 Other surface rod lifting machinery and equipment

57 Rod lifting equipment, subsurface, except pumps

61 Packers

65 Screens, tubing and catchers

71 Oil and gas separating, metering and treating equipment

81 Parts for oil and gas field machinery and tools, sold separately, including parts for portable drilling rigs but excluding parts for other drilling equipment

98 Other oil and gas field production machinery and tools

Product classes generally have the effect of dividing four-digit SIC code classifications into smaller groups. This has dangers as well as advantages. Clearly, much more refined analysis can be done at such a precise level. The other face of this coin reveals that narrowly defined classifications often account for only a small part of the type of production implied by the title. An establishment may also be engaged to a major extent in activities included in other classifications. This reflects the complexity of American industry and will probably not be resolved, but must be understood.

The product classification information is collected every five years and is updated by the Annual Survey of Manufacturers, a mini-census available between census periods.

Within the SIC system the basic unit of classification is an *establishment,* not the legal entity or corporation. A corporation may be a legal association of different businesses located in different areas performing different functions. Suppose the XYZ company has a paper mill, a printing plant, and a (separate) publishing operation. For the purpose of the SIC code, XYZ would represent at least three establishments that would enter into different categories.

An establishment is classified into a code depending on its major economic activity. For manufacturing operations, it is the value of production that establishes the category-classification.

For example, assume that an establishment reported the following:

Total Value of Shipment and Other Receipts	$1000
Miscellaneous Receipts (resales, etc.)	15
Total Value of Products Shipped	985
32721 Concrete Pipe Products	100
32722 Precast Concrete Products	785
32730 Ready Mixed Concrete	100

This plant would be coded into SIC industry 3272, Concrete Products, with a product specialization ratio (see below) of 90% (885/985); it would be subclassed into the five-digit class 32722, Precast Concrete, with a primary product class specialization rate of 80% (785/985).

A difficult problem arises in the fastest growing segment of American industry, the service sector. The way it is currently constructed, the SIC code classifies services in two ways: (a) those that perform a service for a variety of clients are placed in a separate service category; (b) those that provide services for a single clientele are placed in the same category as their customers.

This is only one problem associated with the use of the SIC code. The packaging industry, for example, is scattered through a variety of SIC codes, from Paper and Allied Products to Glass Products to Fabricated Metal. This makes sense for certain types of analysis (physical product analysis) but is contrary to the marketing concept definition of markets. The SIC code is not primarily designed to group products that satisfy similar customer needs. The solution to this problem still lies in the hands of the clever marketing analyst.

Hence, to use the SIC code we must first recognize that each category may comprise a heterogeneous set of establishments, small and large, diverse in manufacturing methods and, perhaps even in products produced. One establishment producing household cooking equipment may also produce microwave transmitters, but a second may not. Certain establishments may be automated; others may use hand labor extensively. Some establishments may have integrated fabrication and production facilities; others may assemble final products from components.

The differences in purchasing needs among these different organizations may be dramatic. In performing analyses with the SIC code, several important assumptions must be checked. The first is that all establishments in the same category engage in similar activities. A check on this assumption is given by the *Specialization Ratio,* the proportion of an industry's output accounted for by the products in the industry's definition.

This can vary dramatically; for example, the specialization ratio for SIC 3822, Environmental Controls, is 86%; for SIC 3691, Storage Batteries, it is 98%; and for SIC 3586, Measuring and Dispensing Pumps, it is 71%. The higher the specialization ratio, the more homogenous the output of the industry, and consequently, the closer it conforms to its SIC classification. The specialization ratio is usually high for most manufacturing industries.

Another key assumption is that the establishments in a given category account for all or a large proportion of the total activity occurring in that category. This assumption can be checked using the *Coverage Ratio,* the share of total national output of a product that is produced by establishments in the industry for which it is the primary product.

Coverage ratios also vary enormously. For example, the coverage ratio for SIC 3822, Environmental Controls is 90%; for SIC 3732, Ship Building and Repairing, it is 98%; but for SIC 3412, Metal Panels, Drums and Pails, it is 11%. The coverage ratio is low when the primary product of an industry is included in the definition of another industry. SIC 3317, Steel Pipe and Tubes, has a coverage ratio of only about 38%. Many establishments in other SIC codes also produce steel pipe and tubes, although not as their major output.

The large variation in these two ratios suggest the caution needed when using such data. The specialization ratio and the coverage ratio are important indicators of analytical reliability. Other problems arise from establishments owned by other establishments that consume their entire output. These interplant transfers, included along with all other shipments, can be an important source of analytical bias.

Another difficulty arises in the All Other or Not Elsewhere Classified categories. Farm Equipment (SIC 3522) is an example of combinations of products that are too small to warrant separate classification.

As a source of data then, the SIC code is an extremely powerful data base, that, like all powerful tools, must be used with care. As discussed in Section 3.3, other countries collect similar information.

But how can you use this data for estimating market demand for your new product? The most common procedure is called the *SIC Search;* where each four-digit SIC code is studied to determine whether establishments making that product or performing that service are potential customers.

This process acts as a screening procedure, eliminating from consideration those codes unlikely to produce significant market potential. Those industries that emerge provide a first, crude definition of the largest market for the product investigated and warrant a more detailed investigation.

3.2 MARKET POTENTIAL EVALUATION

A combination of quantitative assessment and good judgment has led you to the tentative identification of a few SIC codes as prospects for your new product. But all these markets are not equally attractive; industries will differ in the potential for sales and profits that they can offer. An early step in evaluating market opportunities is the development of a *Market Profile,* including those measurable characteristics of a market that have a bearing on the way demand is derived.

If markets are defined in terms of SIC codes, the following characteristics, among others, are available from the U.S. Census:

1. Total Number of Establishments
2. Breakdown by State
3. Value of Shipments
4. Value Added by Manufacture
5. Number of Employees
6. Total Capital Expenditures
7. Specialization Ratio
8. Coverage Ratio

Quantities 3–6 above are often best understood on a per establishment or per employee basis. For example;

- High Value of Shipments per establishment means big firms.
- High Value of Shipments per employee may mean automated facilities, especially if combined with high Total Capital Expenditures per employee and High Per Employee Value added.

The following example illustrates what can be done in constructing a market profile.

Suppose you are the proud inventor of a new separation process that can be used to filter malt beverages, or, alternatively, can be used for milk separation. What did these industries look like in 1972? The 1972 Census of Manufacturers provides the answer in Exhibits 3.3 and 3.4.

Here we have two alternative markets for our product. Milk is more than twice as large as malt beverages according to value of shipments (Exhibit 3.3). But, according to Exhibit 3.4, new capital expenditures are about the same, with no significant difference in trends.

In addition, there are many fewer establishments in the malt beverage industry, geographically concentrated in the Middle Atlantic and East North Central. This may make the malt beverage industry easier, in terms of required selling resources, to enter than the milk industry. As noted in Section 3.3, the exact size and location

Exhibit 3.3   Sample market profile: fluid milk, malt beverages

	2026 Fluid milk	2082 Malt beverages
Total Establishments	2,507	167
New England	252	9
Maine	44	0
New Hampshire	20	1
Vermont	27	0
Massachusetts	94	4
Rhode Island	23	2
Connecticut	44	0
Middle Atlantic	534	42
East North Central	480	41
West North Central	337	15
South Atlantic	228	17
East South Central	123	3
West South Central	141	12
Mountain Division	130	5
Pacific Division	282	23
Number of Establishments with		
20 or more employees	1,287	130
Number of Employees	126,100	51,000
Per Establishment	50.3	308.3
Value Added by Manufacture		
($ millions)	2,552.4	1,993.6
Per Employee ($)	20,241	38,711
Capital Expenditures		
($ millions)	149.2	155.6
Per Establishment	.0593	.931
Per Employee	.0011	.0030
Specialization Ratio	88	100
Coverage Ratio	96	100
Value of Shipments		
($ millions)	9,395.8	4,054.4
Per Establishment	3.74	24.3
Distribution of Establishment Size		
1–4 employees	657	22
5–9	243	3
10–19	320	12
20–49	499	17
50–99	405	18
100–249	313	32
250–499	53	39
500–999	6	15
1000–2499	0	6
2500+	1	3

Source: 1972 Census of Manufacturers.

Exhibit 3.4 Profile trends

	(New) Capital expenditures		Assets/employee	
	2026 Fluid milk	2082 Malt beverages	2026 Fluid milk	2092 Malt beverages
1972	149.2	155.6	–	–
1971	146.3	160.2	12,900	41,020
1970	151.8	177.7	11,900	39,290
1969	119.2	249.8	11,310	36,380
1968	110.4	193.6	10,900	32,340
1967	120.3	140.4	10.280	29,110
1966	105.2	168.8	–	–
1965	114.6	115.4	–	–

Source: 1972 Census of Manufacturers.

of these individual establishments can generally be determined by state industrial directories.

By looking at some of these figures over a period of time we can develop some insight into industry trends. For example:

• Increase in the size of an average establishment is reflected in decrease in the number of establishments accompanied by an increase in employment.

• Automation is reflected in decrease in employment plus an increase in other profile elements.

• Rising prices are reflected in increase in value of shipments with no accompanying increase in value added.

• Position erosion is reflected in decline in coverage ratio – other industries are getting pieces of the pie.

• Rising labor productivity is reflected in increase in value added larger than employment increase accompanied by increase in capital expenditures.

After evaluating market structure, we must quantitatively evaluate market demand. Methods used here fall into three main categories:

1. What customers, in fact, do. This translates into direct product-market testing, impractical on a large scale, for most industrial products. For some industrial products (consumables in particular) direct testing is feasible and is often applied. The methodology appropriate here is well developed for test-marketing consumer packaged goods. See Davis (1970) or Achenbaum (1974).

2. What customers say they will do. This is the focus of the methodology developed in the rest of this volume and will not be addressed here.

3. What people have done. The methods for analysis of past actions and the at-

tempted projection into the future can be broken into two major classes: (a) cumulative (or build-up) methods and (b) aggregate methods. When sufficient cross-sectional and time-series data are available, cumulative procedures relate current or future demand for a product-class to past demand or to related published data. Makridakis and Wheelwright (1978) and Rao and Cox (1978) provide good reviews of these methods.

We will illustrate the first few of these methods using data from the National Bureau of Economic Research data base, MDSMS, shipments for fabricated metal products, given in Exhibit 3.5. Exhibit 3.6 compares the results of the forecasts.

Exhibit 3.5 Fabricated metal product shipments, $ million

Year	Q1*	Q2	Q3	Q4
1969	11,445	11,573	11,516	11,990
1970	11,704	11,050	11,069	10,705
1971	10,729	10,931	11,832	12,172
1972	12,472	12,840	12,865	13,491
1973	14,324	14,684	14,689	15,473
1974	16,483	16,634	17,245	17,177
1975	16,230	16,562	17,614	18,318
1976	19,148	19,730	19,184	19,424
1977	20,774	21,184	21,052	22,121

Source: National Bureau of Economic Research Series MDSMS
*Q1 = Quarter 1, etc.

Exhibit 3.6 Forecasting comparison, fabricated metal products

1978	Actual	Naive	Averaged on four previous quarters, moving average	Moving average with trend adjustment
Q1	22,433	22,121	21,283	22,666
Q2	23,792	22,433	21,698	23,219
Q3	23,980	23,792	22,350	23,772
Q4	25,840	23,980	23,082	24,325

	Exponential Smoothing		
1978	$\rho = .90$	$\rho = .50$	Optimal Box Jenkins
Q1	22,014	21,397	23,168
Q2	22,391	21,915	23,509
Q3	23,652	22,853	24,133
Q4	23,947	23,416	25,141

3.2.1 Cumulative Procedures

Cumulative procedures assume availability of time-series data. A number of such methods exist which differ mainly in the way past observations are related to the forecast value. We present a few of the most widely used methods here and develop them in Appendix 3.1.

Naive Methods: The simplest time series forecasting procedure uses the most recently observed value as a forecast. If one has annual or semiannual data, a naive forecast is equivalent to giving a weight of "1" to the most recent observation and '0' to all previous observations. Other naive methods may modify this procedure by adjusting for seasonal fluctuations. Naive methods are mainly used as a basis for comparing alternative forecasting approaches.

Smoothing Techniques: The notion underlying smoothing methods is that there is some pattern in the values of the variables to be forecast and that past observations represent that pattern as well as random fluctuations. Smoothing methods try to distinguish the underlying pattern from the random fluctuations by eliminating the latter.

First order smoothing techniques include moving averages and exponential smoothing. (See Appendix 3.1 for a more technical review of these methods).

Moving Averages: If a great deal of frequently collected data is available, random fluctuations in the data become important in making short-range forecasts. One way to lessen the impact of randomness in individual forecasts is to average several of the past values. The moving average approach is one of the simplest procedures for doing this. It weights the past n observations with the value $1/n$, where n is specified by the analyst and remains constant. The larger n, the greater will be the smoothing effect on the forecast. If a year's worth of monthly data were available, the moving average method would forecast the next period as $1/12$ of the total for the past year. When new data become available, they are used, with the newest observation replacing the oldest. In this sense, the average is moving. Typically, the method of moving averages is used for forecasting only one period in advance. It does not adapt easily to changes in patterns in the data.

Exponential Smoothing: This approach is very similar to the moving average method, differing in that the weights given to past observations are not constant. The weights decline exponentially so that more recent observations get more weight than older values. Choice of the smoothing factor is left to the analyst. Most often a value is selected experimentally from a set of two or three different trial values. As with moving average methods, exponential smoothing has limitations when basic changes are expected in the data pattern. Exponential smoothing methods cover a variety of procedures, some of which make adjustment for trends and for seasonality. In essence, most adjust the data in some way before applying an exponential smoothing procedure.

Adaptive Filtering: Smoothing methods are based on the idea that a forecast can be made using a weighted sum of past observations. In the case of simple moving averages the individual weights were $1/n$. For exponential smoothing, the analyst has to postulate the declining weighting factor.

Adaptive filtering is another approach for determining the most appropriate set of weights. It is based on an interative process that determines weights to minimize forecasting error.

The Box-Jenkins Method: This method is a philosophy for approaching forecasting problems. It comprises three steps: model identification, estimation and verification. As such, the method allows the analyst to make incremental improvements in his model until error or prediction is minimized with respect to the observed pattern.

The Box-Jenkins approach is the most general of the forecasting techniques and one of the most powerful available today. It can deal with almost any pattern of data and develop an adequate model. Its complexity, however, requires great expertise for use.

Multiple Regression: Regression can be thought of as an alternate way to select the weights that will be applied to the lagged values of variables in making a forecast. As normally used, however, multiple regression typically includes more than the single variable, time.

Typically, a marketer assessing demand may try to link product demand-needs and published data in those SIC codes that are considered high potential. Number of employees is frequently used as the most readily available surrogate for customer size. Multiple regression allows one to determine the relationship between potential demand and other more easily observed variables.

The statistical theory underlying the regression model is well developed. It provides various tests to assess whether the form of the model is supported by the data as well as whether prediction variables exhibit a statistically significant relationship.

The following example shows how internal company data can be used to estimate market potential. Consider the Machinco Company, making a high technology component part. It has, currently, 17 customers for those parts. Exhibit 3.7 gives Machinco's customers along with their number of employees and their volume of purchase from Machinco.

If we use number of employees as a rough predictor of sales potential we might relate

$$\text{Sales} = a_O + a_1 \text{ Number of Employees.}$$

If we do that with our data, then, through linear regression we find that $a_O = 8.52$ and $a_1 = .061$. Now, the U.S. Census of Manufacturers reports that prospective customers for Machinco's product have a total of 126,000 employees. Plugging this into the equation above gives:

$$\text{(Potential) Sales} = 8.52 + .061 \times 126,000 = 7,695.$$

This is nearly 10 times the current sales of Machinco (823) and gives some interesting information about possibilities for expanding sales to other prospects.

Suppose that the company has two prospects. Company A has 1600 employees,

Exhibit 3.7   Machinco's customers and current sales levels

Customer number	Number of employees	Sales in (000's of $)
1	110	9.8
2	141	21.2
3	204	14.7
4	377	22.8
5	395	48.1
6	502	42.3
7	612	27.8
8	618	40.7
9	707	59.8
10	721	44.5
11	736	77.1
12	856	59.2
13	902	52.3
14	926	77.1
15	1045	74.6
16	1105	81.8
17	1250	69.7
		TOTAL = 823.0

(Regression of sales versus employees gives Sales = 8.52 + 0.61 × No. of Employees, $R^2 = .77$)

B has 500 employees. A good guess for the sales potential for Company A is 8.52 + .061 × 1600 or 106 units. Similarly we get 39 units as the potential for Company B.

For a description of analysis similar to this in operation, see Cox and Havens (1977).

Econometric Analysis: Strictly speaking, multiple regression equations fall in the area of econometrics. As generally used, however, econometrics usually refers to sets of two or more regression equations. Thus an econometric model of a company or an industry would include several equations to be solved simultaneously.

Econometric models allow specific modeling of interactions between variables. This is done at the expense of much more analytical complexity and generally more severe data requirements. These models are generally used for aggregated data — industry or national forecasts — or for long-range projections. It is well beyond the scope of this work to compare and contrast quantitative forecasting procedures. Several years ago, econometric models were all the rage — the crystal ball had arrived! But, seemingly, like all cure-alls, the bubble has lost some air, if not burst. The models were not sensitive to recent structural changes in the economy. Even in the stable years of the 1960s, Christ (1975) found that econometric models were not superior to time series approaches to forecasting. Naylor et al., (1972) studied the Box-Jenkins approach compared with the Wharton econometric model of the U.S. economy. Box and Jenkins were clear winners. Another study by Nelson (1972) also picks Box and Jenkins.

Why bother with econometrics then? The answer seems to be that, in addition to giving forecasts, the approach gives important insight into the situation. The evidence on which way to go is not clear, however, and Makridakis and Wheelright (1978) conclude ". . . it is important that each situation be considered on its own merits when trying to decide between a time series technique and a causal or regression technique, rather than always going one way or the other."

3.2.2 Aggregate Procedures

In many instances, sufficient data of the time series variety is not available to use cumulative methods. In this case, aggregate procedures may be used. These link demand to economic factors which reflect the capacity of a market or market-segment to consume a product. A number of such techniques are available that differ mainly in the economic indicators used and in the way the relationships are constructed. The best known and most widely used such technique is input/output analysis, discussed below and in Appendix 3.2.

Input/Output Analysis

In our economy, firms produce products and sell them to other firms that add value and sell the product until at last the finished product is in the hands of you or me — the consumer. Such transactions — a sort of economic system of shipments — are studied in the discipline known as input-output analysis. The father of this discipline is Wassily Leontief who developed the fundamental work in this field in the 1940s (see Leontief, 1951, 1966).

The input-output principle is simple — it is the conservation of mass. Everything that is produced has to go somewhere and when demand for finished products increases, this derives demand for other intermediate (industrial) products. Suppose the government orders a ship to be built. This ship requires (aside from labor) iron and iron requires coal. It requires chemicals in the form of paint and lubricants, and so on in a long, connected chain.

In a highly complex and diversified economy such as ours, direct consumer sales frequently represent only a portion of the output of a given industry. The rest — like the iron needed to build our ship — is an intermediate product used by its purchasers for current input into production processes. Final demand is that output of an industry not sold to another industry but rather to consumers, government, inventory or export. The sum of final demand in a national input-output table is the Gross National Product.

Thus we can develop a series of accounting equations:

Output of Any Industry = Sales to Intermediate Users + Final Demand

Mathematically if we let

X_i = sales of any industry, $i = 1, \ldots n$ industries

x_{ij} = sales of industry i to industry j
$\quad\quad j = 1, \ldots n$ industries

Y_{ik} = sales by industry i to ultimate consumer k
$\quad\quad (k = 1 \ldots K)$

One equation can be written for each industry like:

$$\overbrace{X_i}^{\substack{\text{Output}\\\text{Sector}}} = \overbrace{x_{i1} + \ldots + x_{in}}^{\substack{\text{Intermediate}\\\text{demand}}} + \overbrace{Y_{i1} + \ldots + Y_{iK}}^{\substack{\text{Final}\\\text{demand}}}$$

The system of equations, one for each industry, is called a transactions matrix. It can be understood through an example of a simple economy with three sectors: Agriculture, Manufacture and Consumers: Consider Exhibit 3.8.

These sectors are Agriculture, which produced 200 sacks of flour, Manufacturing, which produced 100 bars of soap and Consumers which provided 600 man-years of labor. The 3 × 3 = 9 elements in Exhibit 3.6 show the intersectoral flows. Agriculture turned out 200 sacks of flour but used up 50 in the process and sent 40 to the soap manufacturers. The consumers got the rest. Manufacturing sent 28 bars of soap to agriculture, used 12 to clean up its own act and sent the remaining 60 bars to consumers.

Each column represents the input structure of the sector. To produce 200 sacks of flour, the farmers needed to consume 50 sacks, get 28 bars of soap and to absorb

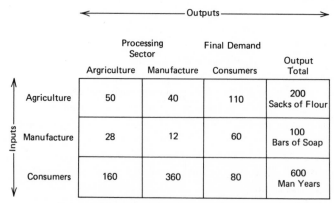

	← Outputs →			
	Processing Sector		Final Demand	
	Agriculture	Manufacture	Consumers	Output Total
Agriculture	50	40	110	200 Sacks of Flour
Manufacture	28	12	60	100 Bars of Soap
Consumers	160	360	80	600 Man Years

Exhibit 3.8.   Transactions matrix example.

160 man-years of labor. Manufacturing needed 40 sacks of flour, 12 bars of its own soap and 360 man-years of labor to produce its 100 bars of soap. And consumers spent the incomes that they received for supplying 600 man-years of labor, on 110 sacks of flour, 60 bars of soap and 80 man-years of direct services of labor.

Of course to be useful, an input-output table must have many more entries. Various countries have developed input-output tables; the most recent include more than 360 sectors in the U.S., 56 (through Eurostat) in Europe. In a larger table, manufacturing would be much more disaggregated: "yards of cotton cloth," "yards of woolen cloth," "reams of newsprint," and the like.

In practice, the intersectoral flows are generally represented in a common unit (dollars) for convenience. If we know the price per unit of each good we can easily translate Exhibit 3.6 into money.

If we now take the output of sector i as absorbed by sector j per unit of total output, we get the input coefficient of a product of sector i into sector j. Mathematically we get

$$a_{ij} = \frac{x_{ij}}{X_j}$$

A complete set of input coefficients for all sectors of a given economy – arranged in the same way as the transactions matrix – is the structural matrix of an economy. Exhibit 3.9 gives the structural matrix for our three-sector economy, assuming a sack of flour = $2, a bar of soap = $5 and a man-year of labor = $1.

Now, to interpret this table, we note that each input coefficient measures the inputs required from each industry to produce a dollar's worth of output from a given industry. For every dollar in manufacturing, we need 16¢ from agriculture, 12¢ from manufacturing itself and 72¢ from consumers (labor). The assumption is that larger outputs need more inputs. In terms of our prior notation:

$$x_{ij} = F(X_j) = a_{ij}X_j$$

This assumes that the relationship between inputs and outputs is linear, at least in a range.

Exhibit 3.9 Structural matrix

From	To		
	Agriculture	Manufacture	Consumers
Agriculture	.25	.16	.37
Manufacture	.35	.12	.50
Consumers	.40	.72	.13
	1.00	1.00	1.00

In the short run, this linearity appears to be a reasonable assumption. See Leontief (1951); Shapiro (1972). There is reasonable evidence that the level of technology for a given industry changes rather slowly. Consequently, if we let

$$Y_i = Y_{i1} + .. + Y_{iK}$$

= sales of industry i to all ultimate consumer groups,

then the following relationship is valid.

$$X_i = a_{i1}X_1 + a_{i2}X_2 + \ldots + a_{in}X_n + Y_i$$

where i = industry.

Thus, once we have the input-output coefficients, we can estimate current demand potential as follows. By reading across the appropriate row (the industry to which the marketer belongs) the marketer can determine the relative importance of different markets for his product or service. When these markets have been identified, the coefficients for each of them can be multiplied by their current dollar output from the most recent census of manufacturers or Annual Survey of Manufacturers to produce dollar estimates of potential by market segment or industry. (Appendix 3.2 gives a more complete, mathematical development of input-output analysis).

Practically, input-output forecasts provide estimates of industrial growth, of the markets that account for that growth, and of the inputs the industry will require if that growth is to be achieved. However, many firms are not in a single industry and must adapt the input-output analysis. One way of achieving this goal, (Tiebout, 1967), is to insert the product or organization as a row in the available tables.

In this case, the company can estimate sales to the various sectors specified in the input-output study, and can calculate how much each industry requires from it per dollar of output. Row coefficients are suitably adjusted. The firm can enter itself as a column and the new structure can be used as an individual company or product forecast. Alternatively, the input-output matrix can be expanded by detailed analysis of a firm's target markets, inserting them, in addition, as sectors in the economy. This may require customized data collection.

Rippe, Wilkinson and Morrison (1976) provide an interesting and useful discussion of input-output demand forecasting with anticipations data. Anticipations data are reports on expected, future sales and capital spending for an industry. The major sources of anticipations data are:

Bureau of the Census; *Manufacturers' Inventory and Sales Expectations Survey,* producing sales anticipations one and two quarters into the future.

Bureau of Economic Analysis; *Plant and Equipment Expenditure Survey,* producing capital expenditures anticipations one quarter, two quarters and one year in advance.

McGraw-Hill, Economics Department, *Business' Plans for New Plants and Equip-*

ment, producing sales anticipations ahead one and four years and capital spending anticipations ahead one, two, three and four years.

The empirical justification for using anticipations data in demand forecasts comes from several sources. Muth (1961) notes that averages of anticipations for an industry are as accurate as elaborate equation models and better than naive models. Rippe and Wilkinson (1974) report that in an experiment involving one-, two-, three- and four-year capital spending forecasts, the McGraw-Hill data generally show smaller root mean squared errors than either autoregressive models of econometric models of investment behavior.

Rippe, Wilkinson and Morrison (1976) also propose an extension of the usual input-output framework by including purchases of goods on capital accounts. Let

$$X_k = S_k + I_k \text{ where}$$

S_k = sales on current account for industry k and

I_k = sales on capital account for industry k.

(Current accounts use the input for each unit of output; capital accounts use the input in production equipment generally, so purchases of capital account inputs are not directly related to output.)

Then, similar to the above,

$$X_i = a_{i1}S_1 + \ldots + a_{in}S_n + c_{i1}I_1 + \ldots + c_{in}I_n + Y_i.$$

The anticipations method of forecasting uses $S_1 \ldots S_n$, $I_1 \ldots I_n$, available at two-digit SIC code accuracy, h time periods, say, into the future.

If X_i^0 is current demand, then X_i^h is demand h time periods in the future. Assume that Y_i^h can be modeled as

$$\hat{Y}_i^h = f(Y_i^0, Y_i^{-1}, \ldots),$$

perhaps as an auto-regressive model. Then

$$\hat{X}_i^h = a_{i1}\hat{S}_1 + \ldots + a_{in}\hat{S}_n + c_{i1}\hat{I}_1 + \ldots + c_{in}\hat{I}_n + \hat{Y}_{ih}$$

where $\hat{S}_1$ and $\hat{I}_n$ are derived from anticipations data.

As an example, the American Iron and Steel Institute (1974) publishes an industry breakdown of shipments each year that can be used as a starting point in the forecast. These numbers need to be adjusted to correspond with two-digit SIC codes. This and complete details of the example are found in Rippe, Wilkinson and Morrison (1976).

Exhibit 3.10 gives the resulting forecasts, four years in advance, using the anticipations-data model. In terms of mean absolute forecast error, the method does

Exhibit 3.10 Steel consumption demand forecast: 1973 (using anticipations data from McGraw-Hill)

Industry	1973	
Capital Account	Predicted	Actual
Mining	807	810
Petroleum	2760	4141
Other Industries	28794	27088
Current Account		
Automobiles	31723	34070
Other Transportation Equipment	4678	4678
Machinery Except Electrical	11652	11381
Electrical Machinery	8528	9242
Fabricated Metals & Instrum.	23252	21167
Other Manufacturing Industries	8024	9951
	120218	122528

Source: Drawn from Rippe, Wilkinson and Morrison (1976).

more than 50% better than a simple model derived by assuming the same change as between the two most recent years.

In sum, this method looks promising. It can be extended to industry sales by product line, company sales, and company sales by product line as long as the appropriate technical coefficients (the a's and the c's) can be estimated at the product or company level. The use of industry anticipatory data allows for more direct and easy use than exogenous forecasts of each industry's demand.

The interested reader might also consult Ranard (1972) for a description of a sales forecasting system using input-output concepts.

However it is determined, then, whether by extrapolations of past demand, detailed regression analysis, input-output analysis or industrial espionage, the size of the potential market for the new product must be determined. This is the first step in assessing the market for the product. A bound on the level of demand for the product as well as an initial targeting of segments of high potential is an important step, prior to detailed analysis. Next comes the identification of potential customer firms in those markets selected as targets.

3.3 IDENTIFICATION OF POTENTIAL CUSTOMERS

You pay taxes. You belong to professional organizations. Your company, your city and your government have libraries. All this buys you data about the firms that are your potential customers, if you know where to find it. Here are some hints.

There are many sources of SIC related data.

U.S. Census of Manufacturers. This is published by the U.S. Department of Commerce and is the most detailed single source of all SIC related data. It is useful for locating market concentration and for determining market potential. It provides data down to five- and seven-digit SIC codes. However, it is published only every four or five years and the current issue may well be out of date.

U.S. Annual Survey of Manufacturers. Published in years when the census is not, it is sort of a mini-census. It can be used in the same ways as the census, although it is not as detailed. It is generally current, more up-to-date than the latest census.

U.S. Industrial Outlook. This is published annually, by the U.S. Department of Commerce. Projections are useful in looking at future market potentials. It is useful in looking at the value of shipments for prospective customers. It also includes references to other current sources about the industries.

County Business Patterns. Published annually by the U.S. Department of Commerce, this source is most useful in determining market concentration (related to number of employees) by state and county.

Survey of Industrial Buying Power. This survey, published annually by *Sales and Marketing Management* magazine, is a good source of market concentration down to individual states and counties. It can help separate small customers from large customers.

Private Industrial Directories. Chief among these are Standard and Poor's *Register of Corporations* and Dun and Bradstreet's *Million Dollar Directory* and *Middle Market Directory*. These are excellent sources of names, locations and buying influences in particular companies within SIC codes. They are published annually. The data are recent, but they do not contain data on smaller companies that may be the key targets.

State, County and Municipal Directories. These directories are published by various government agencies. They provide basically the same information as the private directories, but provide it on companies of all sizes. They are particularly useful when buying power is concentrated in a few states, so that obtaining a few directories is feasible.

Predicasts. Published by Predicasts, Inc., this is a very useful source of projected market growth. It provides growth figures by seven-digit SIC code and, produced quarterly, is very current. It also refers to sources used and is thus a good reference to other information about the market involved.

Market Identifiers. Data can be retrieved from Dun and Bradstreet's continuous file of 3.25 million North American establishments, containing the same information as that in the directories. The data can be obtained very quickly from D & B files and is up to date.

Mailing List Companies. A number of companies provide SIC keyed lists – mailing lists and labels on SIC coded establishments. Many provide additional data such as job titles within company, and the corporate functions. These data can usually be integrated with other data to provide a more complete set of market information.

Several other, miscellaneous (but *useful*) sources include:

International Directory of Published Market Research. This document, available from the Undine Corporation in New York City, contains over 4000 listings of published research broken down by the British Industrial Classification System.

The Encyclopedia of Associations. This encyclopedia covers over 13,000 associations in the United States. It is available from Gale Research and it summarizes current research interests in the organizations and the people in the organizations who can help you with your specific problem.

Ulrich's International Periodicals Directory. This publication, available from RR Boruker in New York, lists over 60,000 titles and gives addresses and editor's name. These trade publication journalists are, potentially, an important source of information or leads.

Guide to American Directories. Similar to the *Encyclopedia of Business Information Sources* by Gale, this guide lists by contents more than 6000 directories. It is available from Klein Publications, in Coral Springs, Fla.

Finally, possible sources of technical research data are research labs.

Industrial Research Laboratories of the United States. It is published by Jacques Cuttell Press in New York. This guide lists facilities by function, by industrial category, by geography and it contains a listing of relevant personnel at each lab and what the lab has recently published. This is a good potential source of early competitive threats.

On top of these sources, there are many foreign or international sources. Many countries maintain and produce data similar to those described above. Most statistical information is still collected by governments either directly or through trade associations. Cross country comparisons are very difficult to make.

One of the most comprehensive reviews of available statistics in both western and eastern Europe is *Statistics Europe: Sources for Social Economic and Market Research* (Beckenham, Kent, England: CBD Research Ltd.). This source gives the address of the central statistical office as well as the addresses of other important organizations collecting or publishing statistics in each country. The list of embassies where a country's major statistical publications are available is provided. Most important, the survey describes every official publication, specifying its content.

The *Directory of European Associations,* also published by CBD Research, Ltd., is a useful source of information about all countries in Europe. It has two parts: the

Directory of National, Industrial Trade and Professional Associations, and the *Directory of Scientific and Technical Societies.* These directories are organized by subject. Within each subject heading, associations are arranged by country, in alphabetical order of international standard country designation. For each association the directory provides a large amount of information including address, telephone number, membership data and a detailed list of publications.

European Companies: A Guide to Sources of Information (Beckenham, Kent, England. CBD Research Ltd.) provides information about business enterprises anywhere in Europe through its guide to available information sources. The survey is arranged by countries in order of international code letters. Information is provided for each country about organizations responsible for business registration, legal form of companies, the number of each form of enterprise in existence, selected general directories of the existence and location of enterprises, directories of directors and executives, and so forth. These sources can therefore be used to identify potential customer firms.

Another interesting source of information is *Marketing in Europe,* (London: the Economist Intelligence Unit Ltd.) which regularly publishes market information on an industry or sector basis within European countries. EIU also publishes *Special Reports* which dissects an industry and describes most of its components in detail. Generally these reports conclude with a review of future prospects for the industry.

In addition to national sources there are a number of international sources of statistical information that might prove useful.

The Statistical Office of the United Nations (UN, New York, USA) collects and publishes data from as many countries as possible in periodic as well as in *ad hoc* publications. On the basis of these statistics, a large number of economic indicators are computed. A number of methodological studies, guides and manuals are also published to assist governments in collecting relevant statistical information. Among its major publications of interest are:

- The Yearbook of Industrial Statistics
- The Yearbook of International Trade Statistics
- The World Trade Annual
- The Commodity Trade Statistics
- The Quarterly Bulletin of Statistics for Asia and the Far East
- The statistical indicators of short-term economic changes in EEC countries.

The Organization for Economic Cooperation and Development (OECD, 75775 Paris, France) collects and publishes a considerable amount of information, supplied by its twenty-four member countries. Special care is taken to make figures as comparable as possible by adjusting, converting and classifying basic data. Among its major publications is an annual survey of industrial sectors such as chemistry, nonferrous metals, electrical components, and the like.

The *European Free Trade Association* (EFTA, 1211 Geneva, Switzerland) is an association of six countries: Austria, Ireland, Norway, Portugal, Sweden and Switzerland. Finland is a close associate. It aims to foster economic activity, full employment, increased productivity, financial stability and the improvement of the standard of living in EFTA countries. Its central statistical office publishes a wide range of comparative information about economic activity within member states.

The *United Nations Educational, Scientific and Cultural Organization,* UNESCO, 75700 Paris, France) has as its objective to contribute to peace and security by promoting collaboration among nations through education, science and culture. It collects many statistics, some of which are included in its statistical yearbook and in other publications.

The *European Economic Community* (EEC, 1049 Brussels, Belgium) groups nine countries: Belgium, Denmark, France, Germany (Federal Republic), Ireland, Italy, Luxemburg, Netherlands and the United Kingdom. Its central statistical office in Luxemburg (STATEC) collects and organizes a range of statistical information about member countries and occasionally about some other countries for comparison.

A major effort has been made at EEC to harmonize industrial classification schemes to allow for cross country comparisons. Not less than four such systems are currently in use:

- The Nomenclature of Goods for the External Trade Statistics of the Community and Statistics of Trade Between Member States (NIMEXE).
- The Nomenclature of Goods for Transport Statistics (NST).
- The General Industrial Classification of Economic Activities with European Communities (NACE).
- The General Classification of Industrial Products (NIPRO).

The statistical publications of STATEC are numerous. Of major interest here are the input-output tables now available for six countries for cross-comparisons. The monthly bulletin provides a summary of all EEC activities as well as an exhaustive list of the publications made available during the period. It should be consulted regularly by any company willing to do business in any of the nine member states.

Finally, the U.S. Department of Commerce produces a series called Overseas Business Reports and Foreign Economic Trends, that are frequently used first sources when starting a study of a foreign market.

We hope this selective review proves useful. Government and industry group sources can be a useful and cost-effective first step in evaluating markets.

3.4 AN ILLUSTRATION: MACROSEGMENTATION FOR SOLAR COOLING

We give a brief sample here of some sources that provided information useful in understanding the cooling market. First, Exhibit 3.11 gives a list of HVAC (*Heating, Ventilating and Air Conditioning*) trade and professional associations, and Exhibit 3.12 gives a set of publications and periodicals. Exhibit 3.13 gives one source used in locating industry concentration: the number of construction and contracting, building or developing firms in the New England area in 1972.

Target market definition in this study was made along three criteria: geographic location, SIC code classification and company size as measured by sales.

Exhibit 3.11   Professional organizations, HVAC consultants/contractors

---

ASHRAE (American Society of Heating, Refrigeration, and Air Conditioning Engineers, 345 E. 47th St., New York, NY 10017)

SMACCNA (Sheet Metal and Air Conditioning Contractors National Association, 8224 Old Courthouse Rd., Vienna, VA 22180)

National Association of Plumbing-Heating-Cooling Contractors (1016 20th St. NW Washington, DC 20036)

American Consulting Engineers Council (and chapters) (1115 15th St. NW Washington, DC 20005)

National Society of Professional Engineers (and chapters) (2029 K St. NW Washington, DC 20006)

Local heating and air-conditiong contractor groups

Exhibit 3.12   Periodicals and publications for HVAC consultants/contractors

---

ASHRAE *Journal* (monthly, see Exhibit 3.11)

Consulting Engineer (Technical Publishing; monthly)

Heating, Piping, and Air Conditioning (monthly; Reinhold Publishing)

The Specifying Engineer (Cahners; monthly)

Engineering News – Records (McGraw-Hill; weekly)

Air Conditioning, Heating, and Refrigeration News (weekly; Business News Publishing Co.)

Air Conditioning, Heating, and Refrigeration Business (monthly; Industrial Publishing Co.)

Heating and Plumbing Merchandiser (bimonthly; Gordon Publications)

Exhibit 3.13   How many HVAC consultants are there?

Numbers of Construction Contracting, Building, or Developing Establishments with Payroll in New England–1972

	General residential contracting/development (SIC 1521, 1522, 1531)	Heating/plumbing/AC contracting (SIC 1711)
Maine	879	325
New Hampshire	949	295
Vermont	668	191
Massachusetts	2739	1763
Rhode Island	545	256
Connecticut	1829	984
Total	7609	3814

Source: U.S. Census Bureau, 1972 Census of Construction Industries

Exhibit 3.14 Sun belt industrial plants

State	Food & kindred products (SIC 20–)		Pharmaceutical preparations (SIC 2834)		Electric components and accessories (SIC 367–)	
	Plants	Employees	Plants	Employees	Plants	Employees
Alabama	357	26,036	–	–	16	1,574
Arizona	166	7,048	–	–	39	13,920
Arkansas	334	25,148	–	–	6	878
California	2,411	147,789	81	6,578	750	67,507
Florida	664	48,506	20	375	83	7,904
Georgia	591	46,724	13	659	11	186
Hawaii	204	11,255	–	–	–	–
Louisiana	507	26,585	8	175	–	–
Mississippi	291	17,061	5	1,750	9	272
Texas	1,371	79,701	26	1,470	95	18,658
New Mexico	122	4,087	–	–	11	186

Source: Dun and Bradstreet

Exhibit 3.15 Installed value of nonresidential air conditioning for 1970 through 1975 with estimates for 1976 through 1985

Year	$ Millions	Field engineered systems	Unitary systems
1970	3,123	68.4%	32.6%
1971	3,216	65.4	34.1
1972	3,298	59.0	41.0
1973	3,539	55.6	41.4
1974	3,838	62.5	37.5
1975	3,845	69.7	30.3
1976	3,850*	65.0	35.0
1977	4,250*	67.0	35.0
1980	4,700*		
1985	5,600*		

*Projection, using exponential smoothing

Geographic location is important for solar cooling market definition since such systems are most efficient in situations where high cooling loads are required and abundant solar energy is available. SIC code classification, the second criteria, was used to eliminate firms that do not require cooling in their manufacturing operations. Exhibit 3.14 gives the number of plants and employees for three key industries in the Sun Belt states.

The third criterion, company size, was used to isolate target-market firms with substantial financial resources, because such firms were more likely to support the additional investment cost required by a solar cooling system.

Exhibit 3.15 gives the evaluation of past expenditures for nonresidential air conditioning systems from 1970 through 1977, according to system type. Sales of industrial A/C systems are expected to rise to over $4 billion for the first time in 1977. As the exhibit indicates, sales of unitary systems grew steadily through 1973, but experienced a rather dramatic downturn in 1974 and 1975. Sales forecasts in that exhibit were developed using exponential smoothing.

3.5 SUMMARY

This chapter is concerned with the first step of industrial market analysis: macro-segmentation. As such, macrosegmentation aims at defining and assessing the target market for an industrial product.

It comprises these tasks:

- The search for markets.
- The assessment of market potential.
- The identification of would-be customer firms.

Many sources of information and methods are available to help perform these tasks. The chapter is selective rather than exhaustive. It reviews only the major information sources about industrial markets and presents some of the forecasting tools available to assess a product's potentials. Since this area of industrial market analysis is the best developed in the literature, the technical reader is referred to other sources for complete details.

CHAPTER FOUR

Industrial

Market Segmentation

You can't satisfy all the people all the time.

So far we have been concerned with understanding organizational buying behavior and with assessing demand potential using available sources of information. Consider Exhibit 4.1. We deal next with an issue of strategic importance: target market segmentation.

The marketing concept suggests that a key to organizational success is the adaptation of products and services to meet customer needs. The marketer requires customers and his most important decision may be the selection of those customers.

This is a crucial problem. Some marketer and customer-prospect matches are better than others. The purpose of market segmentation is to provide a rationale for selecting among customers.

We cannot answer all questions about industrial market segmentation in this chapter. We will, however, delineate the issues and provide methodology for addressing industrial market segmentation problems in a meaningful way.

As an introductory illustration, consider the case of the Divided Aircraft Company (DAC). It is primarily an airline manufacturer and has been quite successful selling passenger planes to commercial airlines for the past 30 years. The company has also developed a sound reputation for the reliability of its aircraft, for minimal cost overruns and for the technical assistance it provides worldwide.

Recently, through its research efforts it became clear to DAC that, because of the soaring price of energy and the steady increase in passenger traffic, most transporters wanted new, wide-body, fuel-saving planes.

After a few months, DAC management started development of a new aircraft. Most technical problems were solved. The plane would incorporate the latest developments in aerodynamics and the engines would use state of the art technologies for fuel injection and combustion. The final configuration of the plane, however, remained to be defined on two key dimensions: capacity (number of seats offered) and range.

The DAC market research department then analyzed the market structure along these two dimensions. The study included both the analysis of current models (Exhibit 4.2) and an estimate of future demand for various configurations of planes (Exhibit 4.3). In marketing jargon, the research department had carried out a segmentation analysis of the airlines market on the basis of the two dimensions of interest. Each cell in Exhibits 4.2 and 4.3 represents a product segment of the market.

Now, which plane(s) should DAC produce? First, note that with the DA10, DA20 and DA30 models, the firm is operating in very competitive markets. The analysis of future purchase intentions indicates that they have no product to offer to segments L and Q, whose potentials are sizeable. Also, some trouble might be in store for model DA20, aimed at segment M, where heavy competition might be expected.

On this information alone, a number of product strategies can be developed for DAC. Here are a few:

• Lengthen model DA20 to increase the passenger payload and aim at segment H.

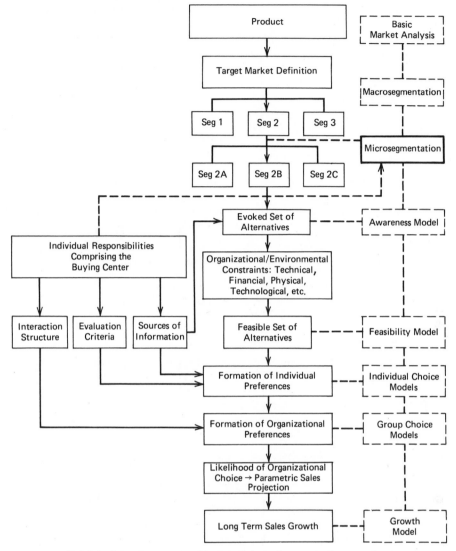

Exhibit 4.1. Structure of industrial market analysis procedure.

- Develop a modified version of the DA30 by increasing the cargo to passenger payload ratio to appeal to segment T.
- Develop a new plane for segment L.

One can identify other possible strategies as well including developing a variable size aircraft that would appeal to other segments.

Clearly, if one is to make a sound decision, additional information is needed about these segments. A key question here is how well can DAC satisfy customer

Exhibit 4.2 Current market structure: the aircraft product offerings by product-segment

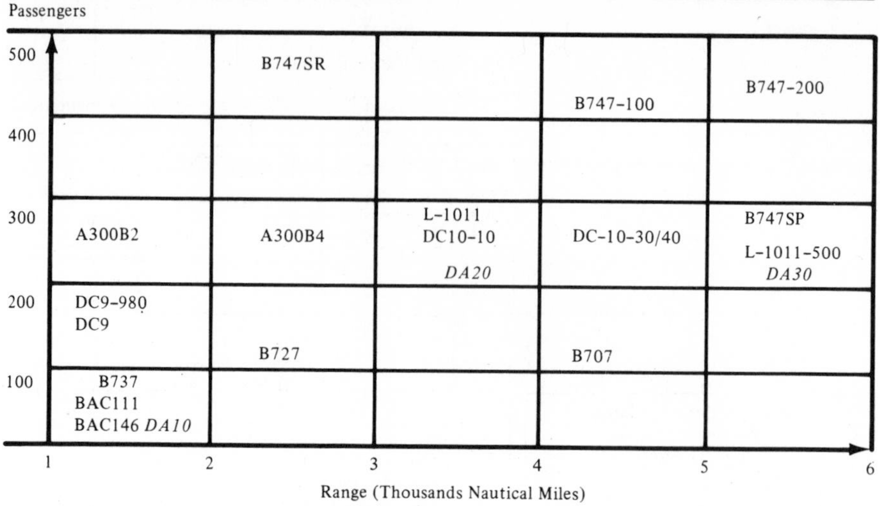

Passengers

Range →	1–2	2–3	3–4	4–5	5–6
500		B747SR		B747-100	B747-200
400					
300	A300B2	A300B4	L-1011 DC10-10 *DA20*	DC-10-30/40	B747SP L-1011-500 *DA30*
200	DC9-980 DC9	B727		B707	
100	B737 BAC111 BAC146 *DA10*				

Range (Thousands Nautical Miles)

Exhibit 4.3 DAC estimates of 1990 market needs (survey of 50 commercial airlines)

Passengers

Range →	1–2	2–3	3–4	4–5	5–6
500	0 (A)	2 (B)	0 (C)	0 (D)	2 (E)
400	0 (F)	0 (G)	60 (H)	10 (I)	0 (J)
300	30 (K)	65 (L)	40 (M)	40 (N)	10 (O)
200	15 (P)	60 (Q)	40 (R)	10 (S)	15 (T)
100	15 (U)	0 (V)	0 (W)	0 (X)	0 (Y)

Range (Thousands Nautical Miles)

needs in each of these segments? One important piece of information is the proportion of expected sales in each segment accounted for by current DAC customers. This information was collected and is summarized in Exhibit 4.4. Now we see that if a new plane is to be developed it might be directed at segment L rather than at segment Q. Segment L includes airlines that are already DAC customers. A strategy aimed at segment R might also be worth pursuing.

Exhibit 4.4 Characteristics of each segment in the aircraft market

Segment	(A) Number of planes expected to be purchased	(B) DAC coverage of column A (number of expected sales by current customers)	(C) market potential coverage (A ÷ B)
A	0	0	–
B	2	0	0
C	0	0	–
D	0	0	–
E	2	0	0
F	0	0	–
G	0	0	–
H	60	25	
I	10	1	10%
J	0	0	–
K	30	15	50%
L	65	50	77%
M	40	27	68%
N	40	10	25%
O	10	3	30%
P	15	4	27%
Q	60	20	33%
R	40	25	63%
S	10	0	0
T	15	2	13%
U	15	0	0
V	0	0	–
W	0	0	–
X	0	0	–
Y	0	0	–

Segmentation and analysis shed light on what products DAC should develop and what markets it should aim at. (We assume here that DAC is already satisfying existing customer needs.) But what type of marketing strategy should go into these (patented) new products? And just how *should* we break up the market?

4.1 THE ESSENTIALS OF SEGMENTATION THEORY

The DAC case illustrates a few ideas about market segementation. Let's review them and broaden them a bit.

Markets, whether industrial or consumer, are heterogeneous. Customers have different constraints, needs, and incentives. As a theory, market segmentation is concerned with grouping potential customers into sets that are homogeneous in response to some elements of the marketing mix. This homogeneity of response allows refinement in the development of marketing strategy.

A *segmentation basis* is a criterion according to which potential customers are grouped. The choice of this criterion is critical. An optimum segmentation basis is one that minimizes the ratio of within segment variance to across segment variance for the response or behavioral variable of interest. Exhibit 4.5 illustrates this concept.

Exhibit 4.5a shows a relevant segmentation basis. There, subgroups of organizations can be separated according to the response variable of interest (likelihood of purchase in the product class; complexity of the purchase decision, etc.). The DAC case might suggest the average age of current fleet as a relevant basis here. In Exhibit 4.5b, the segmentation basis does not lead to homogeneous response groups. In the DAC case, size of purchasing company might provide an irrelevant segmentation basis.

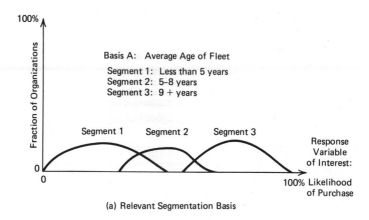

(a) Relevant Segmentation Basis

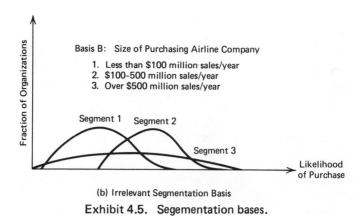

(b) Irrelevant Segmentation Basis

Exhibit 4.5. Segementation bases.

Historically, because of the difficulty and cost of transportation, marketers addressed geographically concentrated groups of customers (geographic segmentation basis). Demographic differences (e.g., age, education) among customers are often associated with different consumption patterns and are used for segmentation of consumer markets as well (demographic segmentation basis). Recent developments in the theory of buyer behavior and in the measurement of customer attitudes have permitted even finer analysis (psychographic segmentation basis). Frank, et al. (1972), provide a comprehensive review of these developments.

A *segment descriptor* is a variable or characteristic that is (a) linked to segment membership and (b) relevant for marketing strategy formulation. For DAC, two descriptors were included in the analysis: the size of segment (potential) and current customer coverage ratio.

In most segmentation studies, descriptors are used for prediction only. First, a segmentation is performed on a representative sample of the potential market. Second, analytical methods (such as regression and discriminant analysis) are used to relate segment membership to descriptors. The model can then be used to predict if a potential customer will belong to a specific segment.

So, the raison d'être of segmentation theory is marketing strategy formulation. Once markets have been segmented, companies can elect to follow any of three strategies:

- Undifferentiated marketing, that is, present one product to the market and support it with the same mix of promotional activities in all segments;
- Concentrated marketing, that is, aim at a single market segment with considerable potential and develop a product and communication mix adapted to the needs of that segment;
- Differential marketing, that is, develop a mix of products and communication strategies that aim at different segments of the market.

For these strategies to be viable, market segments should meet three conditions. The first one is *homogeneity,* a measure of the degree to which potential customers in a segment are similar in terms of some response variable of interest. Unfortunately, there is no perfect segmentation. Very often, there is considerable segment overlap in terms of response to marketing variables.

The second condition is *parsimony,* the degree to which the segments are large enough to be worth considering. An extreme segmentation would have every potential customer as a unique target. To be managerially meaningful, a requirement not met by most segmentation studies — see Guiltman and Sawyer (1974) — a small set of substantial groupings of potential customers should be identified.

The third condition is *accessibility,* the degree to which one is able to characterize segments by observable descriptor variables in order to develop differentiated marketing strategies.

Despite the apparent proliferation of market segmentation studies, many questions are still unanswered. Wind (1978) provides an excellent review of the current status and recent advances in segmentation research.

4.2 SEGMENTATION ANALYSIS AND
INDUSTRIAL BUYING BEHAVIOR

Segmentation methods have developed mainly in the field of consumer marketing. A recent review of the literature on organizational buying behavior indicates that market segmentation theory is not applied at anywhere near the level it has been used in consumer behavior (Sheth, 1976). In fact, most of our literature, unless otherwise noted, assumes that segmentation means consumer market segmentation. Industrial market segmentation is often brought up as an afterthought.

Industrial markets do raise special segmentation issues. Organizations have complex purchasing decision processes and differ markedly from individual consumers. Few industrial market segmentation schemes are available in the literature. Cardozo (1968) identifies only a handful of studies suggesting that industrial markets might be usefully segmented on the basis of (1) industrial buyers' purchasing strategies, (2) buyers' risk tolerance and cognitive styles, (3) differences among purchase requisitions and (4) differences in the environmental forces affecting different buyers. More recently, Wilson et al. (1971) segmented industrial markets on the basis of the decision making styles of individual buyers. These studies, however, are of little direct use, because they do not address practical considerations in implementing the segmentation scheme they propose.

Existing classifications proposed in organization theory are of little help. They lack comprehensiveness and mostly rely on variables that have little managerial relevance. As McKelvey (1975) recently noted, the "study of organizational classification is at such a primitive stage that there is not even agreement about terms, let alone agreement about a theory of classification."

4.3 A STRATEGY FOR INDUSTRIAL MARKET
SEGMENTATION

Wind and Cardozo (1974) review how segmentation analysis is carried out in industrial markets. Their survey reveals that segmentation strategies are used primarily after the fact, to assess products' past performance rather than to develop effective marketing programs. They stress that relevant segmentation methodology is lacking for industrial markets. Segmentation bases most useful for marketing strategy formulation — such as some of the characteristics of the Decision-Making Units (DMU's) — do not lend themselves easily to analysis. So, second choice bases are used instead.

For example, Exhibit 4.6, adapted from Wind and Cardozo, shows how industrial marketing managers view segmentation bases. Organizational characteristic bases are intermediate in terms of appropriateness but highest on ease of implementation. They are the most frequently used criteria.

The DMU characteristics, on the other hand, are viewed as most appropriate, but they are also the most difficult to implement. Here we propose a two-step industrial market segmentation procedure, using DMU characteristics as a basis. Our approach

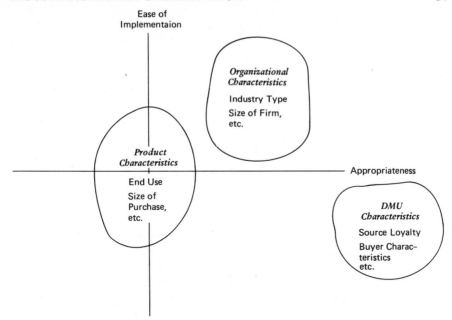

Exhibit 4.6.   How industrial marketers view various segmentation bases.

follows recommendations by Wind and Cardozo (1974). The first step, macrosegmentation, defines the target market and characterizes firms that are likely to react
to a product differently because of their industry, geographic location, or other
easily observable characteristic. Most data needed for this screening is drawn from
secondary sources, as we discussed in Chapter Three.

Second, macrosegments retained as targets are further divided on the basis of
similarities between decision-making units. This step of the analysis, microsegmentation, is the one for which methodology is proposed here. Exhibit 4.7 illustrates
the distinction.

4.3.1 Measuring Decision-Making Unit (DMU)
Composition

Which characteristic of the decision-making unit should we take as a basis for segmentation? A case could be made for using the average age of decision participants
or the number of people in the buying center.

The procedure we suggest, however, uses the pattern of involvement in the buying
decision process. This segmentation basis is both practically and theoretically sound.
In addition, it provides the necessary information for calibrating multiperson choice
models, discussed in Chapter Eight.

Past work on the measurement of purchasing process involvement has generally
been concerned with large cross-sections of firms for which aggregate frequencies
of involvement were computed on an industry or product basis. (Buckner, 1967;

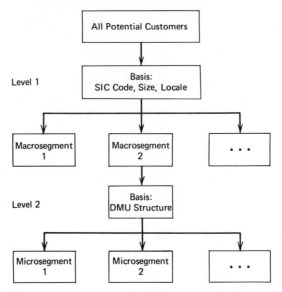

Exhibit 4.7.   A hierarchy of industrial market segmentation.

Scientific American, 1969; Stevens and Grant, 1975). None of these studies, however, dealt with interorganizational variations in that pattern, our focus here.

Our microsegmentation procedure uses a decision matrix to measure each firm's purchasing decision process. As shown in Exhibit 4.8, a decision matrix is a two-way table in which:

- The columns correspond to phases of the purchasing process (needs evaluation, product assessment, etc.).
- The rows correspond to the categories of individuals involved in the process (engineering, purchasing, top management, etc...).

Each respondent indicates the percentage of task responsibilities in each phase of the process associated with each participant category. The request for constant-sum

Exhibit 4.8   Outline of a decision matrix

Phases of purchasing decision process			
Decision participant categories	Description of Phase 1	...	Description of Phase *n*
Decision participant category 1	%	%	%
. . .	%	%	%
Decision participant category *m*	%	%	%
Total	100%	100%	100%

information forces respondents to answer in terms of their perception of the relative influence of each participant category in specific phases of the decision process. It also helps avoid such answers as "in our company, all these categories of participants would be involved through all decision phases."

Development of the matrix (see Appendix 4.1) follows analysis of the purchasing process in a small pilot sample of customer firms. Decision phases and participants' categories are empirically determined each time. A decision matrix is then specific to a product market. Appendix 4.2 discusses use of the decision matrix as a structured measurement instrument to collect information about participants' involvement in the industrial buying process. Appendix 4.3 assesses the convergent validity of the measurements provided.

4.3.2 Microsegmentation Procedure

The procedure for microsegmentation involves four steps as outlined in Exhibit 4.9. First, the pattern of involvement in the purchasing process is measured within a sample of firms in the macrosegment selected as target. Administration of the decision matrix calls for a two-stage sampling procedure. In each firm, a senior management member is identified first. He is asked to name those people in his organization who would be most likely to participate in the decision to purchase a product in the class investigated. Only those individuals identified are contacted and provide the measurements.

Second, we define an index of interorganizational similarity in participants' involvement. This index relies only on the involvement (or noninvolvement) of each category of participants in every phase of the decision process.

Third, we identify groups of organizations homogeneous in the structure of their purchasing decision process. Cluster analytic methods are used for this purpose.

Fourth, we describe each microsegment in terms of the pattern of involvement in

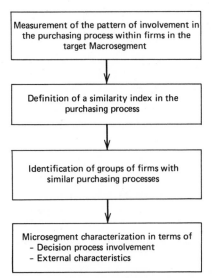

Exhibit 4.9. Outline of microsegmentation procedure.

the purchasing process. We identify categories of individuals most likely to participate in the various stages of the decision. We also characterize each group of organizations on the basis of factors external to the buying center. Multiple discriminant analysis may be used for this purpose.

Appendix 4.2 provides a detailed account of the methodological issues raised by these tasks along with proposed solutions.

Output of the microsegmentation analysis comprises:

1. A set of microsegments along with their relative importance in the target macrosegment.
2. A description of the major categories of individuals involved in purchasing decision making within each microsegment.
3. A microsegment-membership prediction equation. This equation takes characteristics of the firm and predicts the microsegment.

From the relative importance of microsegments it is then possible to assess microsegment potential as follows:

$$M_z = v_z M,$$

where v_z reflects the relative importance of microsegment z in the macrosegment, and M denotes target market potential in the macrosegment as estimated in Chapter Three.

4.4 IMPLEMENTATION OF THE INDUSTRIAL SEGMENTATION PROCEDURE

We now review the microsegmentation procedure as applied in the industrial cooling case.

During open-ended interviews leading to the development of the measurement instruments, we identified five key phases in the purchasing decision process for industrial cooling systems:

1. Evaluation of needs and specification of requirements;
2. Preliminary budget approval;
3. Search for alternatives and preparation of a bid list;
4. Equipment and manufacturer evaluation; and
5. Equipment and manufacturer selection.

We also found that the process involves individuals whose job responsibilities can be grouped as follows:

• Company Personnel — Production and maintenance engineers
                                Plant or factory managers

> Financial controller or accountant
> Procurement or purchasing department personnel
> Top management

- External Personnel — HVAC/Engineering firm
  > Architects and building contractors
  > A/C equipment manufacturers

Exhibit 4.10 outlines the resulting decision matrix.

Information obtained with the decision matrix was used as input to the microsegmentation procedure. First, we identified firms in the sample that fundamentally differed from all others (single linkage cluster analysis was used for this purpose). Ten companies were identified and their decision process information analyzed. These companies formed a heterogeneous group in terms of purchasing behavior; their stated patterns of involvement were significantly different from any other group. Thus, we removed them from the statistical analysis and analyzed them separately, on a case by case basis.

Next, four microsegments were identified. They represent 12%, 31%, 32% and 25% of the total potential of that macrosegment.

Three key questions remain if one is to make managerial use of these results:

- How do the microsegments differ in the patterns of involvement in the purchasing process?
- How does membership in a particular microsegment relate to other characteristics of the organization?
- How can the identification of these microsegments aid in marketing decision-making?

Let's consider the first question; differences in the structure of the decision process across microsegments. We can assess:

1. How many phases each decision participant is involved in?
2. How many participants are involved in each phase?

Exhibit 4.11 summarizes the results of the analysis of the number of decision phases each category of participant is involved in. Important differences are registered among the four microsegments. In microsegment 1, plant managers and top managers are involved in most decision phases, and production engineers and other categories of participants tend to be involved in a substantially smaller number of phases.

Microsegment 2 requires the major involvement of top management. In this segment, decision participants outside the organization, including mainly HVAC consultants and architects, tend to be involved in several phases as well.

In microsegment 3, production engineers are involved in most phases of the decision process. HVAC consultants are also deeply involved, suggesting that some companies in microsegment 3 rely heavily on engineers for guidance in the adoption of such products.

Exhibit 4.10 Decision matrix for the industrial air-conditioning study

| | | Decision phases | | | |
| | 1 | 2 | 3 | 4 | 5 |
Decision participants	Evaluation of A/C needs, specification of system requirements	Preliminary A/C budget approval	Search for alternatives, preparation of a bid list	Equipment and manufacturer evaluation*	Equipment and manufacturer selection
Company Personnel					
Production and Maintenance Engineers	%	%	%	%	%
Plant or Factory Managers	%	%	%	%	%
Financial Controller or Accountant	%	%	%	%	%
Procurement or Purchasing Department Personnel	%	%	%	%	%
Top Management	%	%	%	%	%
External Personnel					
HVAC/Engineering Firm	%	%	%	%	%
Architects and Building Contractors	%	%	%	%	%
A/C Equipment Manufacturers	%	%	%	%	%
Column Total	100%	100%	100%	100%	100%

*Decision phase 4 generally involves evaluation of all alternative A/C systems that meet company needs, while decision phase 5 involves only the alternatives (generally 2–3) retained for final selection.

Exhibit 4.11 Average number of decision phases in which each category of participants is involved. (maximum = 5)

	Micro-segment 1	Micro-segment 2	Micro-segment 3	Micro-segment 4	
Production Engineers	1.91	1.54	4.39	4.67	o o o
Plant Managers	4.39	.57	1.57	2.83	o o o
Financial Controller	1.13	.50	.69	.50	o o
Purchasing Department Personnel	1.43	.71	1.79	.79	o o o
Top Management	2.91	3.68	1.45	1.29	o o o
HVAC/ Engineer Firm	1.48	2.89	3.30	.62	o o o
Architects and Building Contractors	1.35	2.25	1.64	.70	o o
A/C Equipment Manufacturer	.35	.68	.36	.29	

Note 1: for ease of interpretation, the two largest entries in each segment are under-
lined.

Note 2: Differences across microsegments are tested using univariate analysis of
variance.
   o o o means the differences are significant at $\alpha \leq .01$
   o o   means the differences are significant at $\alpha \leq .05$

In microsegment 4, people at the plant level, including production engineers and
plant managers, tend to exert influence in most decision phases.

Thus, differences exist across microsegments in the number of phases in which
each category of participant is involved. This does not directly relate to decision
impact, since some participants who are involved in a small number of phases may
place constraints on the decisions taken in subsequent stages. It is logical to suppose, however, that those participants involved in the most decision phases also
have the most chance to influence the final decision. They therefore deserve special
consideration in the design of industrial marketing programs.

Consider now the number of categories of decision participants involved in each
phase. This analysis considers the amount of interaction evident in each phase of
the process. Exhibit 4.12 summarizes the results; important differences are registered across microsegments.

Exhibit 4.12   Average number of categories of participants involved in each phase
of the adoption process
(maximum = 8)

	Micro-segment 1	Micro-segment 2	Micro-segment 3	Micro-segment 4	
Phase 1	3.56	3.04	3.42	2.75	
Phase 2	2.52	2.11	3.45	2.71	o o o
Phase 3	2.69	2.46	2.69	2.08	
Phase 4	3.04	2.75	2.91	2.12	o
Phase 5	3.13	2.46	2.72	2.04	o o o

Note 1: for ease of interpretation, the two largest entries in each segment are under-lined.

Note 2: Differences across microsegments are tested using univariate analysis of variance.
   o o o   means the differences are significant at $\alpha \leqslant .01$
   o   means the differences are significant at $\alpha \leqslant .10$

For most decision phases, the number of categories of participants involved is consistently larger in segments 1 and 3 than in segments 2 and 4. The number of categories of participants involved does not lessen uniformly as the process moves closer to its final phase (a contention often made in the industrial marketing litera-ture). Phase 1, however, the identification of needs, consistently involves the largest number of decision-participant categories.

Thus, the microsegmentation procedure developed here identifies a number of meaningful microsegments. Differences exist between these microsegments in the pattern of involvement in the adoption process, providing insight into the industrial purchasing process.

The use of these results for industrial marketing strategy depends partly on our ability to characterize the microsegments on the basis of external variables.

Exhibit 4.13 gives a qualitative comparison of characteristics of the organizations found in each microsegment. Companies in segment 4 tend to be smaller, more satisfied with their current air-conditioning system, and more concerned with the economic aspects of industrial air-conditioning. In terms of their purchasing pro-cesses, these companies are characterized by a more frequent involvement of Top Management. Moreover, they rely on external sources of expertise, such as HVAC consultants, to assist them in the assessment of air-conditioning needs, the search for alternatives, and the selection of particular equipment. On the contrary, larger companies represented in segments 2 and 3 use their own engineering capabilities for these same tasks.

The comparison between segments 1 and 3 is interesting because the segments do not substantially differ in terms of size of company. However, companies in seg-ment 3 tend to have more plants, larger cooling needs, and greater concern for the

Exhibit 4.13   Characteristics of organizations in each microsegment

	Micro-segment 1	Micro-segment 2	Micro-segment 3	Micro-segment 4
Satisfaction with current A/C system	Medium High	Low	Medium Low	High
Consequence if A/C system is less economical than projected	Medium High	Low	Medium Low	High
Consequence if A/C system is less reliable than projected	Medium High	Low	High	Medium Low
Company size	Medium	Large	Large	Small
Percentage of plant area requiring A/C	Medium Large	Small	Large	Medium
Number of separate plants	Medium Large	Small	Large	Medium Small

reliability of industrial air-conditioning systems than do companies in segment 1. It is therefore not surprising that companies in segment 3 rely mainly on engineering functions in the process of purchasing an industrial air-conditioning system, while companies in segment 1 involve mainly managerial functions.

Microsegment 2 groups large companies with a small number of plants. These companies view little risk in the purchase of an industrial air-conditioning system. As a result, they generally let these decisions be made at the plant level.

4.5 ADMINISTRATION AND STRATEGY
IMPLICATIONS

The microsegmentation procedure proposed here isolates homogeneous sets of organizations and describes the decision process in each. This information points to strategies aimed directly at those categories of individuals most influential in the various microsegments.

In terms of administration, the decision matrix is included as part of a personally administered or mailed survey instrument, designed to assess the market for a new industrial product. Respondents are identified as those individuals most likely to influence the purchasing decision for a product in that class. More than one individual per organization is studied when appropriate.

The procedure can be used when the potential market for an industrial product contains a small number of customers. Then, the decision matrix would be administered to each customer individually, providing information to develop specific account strategies. For larger industrial markets, the decision matrix would be administered on a sample of industrial organizations. As the industrial air-conditioning study illustrates, implementation of the procedure yields the relative size of the microsegments and describes the structure of the purchase decision within each. This information can be used to:

- Concentrate communication efforts on those categories of individuals most often involved in the purchasing process in the largest microsegments. For air-conditioning, this might lead to a concentration of communication efforts on production engineers and HVAC consultants who are most influential in microsegment 3.
- Predict the structure of the adoption process for a specific firm on the basis of its external characteristics. In this respect, Appendix 4.2 summarizes the results of a multiple discriminant analysis on microsegment membership for the solar cooling study. Promotional material or salesmen calls can then be directed to those categories of individuals most influential in the particular microsegment.
- Select communication vehicles. The categories of individuals involved in the purchasing process differ in their sources of information and communication consumption. In the industrial air-conditioning study, in microsegment 3, production engineers and HVAC consultants were most influential. Because of their common educational background, there is a substantial overlap in their sources of information and communication consumption patterns, suggesting the use of the same communication channels for both groups.

Finally, the microsegmentation procedure provides a better understanding of the industrial purchasing decision process and can help calibrate multiperson choice models (see Chapter Seven).

4.6 SUMMARY

Market segmentation is one aspect of industrial marketing strategy. We have outlined in Chapter One how our approach to segmentation can be incorporated in a quantitative analysis of industrial markets, with associated implications for product design, positioning, and the development of communication programs.

Methodology is developed here to identify segments of organizations with similar purchasing decision processes. The methodology relies on the information collected with a decision matrix from companies in the potential market for an industrial product. It uses cluster analysis to identify homogeneous groups of firms.

Implementation of the methodology in the industrial air-conditioning example identifies four segments of organizations.

Analysis of the relationship between microsegment membership and external characteristics of organizations suggests interesting relationships between the structure of the industrial purchasing process and some generic characteristics of firms, including company size, urgency of the need for the new product, satisfaction with past purchase and the nature of the risks associated with such problems.

This information provides marketers with a better understanding of the purchasing process. It is of immediate use in the development of differentiated communications strategies targeted at key individuals in different segments.

CHAPTER FIVE
Awareness
and Feasibility

Advertising contains the only truth to be relied on in a newspaper.

T. Jefferson

If there were dreams to sell what would you buy?

Beckford

With this chapter we begin the investigation of an organization's procedure for product selection. For the purpose of illustration, we return to our desk-top copier purchase.

Recall that after a few days use of the Samurai, we agreed that we would not go back to our original Copyking 700.

Ethel, our administrative assistant, was put in charge of information gathering. To help her, we discussed what features we would require in a new copier. Dr. Grand insisted that the total budget for the new system should not exceed the present allocation. Operating cost considerations as well as our need for copying on letterhead limited our choice of systems to plain paper copiers.

Ethel and Irma, who wished to eliminate trips to Central Reproduction suggested that the new system should allow copying from bound documents.

Several other selection criteria were set. One faculty member specified that the new system should not require more space than currently allocated. A discussion about the copier incorporating an automatic feed mechanism concluded that the feature was not essential.

What do we see here? After a latent need was uncovered, members of the organization set selection criteria. These allow an initial screening of those choice alternatives of which decision participants are aware, to a smaller number of acceptable choices.

In our copier purchase, we jointly were aware of eight manufacturers offering desk-top models. Our screening criteria eliminated four of the candidates from further consideration. The remaining four candidates: Samurai, Copyking, 4H and Nippon were given attention. Ethel gathered literature and experience from friends in other departments and organizations, and contacted salesmen from all four companies.

Our model parallels this separation, viewing the organizational evaluation process as containing steps of *awareness,* and *feasibility* before *preference formation* and *group interaction.* The disaggregation places emphasis on managerial controls and how they relate to a customer-organization's response.

In this chapter, we treat awareness first and feasibility next. Awareness relates to product recognition and evoking of potential solutions. Feasibility relates to the determination of product requirements and the specifications of purchase conditions. Exhibit 5.1 reviews how these two steps fit into the organizational response model introduced in Chapter Two. Let's analyze each in terms of our market assessment procedure.

5.1 AWARENESS

You may have just invented and produced the best left-handed widget (for industrial use) that the world has ever seen. But you know that if no one ever hears of it, no one will buy it. Awareness — and the consequent role of marketing communication — is a well established concept in the marketing of most consumer products. The concept has industrial relevance as well.

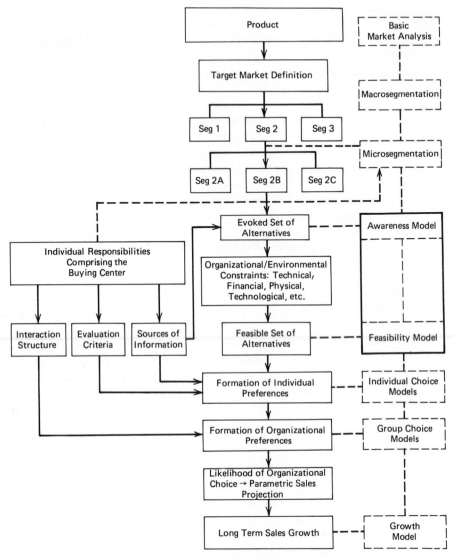

Exhibit 5.1. Structure of industrial market analysis procedure.

Consider Exhibit 5.2, displaying the hierarchy of effects adapted for our industrial purchase environment. This model, portrayed in various forms by Strong (1925), Lavidge and Steiner (1961) and Rogers (1962), suggests that participants go through a number of stages in the purchase process. An early, key movement in the process is this shift from unawareness to awareness and interest. The exhibit also suggests that both personal and impersonal marketing communications contribute to the movement of an individual through that hierarchy of effects. We model awareness by using the following definitions:

Impersonal Marketing Communication (Advertising): Those marketer-controlled messages that reach the customer through various media, primarily print. This category includes space advertising, direct mail, brochures, films, catalogues, and the like.

Personal Marketing Communication (Selling): Those marketer-controlled messages that reach the customer through intermediaries, primarily salesmen and technical service representatives.

Our model is then

$$\text{Probability of Awareness} = f(\text{Advertising, Selling}), \text{ or}$$

$$(1) \qquad\qquad w_d = f_d(A,F)$$

where w_d = Probability of Awareness for participant category d
$\quad A$ = Advertising pressure
$\quad F$ = Sales force pressure

An analytical form for this model is proposed in Appendix 5.1.

Exhibit 5.2 Marketing communications and the hierarchy of effects in an industrial purchase environment.

Stage of personal involvement in industrial purchasing	Influences		
	Impersonal marketing communication	Personal marketing communication	Other influences
Unaware	High	Moderate	Word-of-Mouth
↓			
Aware	High	High	Word-of-Mouth Individual Research
↓			
Interest	Moderate/ Low	High	Word-of-Mouth Individual Research
↓			
Intent	Low	High	Deals/Competitive Terms
↓			
Purchase Recommendation/ Endorsement	Moderate	Moderate	Product Performance
↓			
Post-Purchase Feedback			

Our market assessment procedure explicitly recognizes differences of information sources at the decision participant category level, as well as heterogeneity of response to communication messages. Different awareness functions can be developed for different categories of decision participants.

At the microsegment level, our procedure assumes that once a member of the buying center is aware of a product, he will eventually share his information with other decision participants involved in the purchase. The likelihood that an organization, as a whole, will be aware of the new product is therefore given by the likelihood that at least one member of the buying center evokes this product. Hence we have:

Probability of Awareness at the organizational level,

= Probability that at least one member of the buying center evokes the new product.

$$W = 1 - (1 - w_1)(1 - w_2) \ldots (1 - w_D)$$
$$= 1 - \prod_d (1 - w_d)$$

where

W = Probablility of awareness at the organizational level, and the product (Π) is taken over all decision participant categories involved in the microsegment of interest.

5.1.1 Awareness Models

We noted that function f_d in equation (1) above may be different across decision participant categories. It may also vary across industries. There are several ways to choose reasonable functions: empirically through a field study, or judgementally, using the product manager's past experience.

In the case of a field study, a survey is performed for a sample of individuals from each participant category. They are asked to name the brands or manufacturers that they are aware of, their media consumption patterns, the last time they saw a salesman, and so forth. (Morrill, 1970, describes a large scale study of this nature.)

Various mathematical models can then be used to relate awareness levels to controlled marketing communications variables.

In many cases, however, a second approach will be used because of time and cost constraints. It is based on the concept of judgemental calibration, developed by Little (1970) in his decision calculus approach to the development of marketing decision support systems. This method relies on a manager's experience with the product and its market to infer what the f_d's are for each decision participant category.

Consider Exhibit 5.3. A manager provides a base–level of awareness (Point C) cor-

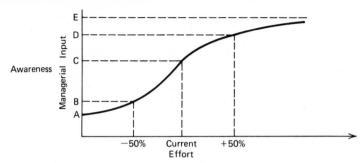

Exhibit 5.3.   Decision calculus calibration.

responding to the current level of marketing effort. The manager is then asked what would happen to awareness for his product:

• With a 50% increase in marketing effort (D).
• With a 50% decrease in effort (B).
• With a level of marketing effort that is essentially unlimited (E).
• With marketing effort set to zero (A).

These measurements provide, as shown in Appendix 5.1., sufficient data to assess an awareness response model. The procedure is repeated as needed, for each category of participant.

Knowing this is the response, by category of decision participant, can then serve as input into a model for communication allocation.

5.1.2 How Much to Spend?

Both of the preceding model-development procedures assume that your spending level is starting somewhere, and that you will go on from there. But where to start?

Two main methods are used for setting communication budgets in industrial markets: rules of thumb and the task method. Lilien et al. (1976) review what is known about industrial advertising effects and budgeting practice.

Rules of Thumb generally request the marketer to specify a percentage to apply against past or anticipated sales. This is easy to use, but does not solve the problem of determining what percent to invest in industrial marketing communications.

The Task Method asks the marketer to set communication goals and develop communication plans consistent with those goals. The problem of advertising response is not resolved here, but the assumptions are made specific.

The ADVISOR studies, conducted at MIT during the last 5 years, have developed some new support for decisions of this type (Lilien, 1979). These studies, covering a cross-section of almost 200 industrial products in a wide variety of industries, have established quantitative industrial marketing budgeting guidelines based on a careful study of practice.

ADVISOR is based on the premises that

1. there are common factors involved in creating marketing budgets for industrial products.
2. the trial-and-error judgements of experienced industrial advertisers and product managers provide a reasonable basis to develop spending levels and allocations.

The ADVISOR studies have isolated a few general characteristics, such as stage in the life cycle, structure of competition, and so forth, that have the most influence on budget decisions. They have also provided the associated equations, so that specific numerical guidelines can be developed.

Discussion of the ADVISOR models is beyond our scope. The important thing to know is that quantitative guidance about what to spend for industrial marketing communications is available, the ADVISOR budgeting norms are situation specific and they explicitly recognize the importance of product, market and company characteristics on marketing spending decisions.

5.1.3 Solar Cooling Awareness

Have you ever heard of solar cooling? Not many of the potential decision participants had either. Our survey indicated that 15% of company people and 41% of air conditioning consultants were aware of solar cooling.

Considering only the two most important decision participant categories in each of the microsegments isolated in Chapter Four, we can estimate current segment awareness as:

	Segment
Awareness = 1 – Probability that no one is aware	
= 1 – (.85)(.59) = .50	1
= 1 – (.85)(.85) = .28	2
= 1 – (.85)(.59) = .50	3
= 1 – (.85)(.59) = .50	4

In this instance, the analysis is performed before any major support program. Once awareness reponse models are calibrated for each participant category, simulation can be used to assess average segment awareness under various communication strategies.

5.2 FEASIBILITY

If you have developed an inexpensive and highly reliable desk-top copier that only produces one copy a minute, there may be only a small segment of the potential buying population that finds the product acceptable. And even if they are aware of it, they won't buy. Feasibility and the associated role of product specifications is a well established concept in industrial purchasing behavior. We now incorporate it in our market assessment procedure.

The model of industrial buying behavior discussed in Chapter Two suggests that when purchasing needs are recognized, organizational purchase criteria reduce the set of product alternatives to a more manageable set of feasible alternatives. Products that are feasible meet an organization's purchase requirements and thus are potential need satisfiers. Our description of the desk top copier purchase at the beginning of this chapter illustrated the concept.

We deal with two issues here that are critical to the industrial marketer:

- What percentage of the potential buying population will find a given product design feasible?
- How do potential customers trade off design criteria? (How much more can be charged for a piece of equipment with a 15 year life than for one with a 10 year life?)

These are the issues we deal with here.

5.2.1 Market Acceptance Functions: Background

When they are placed in a purchase situation, organizations often limit the set of products they consider by setting product standards or limits that they won't exceed (maximum price, maximum delivery time, minimum warranty period, etc.). The way these limits are set varies across organizations. Sometimes, purchase requirements flow from constraints (financial, technological, etc.) that are agreed upon by decision participants. Other times, purchase requirements result from organizational habits.

We suggest that there is a set of criteria that customer organizations use to set product requirements. We call these critera *need specification dimensions;* or from the marketer's standpoint, these can be viewed as *product design dimensions.* The feasibility model specifies the relation between the market acceptance rate and product design dimensions.

The development and calibration of this model requires that we consider two sources of heterogeneity:

- Heterogeneity in *type* of product design dimensions; organizations may differ in the dimensions they use to set requirements. Production constraints, for example, may differ from one organization to another.
- Heterogeneity in *level* of requirement: although organizations may share the same set of need specification dimensions, their requirements along these dimensions may be different. Some companies may find an expected system life of 5–7 years acceptable, but others would not consider adoption of a system whose expected life is less than 12–15 years.

To incorporate these sources of heterogeneity, we follow a three-step procedure, illustrated in Exhibit 5.4.

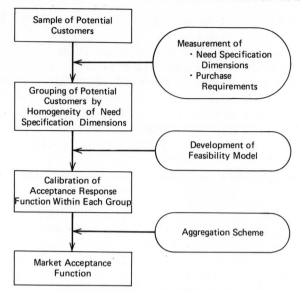

Exhibit 5.4.   Development of acceptance response function.

Step one is concerned with the identification of need specification dimensions, and the measurement of purchase requirements along these dimensions. Methods for collecting these data are discussed in Chapter Nine.

Step two groups organizations that define purchase requirements on the same set of specification dimensions. For example, all organizations that consider first cost and warranty period would be in one group, while organizations that consider operating cost, expected economic life and system back-up would be in another group.

Step three is development and calibration of acceptance functions within each group. The analytical structure of the model is somewhat complex and is discussed, along with the estimation procedure, in Appendix 5.2. Market acceptance functions are then formed, by weighting group acceptance functions by their respective sizes.

Suppose we are interested in determining the best level of some design criterion X. (X may be the length of a warranty period, for example.)

Suppose also that we have developed an acceptance function $R(X)$ where:

$R(X)$ = fraction of the market that finds the product acceptable with design X,

$M(X)$ = contribution margin associated with the product with design X, and

D = market potential,

A = fraction of the market aware of the product,

S = fraction of the market that will actually buy the product if it is acceptable for them.

A gross profit figure for the product is then

$$\text{Profit} = DAS \cdot R(X) M(X)$$

This equation can then be graphed or calculus can be used to find the best level of X.

Consider the following illustration of this approach. (This case covers a real product whose identity is disguised for proprietary reasons.) The company concerned with the product is Teletronique, a French electronic company.

Teletronique is planning to introduce a new piece of electronic equipment and is considering its price and length of warranty period. Our feasibility analysis developed the marginal distribution for price acceptability and warranty period acceptability respectively. (See Exhibits 5.5 and 5.6)

A detailed engineering study that gave production cost as a function of annual volume is displayed in Exhibit 5.7.

We now consider the problem of determining a price level and warranty period for

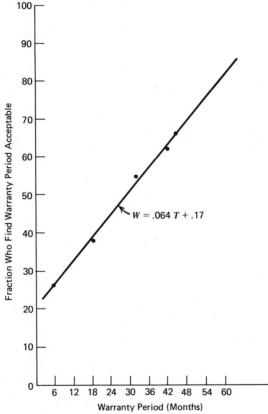

Exhibit 5.5. Warranty period acceptability curve (linear approximation): Teletronique.

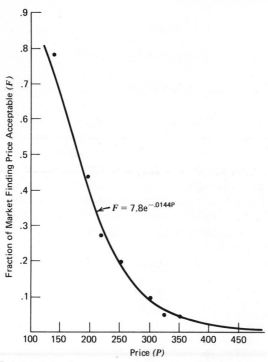

Exhibit 5.6. Price acceptability curve: Teletronique.

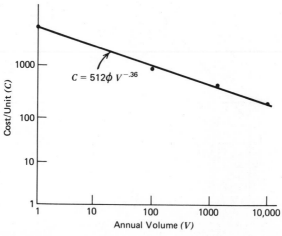

Exhibit 5.7. Production cost as a function of annual production volume: Teletronique.

the new equipment. In developing the solutions (presented in Exhibit 5.8), we assumed distributor margins of 20%, and a market potential = 120,000 units/year.

Following this analysis, a recommendation was made to Teletronique to price its
new product in the $200 range and to offer a 3-year warranty. Note that risk is
greater on the left side of the profit-functions than on the right side, suggesting that
the company might consider a price slightly higher than the model optimum.

Usually, the number of specification criteria is larger than two, requiring the cal-

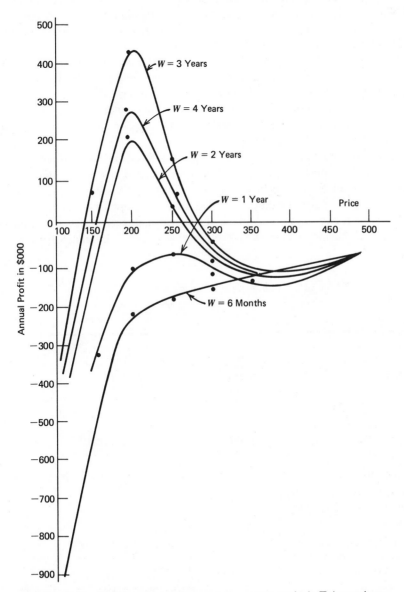

Exhibit 5.8. Profit versus price and warranty period: Teletronique.

culations to be handled by computer. Fast nonlinear programming codes are widely available and can be used here (see Appendix 9.1).

5.2.2 The Solar Cooling Example

Exhibit 5.9 gives the range of company requirements for an industrial cooling system across the entire sample of target companies in the market for solar cooling. The question used for this purpose, discussed in our measurement section in Chapter Nine, requires each company to specify a limiting value (maximum or minimum) beyond which the organization would not consider a product. The data collected with this method is used as input for the acceptance model.

The market acceptance model was developed using methods discussed in Appendix 5.2. The final model had a form that included complex interactions and trade-offs; Exhibits 5.10 and 5.11 illustrate some of the results. Here, we concentrate on trade-offs between design dimensions two at a time, while keeping other system characteristics constant. Higher order trade-offs may be analyzed with the computer, but are difficult to display.

These two figures identify system designs that lead to given market acceptance rates. These combinations of design characteristics we call iso-acceptance curves. For instance, an initial investment cost of $700/ton of cooling with a 9.5-year life define the same feasible market as a $1050 investment and a 12-year life.

These curves also suggest how much of a change in a specific system characteristic is needed to balance a change in another characteristic. Exhibit 5.10 shows that

Exhibit 5.9   Range of company requirements

	Minimum	Mean	Median	Maximum
1. Expected life of the system should be greater than:	5 years	11.6 years	10 years	20 years
2. Initial investment cost of the system per ton of air conditioning should be less than:	$100	$983	$1000	$3000
3. Warranty period should be greater than:	1 month	15.4 months	12 months	60 months
4. The number of successful installations in the field should be at least:	0	17.6	5	100
5. The annual operating cost as a percent of initial cost should be less than:	5%	14%	10%	50%

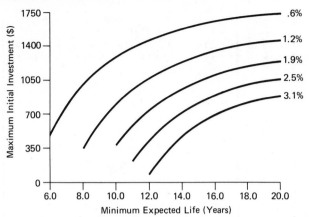

Exhibit 5.10. Solar absorption iso-acceptance trade-off curves — expected life versus initial investment.

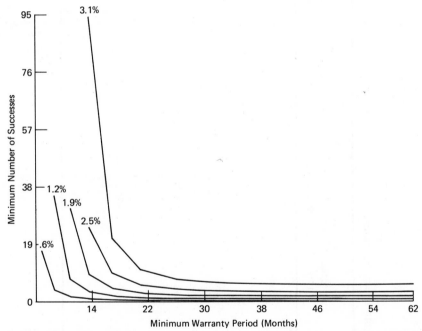

Exhibit 5.11. Solar absorption iso-acceptance trade-off curves — warranty period versus number of successes.

companies will accept higher initial investment costs for longer life. However, it is clear that as expected life increases, the additional money companies are willing to spend decreases.

Finally, the curves can be used to identify thresholds in system designs. Exhibit 5.11 shows that once the warranty period exceeds 22 months, it becomes nearly

Exhibit 5.12 Sample results of multidimensional design tradeoffs based on a computer simulation of market acceptance

	Expected life	Initial investment	Warranty period	Number of successful installations	Operating cost	Expected feasibility
Most Likely Design Characteristics Given Current Technology	15	2000	24	25	7	2.00%
Run 1	20	1000	12	5	10	2.90%
Run 2	10	1000	12	5	10	1.40%
Run 3	15	2500	12	5	10	1.25%
Run 4	15	3000	12	5	10	0.76%
Run 5	15	1500	12	5	10	3.3%
Run 6	15	2000	36	5	10	2.3%
Run 7	15	2000	12	5	10	1.8%
Run 8	15	2000	24	5	10	1.9%
Run 9	15	2000	24	100	10	2.2%
Run 10	15	2000	24	25	10	1.6%
Run 11	15	2000	24	25	5	2.4%

impossible to attract additional customers by further extensions of the warranty period.

Exhibit 5.12 displays some design trade-offs resulting from a computer simulation of market acceptance. We found that:

- Market acceptance for the new system is very low regardless of the configuration considered.
- Market acceptance is sensitive to small changes in expected system life. If the system can be expected to last 20 years vs. 15, projected acceptance goes to 2.9% from 2.0%.
- If investment/ton of cooling can be made as low as $1500/ton, acceptance can go to 3.3%.
- Small changes in operating cost as a percent of initial investment (say from 7% to 5%) lead to substantial increases in acceptance (from 2% to 2.9%).
- As long as the number of successes is in the range of 5 or more, feasibility is not substantially affected by changes in the number of successful installations.

To make best use of these results, we generally need production cost estimates (as with the Teletronique problem). These were not available as part of this project.

Instead, we got experts' estimates of likely system characteristics given present technology. Exhibit 5.13 presents this information. We need it together with the market acceptance function to infer the market acceptance rates reproduced in Exhibit 5.14.

Here the market acceptance function and a systematic analysis of trade-off curves indicates areas of high potential for design improvement. Clearly, present technology and associated high system cost are the major obstacles in the adoption of solar

Exhibit 5.13 Expert estimates of solar absorption system characteristics

	Low	Most likely	High
Likelihood of Occurrence	1/6	2/3	1/6
Expected Life (Years)	10	15	20
Initial Investment ($ per Ton)	1500	2000	2500
Warranty Period (Months)	12	24	60
Number of Successes	5	25	100
Operating Cost (% of Initial)	5	7	10
Payback Period (Years)	10	15	18

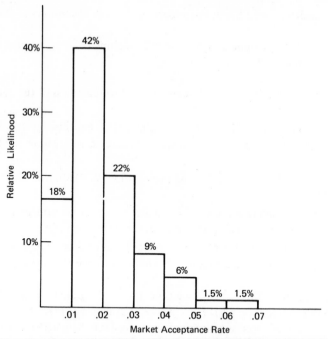

Exhibit 5.14. Simulated distribution of market acceptance for solar absorption air conditioning.

cooling in industrial markets. The market analysis points to alternative system designs that lead to similar acceptance rates. It also provides estimates of what product design modifications it might take to offset incremental initial cost.

5.3 SUMMARY

In this chapter we deal with awareness and acceptability issues. The models we propose assume that, before detailed evaluation of a product, (a) the buying organization must be aware of the product, and (b) the product must meet the organization's requirements. The uncoupling of these two effects gives industrial marketers important leverage to improve product design and communications strategy.

The problems associated with measuring and calibrating these models call for specialized methods of data collection and analysis. These methods, although technical, are not overly complicated, and rewards for performing the analysis are illustrated in two cases.

The cases illustrate that trade-off curves can be developed from survey data and that fairly simple computer-based procedures can give quantitative feedback from the market-place into the R&D function.

CHAPTER SIX

Individual
Preferences
and Choice

In a final analysis, all organizational buying behavior is individual
behavior.

Webster

So far, we have shown how to measure the market potential for a new industrial product. We have presented a procedure that can characterize potential buying organizations in terms of the composition of their buying centers. And we have addressed the issues of organizational requirements and product feasibility. Now we analyze individual choice as suggested in Exhibit 6.1.

Return for a minute to the desk-top copier case, introduced in Chapter Two. Recall that the decision to buy the Copyking 2000 followed an intricate set of activities, and resulted in a purchase commitment. One key aspect of that set of activities was that each individual in the process – Ethel, Irma and Dr. Grand – arrived at a personal position that, after discussion, was resolved in a group choice. Although the Copyking 2000 was finally ordered, two main influences, Ethel and Irma, had strong preferences for the Samurai. We, personally, were indifferent. How did these preferences develop?

Irma and Ethel had identified a number of features or product attributes offered by the Samurai and not by the Copyking. Some of these attributes were tangible; the Samurai, for example, came in a size that would match the available space. Some other attributes were more intangible such as Irma's feeling that they would get more personal attention from the Samurai company after installation. Samurai was obviously trying harder. Dr. Grand, however, did not feel that such differences were substantial enough to justify a change in manufacturer.

As Peter Drucker has pointed out, ". . . what a business thinks it produces is not of first importance. . . . What the customer thinks he is buying, what he considers 'value' is decisive – it determines what a business is, what it produces and whether it will prosper."

The aim of this Chapter is twofold. First, we assess how decision participants in industrial purchasing situations perceive products and differ in these perceptions. That information, combined with our microsegmentation results, allows development of advertising copy or sales messages targeted at issues key to each participant category.

Second, we develop models of individual preference and choice formation that are integrated into our general market response structure. These models allow the marketing decision maker to evaluate and simulate the impact of changes in product positioning on market response within microsegments.

This Chapter, dealing with the concepts and measurements associated with relating product perceptions to individual choice, is structured a bit differently from the preceding ones. Section 6.1 gives a brief, managerial overview of the key concepts. Sections 6.2-6.5 put a bit of flesh around these concepts in slightly more technical terms and illustrate all the concepts with the solar cooling example. The appendices, again, give complete technical details.

The nontechnical reader is advised to cover Section 6.1 carefully and then follow the solar cooling example results through the remainder of the chapter.

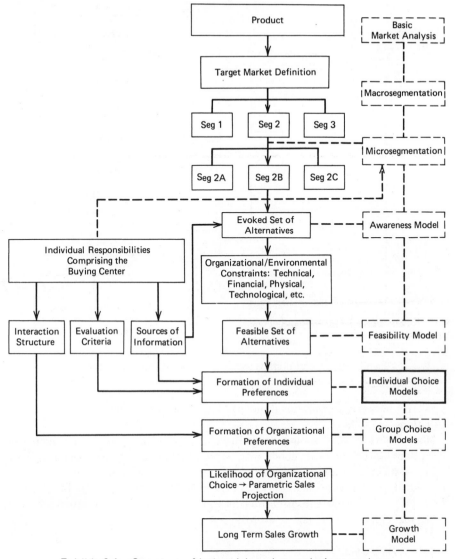

Exhibit 6.1.   Structure of industrial market analysis procedure.

6.1 INDIVIDUAL PREFERENCES AND CHOICE
FORMATION: AN OUTLINE OF OUR
APPROACH

Do industrial purchasing participants use primarily rational or emotional criteria in selecting products? Surprisingly, industrial customers use a number of so-called nonrational criteria in selecting products and services. "There exists a striking

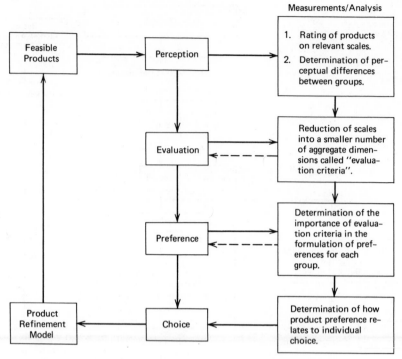

Exhibit 6.2. Major steps in formulation of individual choice.

similarity between organizational buyers and housewives in their respective choice situations." (Sheth, 1973).

Most empirical work about how individuals perceive and evaluate products has been done in the consumer goods area. Several methodologies have been proposed that investigate consumers' product perceptions and the way perceptions relate to individual preferences – Allaire (1973), Hauser and Urban (1977). Exhibit 6.2 outlines the key steps and associated measurements used here to investigate how individual preference and choice evolve.

Step 1. Perception

This step refers to how decision participants perceive a product. We assume that individuals position products in a multidimensional product attribute space. Individual i's perception of an alternative may then be thought of as the coordinates of that alternative on the perceptual dimensions. Operationally, an individual's perception of a product is provided by his ratings of the product on a set of agree-disagree scales that we call perceptual items.

Consider Exhibit 6.3. Here we have two individuals (1, 2), two products (a, b), and two dimensions (value for the money and reliability). (Here the symbol X_{1a} represents individual 1's ratings of product a.) Both individuals

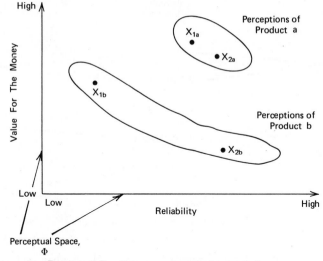

Exhibit 6.3.   Perceptual analysis example.

agree that product a is a good value for the money and quite reliable. However, individual 1 thinks product b is a good value for the money and not
very reliable; individual 2 thinks that the product is quite reliable, but not a
good value for the money.

In industrial purchasing situations product perception differences are likely
to occur among decision participants as a result of differences in background
and job responsibilities – Sheth (1973); Choffray and Lilien (1976a). Consideration of these differences is important in developing carefully targeted
communication programs. Section 6.2 is devoted to that problem.

Step 2. Evaluation

This step deals with the reduction of a perceptual space to a subspace of a
lower dimension, whose axes represent basic performance dimensions used by
individuals to assess products in this class. An individual's evaluation of a new
product may then be viewed as a point in this reduced space.

Exhibit 6.4 illustrates this concept. Here we start with six perceptual dimensions. We find that Engineers really use only three dimensions to characterize
products. A highly reliable product (+) means good service (+) and an attractive product (+) means poor environmental soundness. For Top Managers,
these latter two dimensions are essentially combined. What this means is that
Top Managers do not use as many criteria to discriminate between products
as do Engineers.

A good way to understand this concept is to relate an ordinary layman's
evaluation of wine with that of a wine connoisseur. The wine expert will
taste a number of wines and rate them from good to bad along the dimen-

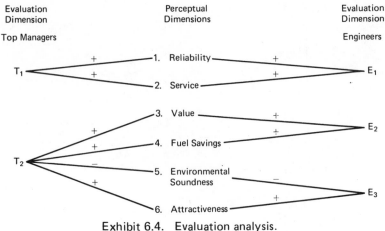

Exhibit 6.4. Evaluation analysis.

sions of color, clarity, dryness, acidity, tannin, nose (or whatever). He will also suggest that a wine has good tannin but a poor finish. Another individual, the nonexpert, only knows whether he likes the wine or not. Thus, if he gives a wine a high rating for bouquet, he probably will give it a high rating for clarity as well. That's the way he thinks. His tastes are not that discriminatory. In our jargon, the wine expert uses many evaluation dimensions, the layman uses fewer. They may both know what they like, but there are more independent controls with the wine connoisseur.

The identification of differences in evaluation criteria across decision-participant groups is important when we try to understand industrial purchasing behavior. We would not expect production and maintenance engineers to use the same criteria as members of purchasing departments when they assess product alternatives. Engineers are more concerned with product reliability and efficiency, while purchasing officers are most concerned about cost.

Section 6.3 of this chapter shows how to measure evaluation criteria and to assess differences across participant groups.

Step 3. Preference

Preference formation deals with the relationship between individual i's evaluation of a product and his preference for it.

Consider two individuals, an Engineer and a Purchasing agent, evaluating three different products, A, B, and C. Assume that we have already determined their evaluation criteria and have developed composite rating scores. Exhibit 6.5 gives the results of the evaluation scores as well as their stated product preferences.

Here we see that the engineer prefers the high reliability product, but the purchasing agent likes the high cost-value product. Through statistical analysis across several Engineers and Purchasing agents, we determine that the relative importance of Reliability to Cost for the Engineer is 5:1 (0.83/0.17 in Exhibit 6.5), but the situation is reversed for Purchasing agents. This type of result is of key importance in determining which issues should be stressed in communications programs targeted at different groups. Here you get five times the preference payout for a convincing reliability story with Engineers than with a cost-value story.

A few industrial marketing studies have addressed the relative power of models of decision participants' preference formation — Scott and Bennett (1971); Wildt and Bruno (1974); Lavin (1969). Although the analytical form of these models is of some interest, their ability to explain preference formation is most important.

Of interest, too, is the ability of models to identify and quantify differences in the relative importance of evaluation criteria across groups. In the example above, knowledge of such differences allowed differentiated positioning of a new product for each category of decision actors and permitted more accurate prediction of the impact on preferences of a product repositioning. Section 6.4 develops preference analysis methods in detail.

Step 4. Choice

Choice formation deals with the mapping of each decision participant's preferences of product alternatives into an estimate of his likelihood of endorsing each. Indeed, individuals do not always choose their most preferred product. It is usually agreed, however, that the higher an individual's preference for a product, the higher the probability that he will choose it when placed in a purchase situation.

As an example, Exhibit 6.6 takes the preference scores from our engineer in Exhibit 6.4 and relates them to his probability of choice for the products in question. Once estimated, individual probabilities of choice for the new

Exhibit 6.5 Preference formation example

	Engineer			Purchasing agent		
	Reliability score	Cost-value score	Preference score*	Reliability score	Cost-value score	Preference score
Relative Importance	0.83	0.17		0.17	0.83	
Product A	6	2	5.33	3	3	3.00
B	3	3	3.00	4	2	2.33
C	1	5	1.67	1	4	3.50

*The higher the score, the better the evaluation of the product

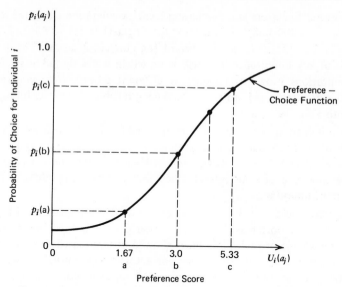

Exhibit 6.6. Relating preference to probability of choice.

product are aggregated within each participant category. This information is then fed into the group decision models discussed in Chapter Seven. The nature of the relationship between preference and probability of choice is discussed in Section 6.5.

So far, our discussion is a bit abstract. However, we have outlined the foundations for assessing individual choice formation in industrial purchasing situations. We next fill in the gaps and flesh out the procedure. Again, we illustrate each step with results from the solar cooling study.

6.2 PRODUCT PERCEPTION ANALYSIS

The analysis performed here assumes a perceptual space common to all decision participants and defined by the set of attributes for the product class under investigation. An individual's perception of a product is a vector of coordinates in this space and is provided by his rating of the product on the corresponding attribute scales.

The first step in the perceptual analysis deals with the identification of key attributes in the product class (salient attributes). Several methods can be used for this purpose. They include focus group interviews, word association and projective techniques. After a scaling procedure has been chosen, a scale is developed and tested for each attribute. Exhibit 6.7 shows the scales used in the industrial air conditioning study.

Then, a survey of a representative sample of potential customers is performed. The product is either presented physically or described in a concept statement, and

Exhibit 6.7 Perceptual scales used in the industrial air conditioning study

	Strongly disagree					Strongly agree	N/A
1. The system provides reliable air conditioning.	1 2 3 4 5 6 7						☐
2. Adoption of the system protects against power failures.	1 2 3 4 5 6 7						☐
3. The effective life of the system is sensitive to climate conditions.	1 2 3 4 5 6 7						☐
4. The system is made up of field proven components.	1 2 3 4 5 6 7						☐
5. The system conveys the image of a modern, innovative company.	1 2 3 4 5 6 7						☐
6. The system cost is acceptably low.	1 2 3 4 5 6 7						☐
7. The system protects against fuel rationing.	1 2 3 4 5 6 7						☐
8. The system allows us to do our part in reducing pollution.	1 2 3 4 5 6 7						☐
9. System components produced by several manufacturers can be substituted for one another.	1 2 3 4 5 6 7						☐
10. The system is vulnerable to weather damage.	1 2 3 4 5 6 7						☐
11. The system uses too many concepts that have not been fully tested.	1 2 3 4 5 6 7						☐
12. The system leads to considerable energy savings.	1 2 3 4 5 6 7						☐
13. The system makes use of currently unproductive areas of industrial buildings.	1 2 3 4 5 6 7						☐
14. The system is too complex.	1 2 3 4 5 6 7						☐
15. The system provides low-cost a/c.	1 2 3 4 5 6 7						☐
16. The system offers a state of the art solution to a/c needs.	1 2 3 4 5 6 7						☐
17. The system increases the noise level in the plant.	1 2 3 4 5 6 7						☐

individuals' perceptions are recorded. Preferences for product-alternatives are also obtained by methods including rankings of constant-sum paired comparisons.

In the industrial air conditioning study, three concept statements were developed, describing a standard compression system, a standard absorption system and a solar absorption system. As we discuss in Chapter Nine, use of concept statements is particularly suitable in industrial marketing since the technical complexity of products and the technical orientation of decision participants make product descriptions a meaningful basis for judgment.

Likely purchase decision participants within firms were grouped on the basis of job responsibility, consistent with a contention by Sheth (1973). Because some variation exists across companies in the responsibility corresponding to different job titles, each respondent was asked to describe his main job responsibilities. This information allowed clustering of respondents into four categories:

	Sample Size
Production Engineers	35
Corporate Engineers	23
Plant Managers	21
Top Managers	41

The aim of the perceptual analysis is to identify perceptual differences across groups of decision participants. After measurement of product perceptions, extent and source of perceptual differences are statistically assessed using a technique known as Multivariate Profile Analysis (see Appendix 6.1). This method allows:

- The assessment of average perceptual scores for each product alternative within each decision group (called a perceptual profile), and
- The overall comparison of perceptual profiles across decision groups.

Exhibit 6.8 illustrates the situations that may arise when there are only two decision groups. In situations 2 and 3 one must further identify the sources of the perceptual differences, that is, the items for which decision groups' perceptions are statistically different.

The results of the industrial cooling perceptual analysis are reproduced in Exhibit 6.9. The Heck Criterion, a measure of the inequality of perceptual profiles, indicates that the hypothesis of parallel perceptual profiles across decision groups can be rejected at the $\alpha < 0.10$ level for each product alternative. The F-ratio for the absorption system suggests differences in profile level across decision groups.

Hence, our analysis suggests important perceptual differences across decision categories for each cooling system. To identify the sources of that variation, we use analysis of variance.

That analysis shows that Production Engineers perceive the solar system more as an energy-saving system than do Plant Managers. They also feel more strongly that it conveys the image of an innovative company than do Top Managers. And they feel it uses available unproductive areas more than do Corporate Engineers — see Choffray (1977).

By aggregating the groups further, we isolated the following interesting patterns of perceptions: Engineers, compared to Managers, feel the solar system:

- offers less protection against power failures and fuel rationing;
- reflects better the image of an innovative company;
- offers less opportunity to reduce pollution;
- is more conducive to energy savings;

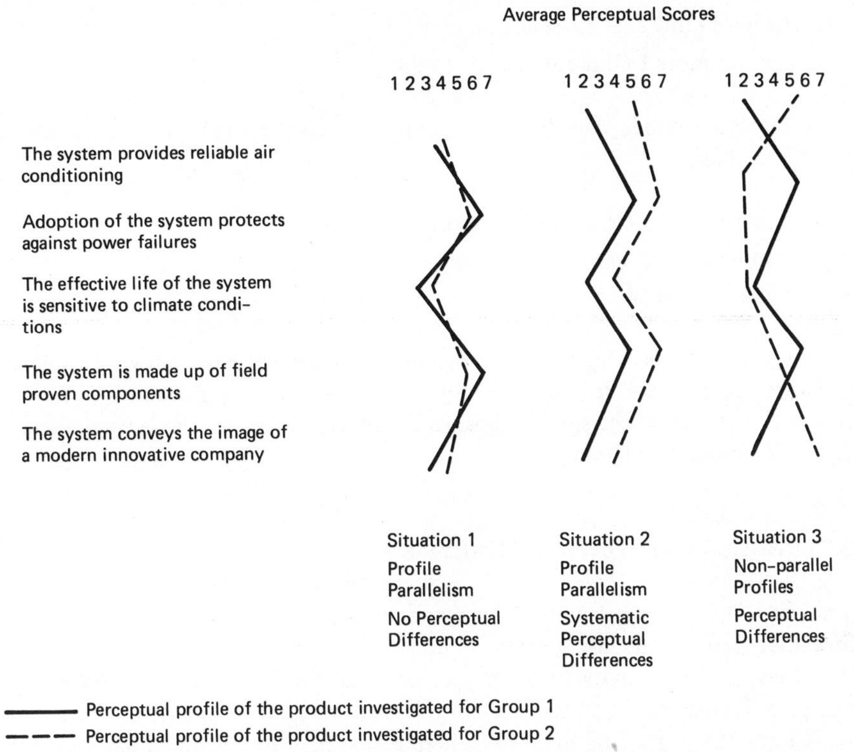

1 2 3 4 5 6 7   1 2 3 4 5 6 7   1 2 3 4 5 6 7

The system provides reliable air conditioning

Adoption of the system protects against power failures

The effective life of the system is sensitive to climate conditions

The system is made up of field proven components

The system conveys the image of a modern innovative company

Situation 1	Situation 2	Situation 3
Profile Parallelism	Profile Parallelism	Non-parallel Profiles
No Perceptual Differences	Systematic Perceptual Differences	Perceptual Differences

——————— Perceptual profile of the product investigated for Group 1
— — — — Perceptual profile of the product investigated for Group 2

Exhibit 6.8. The concept of multivariate profile analysis.

Exhibit 6.9 Multivariate profile analysis for perceptual differences across categories of decision participants

Product concept	Heck criterion for profile parallelism	F-ratio for difference in profile level
Compression System	.294** (S = 3, M = 6, N = 52)	.905 (3,121)
Absorption System	.266* (S = 3, M = 6, N = 51)	2.493* (3,119)
Solar Absorption System	.254* (S = 3, M = 6, N = 50)	.808 (3,118)

*Significant at .10 level
**Significant at .05 level
(This means that at the .10 level, none of the group profiles are parallel and the levels are significantly different for the absorption system.)

- results less in low cost air conditioning;
- contributes more to noise reduction in the plant.

On the other hand, plant personnel, compared to corporate personnel, view the solar system as

- more made up of field proven components;
- more vulnerable to weather damage;
- more state of the art.

Thus, our analysis suggests that perceptual differences exist between categories of participants. These differences point to areas of potential resistance to the solar concept in specific decision groups, and provide input to the development of diversified marketing strategies.

6.3 PRODUCT EVALUATION ANALYSIS

The last section emphasized the importance of identifying the set of product attributes that participants use to assess choice alternatives. When placed in decision situations, however, individuals tend to organize their perceptions hierarchically, grouping various sets of attributes into a few, composite *evaluation criteria*. As Hauser (1975) notes, the hypothesis here is not that an individual has an explicit method to perform such a reduction, but that resulting choice behavior can be described by this process.

We define the evaluation space common to a group of individuals as an R-dimensional subspace approximately spanning the original (K-dimensional) product attribute space ($R < K$). The coordinate axes in this evaluation space are independent. They express how individuals in that group structure basic product attributes into a higher order evaluation dimension. An individual's evaluation of a product may then be viewed as a vector of coordinates in this reduced space.

There are several reasons why such a reduction should be performed before modeling individual choice. First, individuals have limited cognitive capabilities. They can only process a little information simultaneously — Miller (1956). Second, a major objective of our methodology is to elicit creativity in the development of new industrial products. Reduction allows marketers to understand better how decision participants structure perceptions. One can then "visualize" the choice process by geometrically representing product evaluations in the reduced space. Exhibit 6.10 provides the positioning of the three industrial air conditioning systems in the hypothetical evaluation space.

Here, we display two evaluation criteria. The horizontal one is a composite of cost and expected life. Solar is perceived as very costly, but carries with it a connotation of long life. The absorption system is perceived as less costly and lasting longer, but the compression system is the cheapest and shortest-lived.

The vertical dimension is a composite of energy saving and operating cost. The

Exhibit 6.10 Hypothetical evaluation structure for industrial air conditioning systems

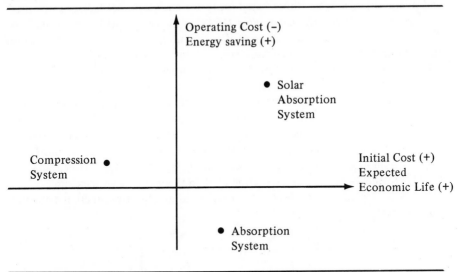

Share of first preferences:
  Compression System : 60%
  Absorption System   : 26%
  Solar Absorption
  System   : 14%

absorption system is perceived as being the least energy saving with the highest operating cost, but the solar system is at the other end of the spectrum.

The display of first preference share at the bottom of the exhibit (read: "60% of the people for whom compression was feasible stated that it was their first choice.") gives some hints about how the positions on these dimensions relate to choice. More about that later.

Two problems concern us here. First, how can we derive the evaluation criteria common to a group of individuals? Second, are these criteria different for different groups?

To investigate if categories of decision participants differ in the way they structure basic attributes into higher-order evaluation dimensions, we assume that individuals in a given category are homogeneous in that respect. Our methodology, then, addresses two questions:

- First, is the dimensionality of the evaluation space the same for different categories of decision participants? Do different groups use the same number of criteria in assessing product alternatives?

- Second, assuming equal dimensionality among different groups, are the evaluation criteria the same?

Several analytical methods can be used to derive evaluation criteria. Decomposition models such as those based on nonmetric multidimensional scaling methods and composition models, those based on factor analytic procedures, can be used.

Nonmetric Multidimensional Scaling (NMS) is concerned with identifying a reduced space of product alternatives so that the interproduct distances best recover (in an ordinal sense) the perceived similarities between these products.

Let $\delta_{i\varrho}$ denote the perceived dissimilarity between product alternatives i and ϱ. This is a measure of how alternative a_i is viewed differently from a_ϱ. It can be obtained either directly or derived from distances on the original attribute scales.

What NMS does is find a configuration of points (the product alternatives) in a space of lowest dimensionality such that the ranking of inter-point distances, $d_{i\varrho}$, is as close as possible to the ranking of the original dissimilarities, $\delta_{i\varrho}$. This is called a monotonic relationship between the $d_{i\varrho}$'s and the $\delta_{i\varrho}$'s. Green and Rao (1972) provide an excellent presentation of NMS theory along with examples.

To reach their objective, NMS algorithms use as an objective function a quantity called stress:

$$\text{Stress} = \left[\sum_{i<\varrho} (\hat{d}_{i\varrho} - d_{i\varrho})^2 / \sum_{i<\varrho} d_{i\varrho}^2 \right]^{1/2}$$

where $\hat{d}_{i\varrho}$ is a distance as close as possible to the $d_{i\varrho}$, but which is monotone with the original dissimilarities, $\delta_{i\varrho}$.

For a given dimensionality the configuration retained is the one that minimizes the stress function. Nonmetric Multidimensional Scaling methods have been used with some success in industrial marketing. See for instance Ford (1975) and Gibson et al. (1972).

Factor Analysis starts with the original perceptual ratings. Its objective is to reduce the perceptual variables *linearly* into a smaller set of independent composite dimensions. Harman (1976) and Rummel (1970) provide excellent reviews of these methods.

The classical factor analysis model considers that the variance observed in each original variable is partly accounted for by a set of *common factors*, and partly by a factor specific to that variable. The common factors account for the correlations observed among the original variables.

The model can be written as:

$$x_{ki} = \sum_{r=1}^{R} a_{kr} f_{ri} + \mu_k y_{ki}$$

where

$\quad r = 1, \ldots R$ factors

$\quad i = 1, \ldots I$ individuals

$\quad k = 1, \ldots K$ original variables

So, each of the K observed variables x_k is described in terms of R (usually $R < K$) common factors f_r, and a unique factor, y_k, with weight μ_k.

The quantity a_{kr} is called a *loading*. It expresses the correlation between the hypothetical factor r and the variable k; $(a_{kr})^2$ therefore represents the fraction of the variance in variable k accounted for by factor r.

Two quantities are important in interpreting the results of a factor analysis:

• the *communality*, h_k^2, expresses the percentage of the variance in variable k accounted for by the R common factors. Hence

$$h_k^2 = \sum_{r=1}^{R} a^2_{kr}$$

• the *eigenvalue*, λ_r, represents the contribution of each factor in explaining the total variance in the original variables. Hence,

$$\lambda_r = \sum_{k=1}^{K} a^2_{kr}$$

In a specific application, it is not uncommon to extract a small number of factors (2-3) that account for the major part of the total variance (80-90%). If such is the case, the factor analysis model has been successful in identifying a smaller set of independent, composite dimensions that accurately reproduce the patterns of intercorrelations among original variables.

Here, we suggest using factor analysis to investigate the structure of the evaluation space common to a group of decision participants. Factor analysis has three main advantages over nonmetric multidimensional scaling:

• First, it provides a framework within which both objective and subjective product characteristics can be combined into meaningful evaluation criteria. NMS methods do not provide any tangible way of interpreting their dimensions.

• Second, factor analysis is suitable when the number of product alternatives is small (less than 4). In such situations, NMS solutions are typically indeterminate.

• Third, factor analysis methods provide better criteria for comparison than do other methods of reduction. We develop in Appendix 6.2 a test to assess the similarity between factors extracted from different groups. The appendix also gives the details of the product evaluation procedure.

Finally, a recent empirical study by Hauser and Koppelman (1978) concludes that factor analysis is superior to nonmetric multidimensional scaling from the standpoint of predictive ability, interpretability, and ease of use.

6.3.1 Application

In the solar cooling study (see Appendix 6.2 for the procedure) we found that the number of criteria retained by these groups differ (see Exhibit 6.11). Production Engineers and Top Managers have a three dimensional evaluation space; the other two groups have a two dimensional space. This suggests that Production Engineers and Top Managers, reported to exert more influence in the purchase of industrial air conditioning systems – see Cheston and Doucet (1976) – use more evaluation criteria to assess these alternatives.

Separate principal factor analyses were run for Corporate Engineers and Plant Managers, and for the pooled sample. A varimax rotation was performed in each case. Most similar factors were identified and their equivalence tested using the test described in the Appendix 6.2; the hypothesis of equality of the evaluation criteria used by Corporate Engineers and Plant Managers was rejected. The procedure was repeated for Production Engineers and Top Managers with similar results.

As both pairs of decision groups show different evaluation criteria let us examine these differences. Exhibit 6.12 interprets the evaluation criteria for Corporate Engineers and Plant Managers.

Managers appear to group operating costs, the system's use of currently unproductive areas, and the protection the system offers against irregularities of supplies of traditional energy sources in their first evaluation dimension. Corporate Engineers, on the other hand, include the system's first-cost, its vulnerability to weather damage and its complexity.

Exhibit 6.13 interprets factor solutions for Top Managers and Production Engineers. Here, too, substantial differences in the composition of the respective evaluation criteria of the two decision groups are apparent. Top Managers group the system's protection against power failures, its use of currently available, unproductive areas, its vulnerability to weather damage and its impact on the noise level in the plant. Production Engineers include the system's complexity and the substitutability of major components.

In sum, the evaluation space analysis performed for industrial air conditioning systems shows that groups of participants differ not only in the number of evaluation criteria they use to assess product alternatives, but also in the composition of these criteria.

Exhibit 6.11 Evaluation space dimensionality for decision participant groups

Decision participant group	Dimensionality of evaluation space
Production Engineers	3
Corporate Engineers	2
Plant Managers	2
Top Managers	3

Exhibit 6.12 Comparison of factor solutions for plant managers and corporate engineers

	Factor 1	Factor 2
Plant Managers (PM)	(+) Energy Savings (+) Low Cost a/c (+) Fuel Rationing Protection (+) Use Unproductive Areas (+) Reduce Pollution (+) State of the Art Solution (+) Modern Image (+) Power Failure Protection	(−) Field Proven (−) Reliability (+) Not Fully Tested (−) Substitutability of Components (−) Climate Sensitivity
Corporate Engineers (CE)	(+) Not Fully Tested (−) System's Cost (−) Field Proven (−) Reliability (+) Vulnerability to Weather (+) Complexity	(+) Reduce Pollution (+) Fuel Rationing Protection (+) Energy Savings (+) Modern Image

Notes:
- Based on factor loadings greater than .50 presented in decreasing order of importance.
- Underlined items appear in the corresponding group of decision participants and not in the other.
- The sign appearing on the left hand side is the loading's sign.

6.4 INDIVIDUAL PREFERENCE FORMATION

Is there a relationship between an individual's evaluation of product alternatives and his preferences? Usually, there is. We now explore methods of determining a quantitative form for that relationship.

Compaction is our term for the process of developing a quantitative relationship between product evaluations and preferences. We relate individual i's evaluation of alternative a_j (the vector X_{ij}) to his preference U_{ij} for that alternative. Analytically:

$$U_{ij} = C_d(X_{ij}; \lambda_d)$$

where λ_d is the vector of preference parameters. You can think of the λ's as weights associated with evaluation criteria.

The expression for U_{ij} implies that the form, C_d, as well as the preference parameters, λ_d, are common to all individuals in participant category d. This assumption can be relaxed, however, and we can allow for additional sources of heterogeneity within each participant category.

Exhibit 6.13 Comparison of factor solutions for top managers and production engineers

	Factor 1	Factor 2	Factor 3
Top Managers (TM)	(+) Fuel Rationing Protection (+) Reduce Pollution (+) Energy Savings (+) Low Cost a/c (+) Modern Image (+) Power Failures Protection (+) State of the Art Solution (+) Use Unproductive Areas	(+) Vulnerability to Weather (−) Reliability (+) Climate Sensitivity (+) Not Fully Tested (−) Field Proven	(+) Noise Level (+) System's Cost (+) Field Proven (−) Not Fully Tested
Production Engineers (PE)	(+) Low Cost a/c (+) Energy Savings (+) Reduce Pollution (+) Fuel Rationing Protection (+) Modern Image (+) State of the Art Solution	(+) Field Proven (+) Substitutability of Components (+) System's Cost	(+) Not Fully Tested (−) Reliability (+) Climate Sensitivity (+) Complexity

Few empirical studies have dealt with preference formation in industrial markets. Lehmann and O'Shaughnessy (1974) report significant differences in the relative importance of several evaluation criteria, both among industrial buyers and across categories of products purchased. Wind (1970) investigates source loyalty and assesses its importance in the purchasing decision for industrial components. Cardozo and Cagley (1971) analyze procurement managers' preferences for specific bids and bidders that involve different levels of risks. Hakansson and Wootz (1975) investigate a similar problem but in an international environment. Both studies note the importance of perceived risk in individual buying behavior. Wilson (1971) finds evidence of individual decision-making styles that are related to buyers' personality traits such as need for certainty, need for achievement and level of self-confidence.

There have been several assessments of the ability of attitude models to explain the way decision participants form preferences. Scott and Bennett (1971) study linear attitude models used to account for engineers' preferences for different brands of resistors. Wildt and Bruno (1974) use a linear model to predict rank ordered preferences for capital equipment. Lavin (1969) investigates the power of several models to explain the adoption of data processing equipment. Scott and Wright (1976) analyze decision participants' product evaluation strategy for component parts.

We perform two tasks here in this section. We

- develop models of individual preference formation, and
- assess the importance of differences in evaluation criteria across decision groups in the formation of individual preferences.

These two issues are linked. After selecting a single preference model, we see if we can get better insight into the process of preference formation by considering the heterogeneity we have isolated already.

6.4.1 Models of Preference Formation

We are concerned with models of preference formation that deal with multiattributed product alternatives. In our case, these attributes represent an individual's evaluation of the product on his set of evaluation criteria.

A distinction must be made between compensatory and noncompensatory models:

- Compensatory models allow trade-offs between attributes (we would be willing to pay $2000 more for a cooling system with a 10 year warranty period than for one with a 5-year warranty).
- Noncompensatory models do not admit such trade-offs. Three types of noncompensatory models are:

  1. Dominance models: these assume that when comparing alternatives, individuals identify the subset of them that dominate all others on all evaluation criteria simultaneously.

2. Conjunctive-disjunctive models: conjunctive models assert that a product to be considered for final choice has to meet minimum requirements on all evaluation criteria simultaneously. Disjunctive models evaluate product alternatives on the basis of their maximum level on some criteria. To be considered for choice a product has then to exceed the requirement on some, and not all, evaluation criteria.

3. Lexicographic models: these process attribute levels sequentially. First, product alternatives are ranked in accordance with the most important evaluation criteria. If all of them can be ranked along that criterion, the remaining evaluation criteria are not considered. However, if tied alternatives are encountered on the most important criterion, the next one is considered and so on until all are ordered or all evaluation criteria have been considered.

So, with noncompensatory models, comparisons are made criterion by criterion. Therefore, a product profile cannot be compacted into a single performance.

Compensatory models have been used extensively in marketing for analyzing consumer preferences. These models provide a single measure of preference or utility for each multidimensional product evaluation. In their review of available techniques of consumer preference determination, Hauser and Urban (1979) distinguish five such models: (1) Expectancy value; (2) Preference regression; (3) Conjoint analysis; (4) Logit; (5) Utility theoretic.

Some empirical studies of the accuracy of these models are available. Lavin's (1969) analysis of the adoption of data processing equipment suggests that, although lexicographic models describe a manager's decision processes more accurately, they are inferior to simple compensatory models in predictive ability. Allaire (1973) draws similar conclusions from his analysis of the adoption of a new consumer product. His results indicate that preference models should be estimated by statistical methods on groups of individuals sharing a similar evaluation space. Hauser and Urban (1979) could not discriminate in terms of preference recovery between complex utility models and a simple linear additive model estimated by preference regression.

Following these studies, our approach suggests that several models, some linear and some nonlinear, should be estimated, and the one that works best in terms of preference recovery, interpretability, and parsimony should be retained.

6.4.2 Application

We apply our concepts to the industrial cooling case. Earlier we found substantial differences between participant groups in the way individuals structure product attributes into higher order evaluation criteria. We now relate these perceptions, as measured by the appropriate factor scores, to preference.

We use a linear regression model for this purpose. Following an approach suggested by Urban (1977), for each category of decision participants, a regression is performed across choice alternatives and individuals. This significantly increases the number of points available for estimation.

To see if our heterogeneous results add to our understanding of preference formation and evaluation criteria importance, we perform this analysis under three different sets of assumptions:

A1: Evaluation criteria and preference parameters are the same across all decision groups.

A2: The evaluation criteria (but not preference parameters) are the same across all decision groups.

A3: Both the evaluation criteria *and* the preference parameters differ across groups.

(Note here that if our model is Preference = $a_1 F_1 + a_2 F_2$, then the a's are preference parameters and the F's are evaluation criteria.)

Assumptions A1 and A2 need an evaluation space common to all participant categories. Hence, a principal factor analysis was performed for the total sample. Three factors were retained using the parallel analysis method criterion, and a varimax rotation produced a simple structure.

The two measures of individual preferences requested in the survey — ranks and constant-sum paired comparisons — were compared and individuals inconsistent in their preference judgements were eliminated from the analysis.

Two sets of regressions were run. First, actual rank-order preferences was used as a dependent variable. Although this dependent variable is only ordinal, Hauser and Urban (1979) suggest that least-squares regression closely approximates monotone regression for integer, rank-order preference variables. Second, the constant-sum paired comparison preference data were transformed to a ratio-scale via Torgerson's (1958) method, and used as dependent variables. In both cases, factor scores were computed for each individual and each product alternative. These factor scores represent each individual's evaluation of the three alternatives and were used as independent variables.

Preference recovery (for both first preference and the actual rank order of each individual's preference) is a sensible goodness of fit measure for preference regressions — Hauser and Urban (1979); Wildt and Bruno (1974). With three alternatives, a random model would recover first preference one-third of the time and would recover full rank-order preferences one-sixth of the time.

Exhibit 6.14 summarizes the preference recovery results under all three sets of assumptions. It appears that preference recovery is best when heterogeneity of evaluation criteria and preference parameters is considered (assumption A3). First preference recovery can be compared with the percent of correct first choice predictions for a model that equally weights all evaluation criteria: 31% under assumption A1 and A2 and 35% under assumption A3.

The numerical results of the regression analysis give little intuitive information without further analysis. Choffray (1977), gives a complete display of the results. However, the resulting conclusions were quite interesting:

1. Comparing the results under A1 with A2, a test of the equality of preference parameters across all decision participants cannot be rejected at the 0.05 level.

Exhibit 6.14 Preference recovery analysis

| | Homogeneous evaluation criteria | | Homogeneous evaluation criteria | | Heterogeneous evaluation criteria | |
| | Homogeneous preference parameters | | Heterogeneous preference parameters | | Heterogeneous preference parameters | |
	Rank Order Preferences	Cst. Sum Preferences	Rank Order Preferences	Cst. Sum Preferences	Rank Order Preferences	Cst. Sum Preferences
1st Preference Recovery	.65	.63	.61	.60	.69	.66
Full Rank Order Preferences Recovery	.42	.44	.41	.39	.49	.47

130

2. Under A3, it appears that production engineers weight reliability and complexity issues heavily. This was not seen under A2. Also not seen under A2 was that this result was in a counter-intuitive direction (the more complex, the *more* the system is preferred). This result is explained by the job enhancement seen by the production engineers working with a new, challenging system.

3. Another divergence exists for Top Managers. Under A3, they make trade-offs between reliability and fuel-use efficiency. This was not seen under A2.

Hence, the preference regressions run under assumption A2 (common evaluation space) not only lead to a poorer preference recovery, but also overlook some key issues of importance in the construction of these preferences. Thus, the consideration of different evaluation criteria across decision groups leads to a better understanding of how decision participants form preferences.

6.5 ASSESSING PROBABILITY OF CHOICE

After assessing preference, we next consider product choice. The prediction of choice from individual preference scores is not a trivial problem. Preferences are often inconsistent and unstable. At best, preference scores can help us assess choice probabilities.

Let $p_i(a_j)$ denote the probability that individual i chooses product alternative a_j. We have:

$$p_i(a_j) = P_d(a_j/U_{i1}, U_{i2} \ldots U_{iJ})$$

where P_d is a function that maps preference scores ($U_{i1} \ldots U_{iJ}$) for individual i in decision group d into his likelihood of purchase $p_i(a_j)$.

This expression implies that the analytical form P_d is the same for all individuals in participant group d. This assumption, however, can be relaxed if needed.

6.5.1 Probabilistic Models of Choice

Several models of individual choice have been proposed that explicitly recognize the probabilistic nature of human choice behavior. Probabilistic theories of individual choice differ about the locus of the random element in the decision process. Luce and Suppes (1965) provide an excellent review of these questions.

In random utility models, the preference scores, or subjective utility values, undergo random fluctuations, and the choice mechanism is completely deterministic. The individual chooses the product alternative that has the highest momentary utility.

Constant utility models, on the other hand, consider that the decision rule itself is subject to randomness, but individuals' subjective evaluations of the alternatives are constant. According to constant utility models, choice probabilities are defined by a function of the distance between the preference scores of the product alternatives that form an individual's choice set.

Luce's (1959) model of individual choice is an example of the latter approach. It states that

$$p_i(a_j) = \frac{U_{ij}}{\sum\limits_{k=1}^{K} U_{ij}}, \; U_{ij} > 0$$

where $p_i(a_j)$ = probability that individual i chooses brand j

$\quad$ U_{ij} = consumer i's ratio scaled preference for brand j and the summation is taken over individual i's choice set.

A model that has received considerable attention in the marketing literature (Pessemier et al., 1971; Silk and Urban, 1978) is the multinominal logit. This model states that measures of preferences are related to choice probabilities by:

$$p_i(a_j) = \frac{(U_{ij})^\beta}{\sum\limits_{j(i)} U_{ij}^{\beta}}, \; U_{ij} > 0$$

where $j(i)$ is that set of brands that individual i considers.

Other models of individual choice used in the marketing, econometric and transportation sciences areas include multinominal probit, conditional probit, elimination by aspects, generalized extreme value (generalized logit) models and various hybrids. It is beyond our scope to deal with these different formulations here. The interested reader is referred to McFadden (1976, 1978) or Hartman (1978) for more detail.

Some statistical methods provide a direct solution to both the compaction and the individual choice probability assessment parts of the methodology. Discriminant analysis is such a method. It could be used with ranked individual preferences for the new product alternative as a dependent variable and with individual product evaluations as predictors. Classification probabilities can then be taken as estimates of each individual's likelihood of endorsing the new product, based on his evaluation.

6.5.2 Implementation: Solar Cooling Study

In our solar cooling problem, individual choice probability was estimated for the new product as well as for its main competitors and aggregated within each decision participant category. Exhibit 6.15 reproduces average probabilities of choice for each category of participants in the purchase of an industrial air conditioning system.

Exhibit 6.15   Average probabilities of choice

	Absorption System	Compression System	Solar Absorption System
Production Engineers	.03	.47	.50
Corporate Engineers	.04	.77	.19
Plant Managers	.04	.50	.46
Corporate Managers	.07	.49	.44

This information, along with the results of the microsegmentation analysis, provides the foundation for the estimation of organizational response discussed in the next chapter.

6.6 SUMMARY

This chapter presents methodology to assess how decision participants perceive, evaluate, form preferences, and make choices between feasible product alternatives.

The methodology identifies major sources of perceptual differences across decision groups as well as differences in evaluation criteria. The relationship of these differences to individual preferences is assessed.

Implications of this analysis for marketing strategy are most powerful when considered in conjunction with the microsegmentation procedure. The microsegmentation analysis shows the different patterns of involvement in the decision process, but the perceptual analysis uncovers different information needs for these microsegments.

Analysis of product perceptions across categories of decision participants allows identification of those attributes of a new product that are not perceived as management wants, so that corrective action can be taken. In the case of a solar air-conditioning system, differences in product perceptions were identified among the four categories of participants investigated and have been used for market entry strategy formulation.

Analysis of differences in evaluation criteria among categories of decision participants shows how preferences relate to product characteristics. Such analysis allows:

- Identification of potential problems in a new product's design by assessing its position relative to those of competitors on the evaluation criteria of each category of decision participant.
- The development of salesmen's presentation strategies that address the requirements of each category of decision participant.

- The simulation of the impact that changes in the new product design or positioning will have on preferences of each category of individuals.

In sum, the methodology developed here provides information for industrial product positioning decisions. It is based on sound, quantitative criteria to assess product strengths and weaknesses. Used normatively, the models allow us to assess how product positioning changes are likely to affect product perceptions, preferences and choices.

CHAPTER SEVEN

Group

Choice Behavior

It is essential in building any market research information system for industrial goods that the process
of conflict resolution among the parties and its impact on supplier or brand choice behavior is carefully
included and simulated.

Sheth

Who makes industrial buying decisions? Our literature review in Chapter One, as well as our experience with industrial markets, suggests that there are frequently several people involved. These individuals have their own preferences for organizationally feasible alternatives. Individual preferences then are translated into organizational choices.

Empirical study of joint decision making has been difficult, since neither a theoretical framework nor research tools in marketing appear geared to group decision processes. As a result, marketing practitioners and researchers have generally considered group decision making as a process that cannot be observed or measured but which must be inferred from observations of response to specific marketing stimuli. There are no formal models that we know of that are being used to characterize and understand organizational buying interaction, although some progress has been made recently in this direction — Spekman (1978), and Krapfel (1978).

What is organizational buying interaction? Return to our office copier example, where the actors are Ethel, Irma, Dr. Grand and us. After they had prepared a list of credits and debits comparing the two feasible alternatives — Samurai and Copyking — Ethel recommended the Samurai, preferring some of its features. We were indifferent. The final choice was the Copyking. What happened?

After the recommendation by Ethel, we met briefly. Dr. Grand suggested to Ethel and Irma that it would be better to stay with the same manufacturer, as the current manufacturer had a reasonable service record and we generally got a repairman within a day. A decision to switch would involve some risk that Dr. Grand did not feel was justified. What, then, did Ethel and Irma think? Put in that position, Ethel and Irma concurred and a decision was made — Copyking.

What does this show? After members of the decision unit had evaluated and expressed their own preferences for feasible alternatives, they interacted. The organizational position was no doubt important: Dr. Grand is faculty chairman and carries important weight in the process.

Here, we define the interaction process in organizational buying as those activities that eliminate conflict between individual preferences and lead to a choice for the organization. In this chapter, we seek a formal structure to characterize this process.

Refer back to the structure of our model to assess industrial market response (Exhibit 7.1). Here, we concentrate on the buying center's selection of a specific alternative from a firm's feasible set. Our goal is not to explain, but, rather, to predict organizational response to industrial marketing activities by making formal assumptions about the kind of interaction that might occur.

We model the interaction process within each microsegment of the target market for the new product. As we discussed in Chapter Four, a microsegment comprises firms that show substantial homogeneity in the composition of their decision-making units. Based on management's prior experience, one or several models of group interaction will be used to simulate decision behavior within a microsegment.

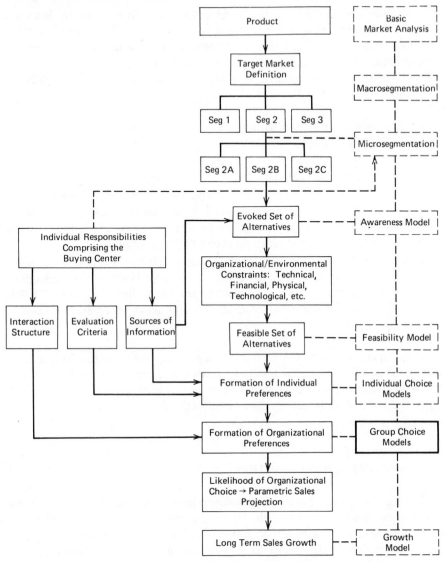

Exhibit 7.1.   Structure of industrial market analysis procedure.

7.1 CRITERIA FOR MODELS OF THE PURCHASING
   INTERACTION PROCESS

As we detail in Appendix 7.1, there is little empirical research on the interaction among organizational members who participate in the purchasing process: definitive, usable models of group choice are not available. Our objective here is to suggest criteria that usable descriptive models of group choice should satisfy and then to develop several models that meet them. We do not intend to develop a model of organizational choice that would be applicable in all product and market situations. Rather, we suggest alternative ways to structure that process, based on different assumptions about the nature of group interaction.

The following criteria are used to develop the models of purchasing decision interaction. These models should be

- *Understandable:* The general nature of the model must be easy to grasp by those involved in industrial marketing activities (e.g. the manager in charge of the new product).
- *Extendable:* The model structure must be broad enough to handle a varying number of decision participants as well as a varying number of choice alternatives.
- *Probabilistic:* Even if the preferences of all decision participants were completely determined, our knowledge about group decision processes is so limited that we can at best expect to reproduce group choice probabilistically.
- *Heterogeneous at the Individual Level:* Decision participants have different backgrounds, expectations and product evaluation criteria. They can also have different choice probabilities for organizationally feasible product alternatives. Models of organizational choice must recognize this and allow for heterogeneous individual choice probabilities.

In developing models of the organizational choice process, we implicitly assume that industrial purchases are the result of a systematic decision process. This assumption is quite reasonable for most purchases. Situations may occur, however, in which organizational choices are mainly driven by situational factors – Sheth (1973).

7.2 DESCRIPTIVE MODELS OF BUYING CENTER INTERACTION

Four models of group choice are introduced here. Each corresponds to different assumptions about the nature of the interaction process. We distinguish a Weighted Probability Model, a Voting Model, a Minimum Endorsement Model, and a Preference Perturbation Model. Appendix 7.2 reviews the analytical structure of each of these models.

7.2.1 The Weighted Probability Model

The Weighted Probability Model assumes that the firm as a whole is likely to adopt a given alternative among the feasible ones, proportional to the relative importance of those participants who choose it.

This model views the group decision as a two-step process. In step one, a member of the buying center is chosen as decision–maker, based on his relative importance in the choice process. In step two, the decision maker retained selects an alternative according to his choice probabilities. Conceptually, this model considers that a single decision participant is responsible for the group choice. Who that decision maker will be however, is unknown.

There are two interesting special cases of this model. First, *autocracy* in which a single decision participant is the only one responsible for the group choice. Second, *equiprobability,* where all decision participants have the same likelihood of becoming the decision maker.

The equiprobability model has received some empirical support, both in dyadic decision making (Davis et al. 1973) and in group decisions involving more than two participants (Davis, 1973). It has also been found to accurately describe risk shifts in group decision making (Davis, 1973).

7.2.2 Voting Model

The Voting Model attributes the same weight to all individuals involved in the decision process. It states that the probability that the organization will choose an alternative among those feasible is equal to the probability that the alternative receives the endorsement of the largest number or majority of decision participants.

Conceptually, the model states that whenever decision participants disagree as to the alternative to be adopted, the majority or a plurality rules. The model has received some empirical support (Davis, 1973). Although the equiprobability version of the weighted probability model was found to be a little more accurate than the voting model in accounting for the risk shift phenomenon, Davis concludes that, "Clearly, larger groups, and/or tasks with more alternatives are required in order to distinguish between the equiprobability and [voting] models for risk-taking tasks."

7.2.3 The Minimum Endorsement Model

This model assumes that in order to be accepted by a firm, a product alternative has to be the choice of a *prespecified* number (quota) of participants involved in the process. Conceptually, the model considers interaction in the purchasing process as a dynamic voting scheme in which participants vote over and over again until the quota is reached.

The Minimum Endorsement Model therefore states that the probability that the decision group will choose a given alternative is equal to the probability that this alternative is the one that reaches the minimum endorsement level first.

Specification of the quota, or minimum endorsement level allows considerable flexibility in the use of this model. Possible rules are *unanimity* and *simple majority.* But in no way do these two rules exhaust the possibilities offered by the model. The unanimity rule, however, appears to capture some of the essence of the multi-person choice involved in industrial purchasing situations (Buckner, 1967).

The conditional nature of the Minimum Endorsement Model allows dynamic changes of individual participant choice probabilities. Indeed, if the quota is not reached at the first vote, group members might update such probabilities on the basis of past individual or group behavior.

7.2.4 The Preference Perturbation Model

This model assumes that a group is most likely to choose the alternative that perturbs individual preferences least. The probability that a given product be chosen by a firm's buying center is inversely proportional to the number of preference shifts that would be needed to make that alternative the first choice of every decision participant.

Conceptually, this model follows from the observation that many decision groups seem to choose everybody's second choice. This mode of group behavior also recognizes the existence of satisfaction seeking decision participants rather than preference maximizers.

Thus the four models correspond to substantially different assumptions about group choice behavior. Appendix 7.3 presents the results of a simulation study in which group choice probabilities were computed in parallel with the four models for a range of decision participant categories and a range of choice alternatives.

7.3 USE OF GROUP CHOICE MODELS: PUTTING THE PIECES TOGETHER

How are these models used?

Starting with the microsegmentation analysis performed in Chapter Four, we characterize each microsegment by a set of decision participant categories, along with their relative involvement in the purchasing decision process. Let these microsegments be denoted:

$$z: z = 1 \ldots Z$$

and the volume-weighted percentage of companies in the target market that fall in each of them:

$$\Psi_z: z = 1 \ldots Z$$

The individual choice models provide the distribution of individual choice probabilities, $P_d(a_j)$, for organizationally feasible alternatives within each category of decision participant.

Then, the manager in charge of the new product specifies for each microsegment what models of multiperson interaction best reproduce his understanding of the adoption process there. This method of judgemental calibration guarantees that the manager's prior knowledge of the market is incorporated in the market assessment procedure.

For segment z his estimates might be:

Weighted Probability Model: ω_{1z}

Voting Model : ω_{2z}

Minimum Endorsement Model $\qquad$ $:\omega_{3z}$

Preference Perturbation Model $\qquad$ $:\omega_{4z}$

With $\sum_{\ell} \omega_{\ell z} = 1$ for microsegment z. In a specific case, one ω may be 1 and the rest 0, suggesting that the manager views that microsegment as quite homogeneous in terms of the interaction process taking place within potential customer firms.

If we let $S_z(a_0)$ denote the estimated market share of microsegment z that finally adopts new product a_0 we get:

$$S_z(a_0) = \sum_{\ell} \omega_{\ell z} P_g(a_0 | \ell)$$

where $P_g(a_0 | \ell)$ is the probability that a_0 is the organizational choice given interaction model ℓ.

Microsegment response can then be aggregated by computing

$$M(a_0) = M \sum_{z=1}^{Z} \Psi_z S_z(a_0),$$

where M is the market potential estimated in Chapter Three.

7.4 SUMMARY AND CONCLUSION

In this chapter we propose four classes of descriptive, probabilistic models of group choice. These models, used in conjunction with the microsegmentation results and the individual choice models, simulate industrial purchasing interaction within each microsegment.

The specification of the model that should be used in a specific situation is left up to the manager's judgement. This allows incorporation in the procedure in management's prior experience with the market or product class.

The four models proposed are by no means exhaustive. An alternative to explicit modeling of group choice is to simulate the impact of different interaction assumptions on group response. This approach is particularly suitable when neither the manager in charge of the product nor sales people have an accurate understanding of the interaction process that characterizes decision making within each microsegment, and they want to test the sensitivity of market response to various interaction assumptions.

CHAPTER EIGHT
Dynamic Extensions

It is easy to see, hard to foresee.

B. Franklin

Time is money, and many people pay their debts with it.

Josh Billings

The market assessment procedure developed so far is missing one important dimension — time. This is partially by design. It is difficult enough to assess the market at a single point in time; projecting growth is hazardous at best and is frequently astrology. The last part of our market assessment procedure incorporates a time-dependent demand projection seen in Exhibit 8.1.

Before proceeding, we need a few words about the wisdom of hindsight. After the fact it is clear that xerography was an innovation of great potential. How could

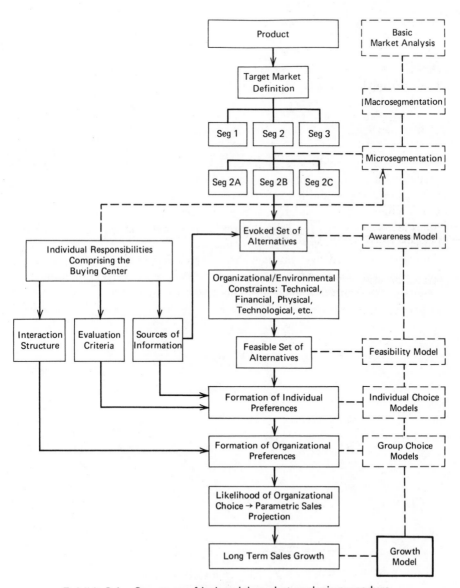

Exhibit 8.1.   Structure of industrial market analysis procedure.

some of the most astute corporations in America miss it? It will be clear, in retrospect, 10 years from now, which of the many solar technologies was to be the inevitable winner.

The field of economics has provided a number of models that have been able to trace the time-path of new innovations after the fact. But you are a product manager for bubble memories. The only difference to you whether bubble memories make it this year or next year is that if they don't make it this year, you won't have a job next year. So timing is important and you need this information before the fact.

The model that we propose here is a dynamic multimarket extension of the model developed earlier. The mathematics of growth models is somewhat arcane and many of the details of this Chapter are relegated to appendices. We will motivate the developments here, give some background in substitution theory, and then discuss the application to an emerging technology, photovoltaics.

8.1 NEW PRODUCT GROWTH AND EPIDEMICS

New products are like diseases. Some catch on and infect everyone. Others are like the swine flu of 1975 — lots of noise and no action. The difference between a product's catching on and not catching on is often subtle (though painful). Models of new product growth are realistically unstable; small changes in model conditions are often reflected in large changes in projection. This mirrors the processes modeled — these processes are inherently unstable.

Few new product innovations immediately capture their entire market potential. Usually the penetration rate, over a period of time, tends to take the form of an S-shaped curve shown in Exhibit 8.2. This process — substitution — is characterized

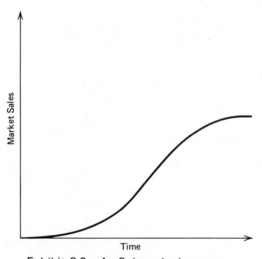

Exhibit 8.2. An S-shaped sales curve.

by a slow initial rise, followed by a period of more rapid growth, finally tapering off to a fixed saturation value.

The S-shaped hypothesis is supported by much empirical evidence. Fisher and Pry (1971) have shown that for seventeen cases of substitution there is good support for this hypothesis. Exhibit 8.3 reproduces the cases they studied and Exhibit 8.4 plots the so-called Fisher-Pry model on semilog paper, showing the fit for four technologies.

The model that Fisher and Pry use hypothesizes that the rate of adoption of a new product or process is proportional to the fraction of the old one still in use. Mathematically, if we let:

$$f = \text{fraction of the market captured by the new product}$$

and

$$t_o = \text{time when } f = 1/2,$$

we get

$$f = \frac{1}{1 + \exp(-b[t - t_o])}$$

or

$$\frac{f}{1 - f} = \exp(-b[t - t_o]) \tag{1}$$

Here b is the growth constant, characterizing the growth to potential associated with a particular technology and equation (1) is log-linear, leading to the straight line plots of Exhibit 8.4.

It turns out, however, that many different mathematical forms can be used to represent such a time pattern. Sahal (1976) discusses four separate reasons for these growth processes to conform to S-shaped trends. These reasons lead to (a) logistic formulations, (b) cumulative normal, (c) gompertz and (d) various mixed formulations. Sahal indicates that, after the fact, one or another S-shaped curve will be shown to describe the time path of sales well. However, he concludes that the

". . . value of such a model is limited because it sheds little light on the nature of the underlying mechanism. More important, such a model is likely to be of little help in prediction because of the difficulty (especially at an early stage in the process of diffusion) of choosing a specific form from a variety of S-shaped curves that would be appropriate." p. 230.

Exhibit 8.3 Takeover times (Δt) and substitution midpoints, t_0, for a number of substitution cases

Substitution	Units	Δt Years	t_0 Year
Synthetic/Natural Rubber	Pounds	58	1956
Synthetic/Natural Fibers	Pounds	58	1969
Plastic/Natural Leather	Equiv. Hides	57	1957
Margarine/Natural Butter	Pounds	56	1957
Electric-Arc/Open-Hearth Specialty Steels	Tons	47	1947
Water-Based/Oil-Based House Paint	Gallons	43	1967
Open-Hearth/Bessemer Steel	Tons	42	1907
Sulfate/Tree-tapped Turpentine	Pounds	42	1959
TiO_2/PbO-ZnO Paint Pigments	Pounds	26	1949
Plastic/Hardwood Residence Floors	Square Feet	25	1966
Plastic/Other Pleasure-Boat Hulls	Hulls	20	1966
Organic/Inorganic Insecticides	Pounds	19	1946
Synthetic/Natural Tire Fibers	Pounds	17.5	1948
Plastic/Metal Cars	Pounds	16	1981
BOF/Open-Hearth Steels	Tons	10.5	1968
Detergent/Natural Soap (U.S.)	Pounds	8.75	1951
Detergent/Natural Soap (Japan)	Pounds	8.25	1962

Note: Δt is the time from 10% to 90% takeover.

Appendix 8.3 provides an overview of the state of the art in the area of diffusion and substitution models.

Should we give up? We think not. The problem is that these models all call for a prior selection of a function form. We suggest an alternative: first, study the process in the particular market, and then model it, as appropriate. We use the same philosophy here, with the S-curve as the output, not the input, of the analysis.

Let us return to the analogy between epidemics and innovations. The key is the imitation-effect, the influence that past, satisfied users (infected) have on prospective buyers (uninfected). Marketers try to accelerate the process by constructing satisfied users through reference plants — those product installations constructed at a reduced cost to the user for the major purpose of gathering a reference for the product. This effect was measured through the influence of prior successful installations in our feasibility model developed in Chapter Five. Thus we explicitly incorporated this interaction effect; what remains is to lay out a model that by making explicit assumptions about market behavior allows estimation of new product share for each of a number of future time periods. This model is somewhat complex, however. For a simpler approach approximating this procedure consider the following.

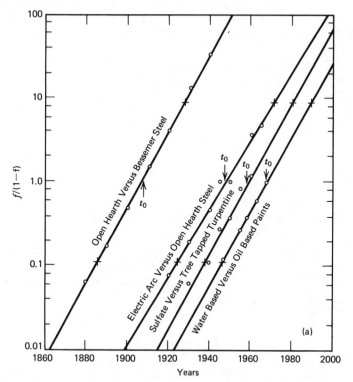

Exhibit 8.4. Fig. 2. Substitution data and their fit to model for a number of products and processes. Reprinted by permission of the publisher from "A Simple Substitution Model of Technological Change," by T. C. Fisher and R. H. Pry, *Technological Forecasting and Social Change,* Vol. 3, pp. 75–88. Copyright © 1971 by Elsevier North Holland, Inc.

8.2 A SIMPLE APPROACH AND A SIMPLE MODEL

Mansfield (1968b) has studied new product diffusion in retrospect and found that a logistic curve tracks innovations very well. In terms of the notation above, he also found that its particular growth constant could be modeled quite well as:

$$b = a_1 + a_2 \pi + a_3 S$$

where

π is the profitability or value of introducing the new product, by a customer,

S is the size of the referred customer investment, and

a_1, a_2 and a_3 are constants.

If we can estimate π and S for our new product, then the only unknown is the ultimate market penetration level. But that is a key result of Chapters Three and Five in particular.

Life is not that easy, however, and other factors should be considered in a dynamic model of industrial market behavior, including:

- Experience curve cost economies,
- Variation in market potential over time,
- Multiple macrosegments, and the like.

The diffusion model we propose incorporates customer heterogeneity and the dynamics of the marketplace drive time-varying product perception and acceptability functions. The model accounts for cost variability over time through the application of a learning or experience curve when appropriate.

Exhibit 8.5 sketches the structure of the model. The model resembles several of our organizational adoption models from Chapter Two placed side-by-side, over time. Demand potential is assumed to grow according to a (situation-specific) growth model as we discussed in Chapter Three. The two macrosegments here

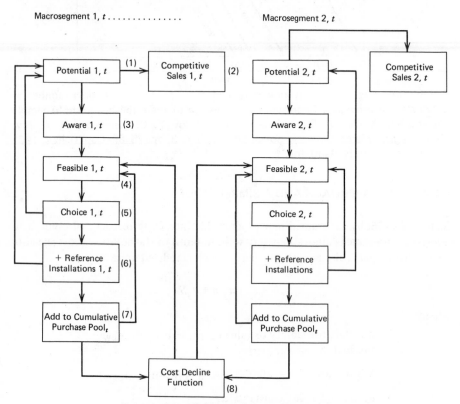

Exhibit 8.5. Outline of dynamic model.

suggest the interdependency found in a multisegment model: beer brewers are interested in successful installations of separation equipment in factories and may not be impressed with oil/water separation on diesel tankers. But, from the manufacturer's standpoint, sales anywhere add to its experience pool and learning effects may take place.

Market potential is translated into expected demand through a macrosegment model that parallels our model in Chapter Two. Step (1) calculates market potential as a dynamic input. A market potential growth model is appropriate here. That potential must be decreased by (a) sales to potential customers of the product and (b) sales of competitive products at t (Step (2)).

The market potential is factored down by the fraction of the market aware of the product. As we noted in Chapter Five, this awareness is related to the level of marketing communications.

Step (4) deals with product feasibility. In most cases, two key dimensions will be cost and prior product successes. Thus, the feasibility screen here has feedback from the cumulative purchase pool and from a cost-decline function.

Choice given feasibility is Step (5). Chapters Six and Seven deal with choice given product feasibility. For the purpose of this dynamic model, the choice given feasibility can be summarized as a fraction of potential to be purchased in any given year.

Step (6) adds reference installations to the cumulative purchase pool. The company may decide to place test versions of the product with several potential customers. This raises the level of successes and adds to the cumulative purchase pool in Step (7).

Step (8) deals with cost decline. There exists much evidence that production costs decline in a certain, well behaved manner as cumulative production increases (see Andress, 1954; Boston Consulting Group, 1970). Since the same physical product is sold to more than one market or sector, all purchases affect the cost decline function.

Thus, the first dynamic input for the model early in the life of the product would be the building of reference installations. Note the similarity here with sampling in consumer markets. This starts the marketing process going. Cost declines can be modeled as exponentially decreasing functions of the cumulative number of products sold or as a more arbitrary decline, perhaps allowing for no cost decline at all.

This structure, illustrated in Appendices 8.1 and 8.2, adds the key dimension of time to the market assessment procedure we have been developing. The final model allows for detailed sensitivity analysis not only on demand potential, but on the time path of demand as well.

For example, the effect of an advertising program, raising the level of awareness by 20% in the first year of a product's introduction, can be played out over the lifetime sales path of the product through the use of this model.

Two results of the analyses we have made so far with a simplified version of the model are especially important in the planning of marketing activities for new industrial products:

1. Delaying allocations for reference plants is unlikely to be more effective than are heavier, front-end allocations. This means when the product is ready to go, push it as hard as possible as early as you can (unless it is not fully developed or demand cannot be met).

2. If increase in market receptivity following successful installations is S-shaped (i.e., the first 3-4 successes gives proportionally more credence to the product, but installation 100 has less incremental effect than installation 99), then, an optimal market development strategy is to develop one area or segment at a time until it reaches a certain, initial size, and then develop a second segment, and the like. This sensible, roll-out strategy is the best use of marketing resources.

These results are fairly general output from our models and suggest rules to be followed if no situation-specific factor suggests otherwise.

8.3 CASE APPLICATION: PHOTOVOLTAIC DIFFUSION

This application of the dynamic model discussed here is a little different from the solar cooling case. The decision-maker is the United States government, and the product is an alternative energy device: photovoltaic cells. The problem is analogous to that faced by an industrial marketer who wishes to get a new product designed, accepted and diffused. Viewing the government from a marketing perspective can be an important aid in the management of emerging technologies.

The Energy Transition and Photovoltaics: The United States appears to be undergoing a transition from petroleum and natural gas to an eventual reliance on new sources of energy. Such a transition has occurred twice before in our history: once from wood to coal between 1850 and 1910 and then from coal to oil and gas between 1910 and 1970. This current transition is stimulated not by the discovery of a new primary fuel, as in the past, but rather by depletion of resources.

Photovoltaic cells (solar batteries) have emerged in the latter half of the 1970s as a potential source of electrical energy for the 1990s and beyond. They are soundless, nonpolluting and are powered by a free, renewable energy source – the sun.

Government and private interest in photovoltaics has been stimulated by the rising cost of producing electricity from conventional energy sources and by the fact that photovoltaic cells can become commercial now with existing technology. A major barrier to commercialization is the high current cost of these products.

In hopes of accelerating PV commercialization, the U.S. Department of Energy has created the National Photovoltaics Program. The program's objectives include lowering PV costs, demonstrating to potential users the viability of PV as an energy source, and identifying conditions under which adoption of PV will be most rapid.

Our analysis is focused on the determination of a level and allocation of government demonstration program resources and the specification of a product design/ strategy that will most efficiently accelerate PV diffusion.

PV Markets: Because of the current high cost of PV, between $12 and $20 per peak watt (about 10 times higher than cost-effective levels), current markets are limited primarily to space and remote terrestrial applications. Three important, larger macrosegments have been isolated by the PV program for intensive analysis.

1. *Agricultural Macrosegment:* Power for irrigation systems is a good application for PV because demand coincides with sunny periods – the period when PV array output is highest. This coincidence eliminates the need for storage systems. The current lack of power in crop fields as well as the possible use of PV's for crop drying as well as irrigation increases PV's attractiveness. Also, utilities are not interested because the demand in this sector is intermittent and increases load requirements in the peak summer months. PV will be cost effective here first.

   Because of its low power requirement, drip or trickle irrigation is an attractive prospect for near-term photovoltaic applications. In 1975, drip irrigation was irrigating 133,000 acres. A 30% growth rate has been predicted for drip irrigation, and by 1985 drip-irrigated acreage could reach 1,800,000. A drip-irrigation system would require about 60 peak watts per acre, making the drip irrigation market for photovoltaics about 50 million peak watts in 1985, assuming a 50% market penetration rate.

2. *Central Power Macrosegment:* Central power applications are clearly of interest because of the enormous size of the market. However, in central power, PV applications will be competitive only at very low unit prices. Even at low prices, PV's will likely be used as an auxiliary source of power in areas of the country where peak demand coincides with peak system output.

3. *Household Macrosegment:* PV arrays can become competitive in the household sector at about 50 cents per peak watt. Consumer purchase of PV, strongly influenced by actions in the building trade, will be a function of cost, convenience, reliability, and technological acceptance. Critical to adoption in this segment is development of aesthetically pleasing housing designs which use PV cells, and the development of technology for installations in existing homes.

   Acceptance of this technology by consumers can be accelerated through the federally funded PV demonstration program. Maximum impact on market demand can be achieved by the selection of sites that hold the greatest probability of demonstrating the economic benefits of PV technology.

   The household sector could account for as much as 8000 megawatts of PV arrays by the year 2000. (Bereny, 1977).

Analysis

To date, the PV concept has been field tested in the agricultural and residential sector. A pumping installation was opened for viewing in Mead, Nebraska, on July 21, 1977, during Farm Tractor and Safety Day at the University of Nebraska's experimental farm. Two groups of farmers were tested: those who had not been exposed to the exhibit (but were given a PV concept) and those who did see the exhibit, (with a before-and-after test on a cooperating subgroup). A total of 296 interviews were made.

The results (see Lilien, 1978,) can be summarized as:

- Exposure to an operational PV site (as opposed to a concept statement only) had a significant impact on the way farmers think about photovoltaics but not on their preference for the system relative to electric or combustion powered systems.
- Key factors associated with preference/perception are:

  newness and expense,

  complexity and untried concepts,

  independence from traditional fuel sources.

- Individuals who had been exposed to the site showed greater understanding and ability to comprehend system trade-offs than those who had only seen the concept.
- Exposure to the working PV site made individuals aware of the energy savings potential of the PV system.
- Expected payback of PV systems is the single most important factor limiting marketability.
- Only 3-4 demonstration sites are needed in an area to foster new product adoption and lead to positive PV perception among farmers.

A variety of current and prospective homeowners saw a model of a PV display at the State Fair in Nebraska in September, 1977. These people were contacted later with two concepts: one energy independent (isolated from the utility), the other energy dependent ("run your electric meter backward when your production exceeds your consumption").

Another, matched sample of homeowners and prospects was also contacted who had not seen the display. A total of 252 people were contacted.

The key findings for the residential sector were:

- Exposure to a PV site alleviates the need to gain expert approval before accepting PV as a viable alternative to traditional energy systems.
- Exposure to a PV site increases preference for the system.
- Exposure to an energy independent concept brings out concerns about system reliability.
- Exposure to a utility dependent concept brings out ecologically oriented concerns.
- Key factors associated with PV are:

  complexity and untried concepts

  reliability and safety

  pollution reduction and energy conservation.

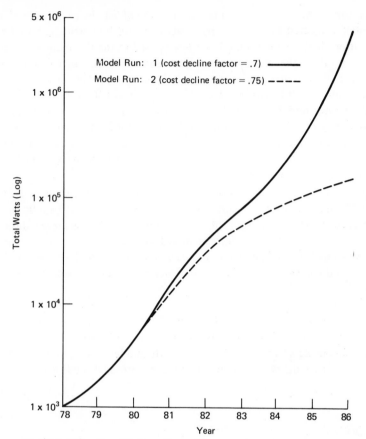

Exhibit 8.6. Sensitivity of model to changes in learning curve.

A third sector for the model — central power — was calibrated judgementally, using expert opinion to develop model parameters.

The government is proposing to spend $286 million over the next 8 years on market development. The allocation of this investment was investigated using the PV model (Appendix 8.1). The major results of initial model runs are:

1. Allocate resources, physical region by region, in agriculture first, until it gets going — then move on to residential. Finally, allocate to central power. This reflects the marketing concept: concentrate your efforts in those areas where you can do the most good for your customers. Some important members of the Department of Energy wished to go directly to Central Power, since "that's where the big market is." Our analysis shows it is best to go to Central Power after several steps.

2. Final demand projections are most sensitive to the rate of cost decline — the

learning curve effect. A change in the decline rate of 7% changed the cumulative number of projected installations by a factor of 20. Interestingly, an intensive investigation of this supply function was proposed to the Department of Energy but was cut from the program of analysis as being of insufficient importance. Exhibit 8.6 displays the results of varying the learning curve. The sensitivity of market demand to the learning factor leads to two conclusions: (1) Unless cost for PV declines rapidly over time (i.e. by a factor greater or equal to 30% for every doubling of output) the proposed level of funding is insufficient to meet the Department of Energy's price and market goals; and (2) a detailed study of the supply curve must be completed before beginning an analysis of the benefits of a government procurement program.

3. Finally, we investigated the impact of an improvement in consumer attitudes toward PV on one of two questions: perception of PV cost/benefit or PV's sensitivity to weather damage. This improvement could be achieved through a government or private sector information dissemination program. The results of this analysis are that the change causes an increase in total wattage of 13.1%, decreases end-period price by 6.1%, and increases private investment level by 11.1%.

Many other runs were made with the model. The results show that the model provides a tool to look not only at the effect of particular marketer actions but also at the proper sequencing of those actions on the rate and level of market penetration. The same type of results would be available were the model modified for another technology.

8.4 SUMMARY

This chapter added the key dimension, time, to the market assessment procedure. The development is conceptually straightforward though the procedure requires somewhat more data and assumptions to develop than do the static models.

The key point about most diffusion models is that, although they are useful descriptors after the fact, they are not valuable as predictors. With that motivation in mind, we developed an extension of the market assessment procedure that incorporated the time dimension. That extension was described in some detail and applied to the case of analyzing the market for photovoltaics.

We were also able to show some important conclusions from diffusion models about the timing and allocation of marketing program resources. In particular, we indicated that policies that (a) concentrate efforts early in the program and (b) concentrate efforts in one area or macrosegment at a time before proceeding, are most likely to be cost-effective, depending upon the shape of the imitation function.

CHAPTER NINE

Research Support and Industrial Market Information

Half the information a manager has is irrelevant for decision making. The problem is to know which half.

The last chapter completed the presentation of our model-based methodology to assess market response to new industrial products. We've said little so far about the logistics of performing such an analysis. This chapter addresses that issue.

We all hear repeatedly that the real problem in industrial marketing is the lack of information about markets. Typically, managers do not know what their market share is, who their customers are, what their needs are, who their competitors are, and so forth. Our experience with industrial markets, however, suggests that much information is actually available: companies have plenty of information, sometimes too much. But it is scattered across several departments or divisions and usually available in a form unsuitable for decision making. Most often, industrial marketing managers lack the tools to collect and process available information to make it relevant for use in their decisions.

This need for more reliable and relevant information is so important that some American companies are currently developing sophisticated product information systems.

The aim of this Chapter is to present the structure of an industrial market research and control system. Such a system comprises a set of procedures that make product-market information available in a suitable form at the time needed for decision making. We discuss how the methodology developed here meshes with that structure.

9.1 STRUCTURE OF A MARKET RESEARCH AND CONTROL SYSTEM

Exhibit 9.1 reviews the general structure of an industrial market research support system. It is derived from the Decision-Information scheme found in Montgomery and Urban (1968).

The aim of the system is to satisfy the information needs of the manager when he is faced with decision making. It translates rough market information into a more relevant form. The system may be viewed as a manager's assistant who promptly

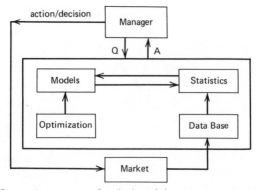

Exhibit 9.1.   General structure of an industrial market research support system.

answers questions about the market. Nowadays, such systems are computer-based. Programs are interactive, and they allow sophisticated information manipulations. The market research support system comprises four elements: (a) a data base; (b) a set of statistical methods; (c) models; (d) optimization procedures.

The *data base* is really a storehouse for the market information that the firm considers relevant for decision making. It contains both raw data, such as that collected from the market, and processed data resulting from previous manipulations. The data base's usefulness depends on its accuracy; errors in the measurement, collection and recording processes must be minimized. Cleaning activities are then an important part of data base creation.

The *statistics box* refers to programs that enable the manager both to test for the significance of relationships between product and market variables as well as to calibrate the models. A well designed market research support system should provide econometric capability, a battery of univariate and multivariate statistical methods, and time series procedures. Illustrations of several of these methods have appeared in the preceding chapters. Appendix 9.1 gives an overview of some available computer codes.

The *models box* refers to the set of models that can be used to solve a manager's problem. These models are of a predictive or normative nature according to whether the manager wants to anticipate the phenomenon of interest or control it. Several models can be used in a given situation. The best one is that which answers the manager's needs most efficiently. The methodology we developed here rests on a number of such models. We have distinguished the awareness model, the feasibility model, the individual choice models, the group decision models and the share projection models. For each of these, several analytical forms could be postulated and calibrated.

The *optimization box* refers to the use of models for decision-making improvement. Once a model has been postulated and satisfactorily calibrated, it may be used for simulation and optimization. A set of mathematical programming procedures must then be incorporated in the market research support system. Some of these are used in the framework of our methodology for product design and positioning optimization. In the first case, the feasibility model can be used in parallel with cost information to infer optimal product designs. In the second case, individual evaluation models can be used to simulate the impact of changes in product positioning on preference formation. This analysis allows consideration of positioning trade-offs in the development of differentiated marketing programs.

A characteristic of this system is the interaction among its components. In a given application of the system the manager defines the decision problem and specifies his assumptions. This step allows development of a model that incorporates hypotheses and constraints.

Parameters of the model and constraints are estimated using statistical tools based on information provided by the manager's experience or the data base. This step is called calibration. It is followed by optimization which may use mathematical programming routines to develop recommendations for actions, based on the problem specifications.

The development and use of marketing research support systems has received increasing attention during recent years (Schewe and Dillon, 1978). Decreasing computation costs coupled with greater staff capability and the wider availability of computer codes have accelerated this trend. And Little (1979a) suggests the trend is likely to continue: "Where marketing decision support systems have taken root, they have grown and become increasingly productive for their organizations."

9.2 INCORPORATING OUR RESPONSE MODEL
IN AN INDUSTRIAL MARKET RESEARCH
SUPPORT SYSTEM

How does the response model developed here combine with an industrial market research support system? So far, the book has concentrated mainly on the statistics, the models, and the optimization components of such systems. We now describe the data base needed to perform the analysis.

Exhibit 9.2 presents the major measurements needed for calibrating the industrial market response model in a typical implementation. We review each of these measurements in turn.

9.2.1 Market Measurements

The first measurement step aims at specifying the target market for the product investigated. The purpose is to narrow the scope of the analysis only to those

Exhibit 9.2 Major measurements for calibrating the industrial market response model

Data Type	Source	Measurements	Use
Hard	Market	Target Market Description	Macrosegmentation
	Organizations	Need Specification Dimensions and Organizational Requirements	Calibration of Feasibility Model
		Buying Center Composition	Microsegmentation
	Decision Participants	Product Awareness and Communication Consumption Patterns	Calibration of Awareness Model
		Product Concept Evaluations and Preferences	Calibration of Individual Choice Models
Soft	Industrial Marketing Manager	Judgmental Estimates of Interaction Process	Calibration of Group Decision Models

organizations most likely to purchase the product. This step of the analysis, which we call macrosegmentation, was discussed in Chapter Three. It contains two phases.

- *Target Market Descriptor Definition:* Relevant target market descriptors have to be selected. Managerial experience can be tapped for that purpose. For example, in the industrial cooling case, three target market descriptors were used: geographic location, size, and activity.
- *Market Potential Assessment:* Once target market descriptors are selected, secondary sources of information, mainly published sources, are used to assess market potential for the product. In the industrial cooling study, only firms that required space cooling for in-plant processes (mainly food processing, electronics, pharmaceutical, printing trades and apparel manufacture), had actual sales larger than $5 million and owned production facilities in the Sun Belt states were retained as potential customers.

9.2.2 Customer Organization Measurements

Two major types of measurements have to be obtained at the customer-organization level:

- Product specification requirements.
- Buying center composition.

Measurement Method: The development of reliable survey questions to measure the two variables of interest follows several steps.

First, a series of open ended interviews or group interviews (see Wells, 1974) are conducted with members of the buying center in a small number of target companies. Our experience indicates that such interviews with 3–5 firms generate much of the information necessary to develop prototype survey questions.

These interviews aim at identifying:

- Organizations' need specification dimensions, that is, those dimensions along which they specify purchase requirements.
- Buying center composition, that is, the individuals, along with their major organizational responsibilities, who are involved in the various phases of the decision process.

Careful content analysis of these interviews allows development of prototype survey questions for assessing organization specification requirements. For this purpose, we have used questions requesting the maximum (or minimum) value along each specification dimension beyond which the firm would reject a product out of hand. To reduce individual response bias, respondents were allowed to use any information sources in their organization (including colleagues) to provide their answers. Exhibit 9.3 provides sample questions used in the industrial air conditioning study.

Exhibit 9.3 Sample questions used to measure target companies' requirements for industrial cooling systems

---

Suppose your company has decided to install an air conditioning system in a *new* plant and has identified several different systems for consideration. In screening these alternatives, your company *will eliminate* any system,*

a. If its expected life is *less than* _____ years. NA _____
b. If its initial investment cost is *more than* _____ $/ton of cooling. NA _____
c. If it is covered by a complete warranty of *less than* _____ months. NA _____
d. If it is successfully operating in *less than* _____ other industrial installations. NA _____
e. If its annual operating cost (maintenance included) is *more than* _____% of its initial investment cost. NA _____

---

*Answer NA if the question is not relevant for your firm.

These interviews also provide decision process information needed for developing a prototype decision matrix. This measurement tool, which we discussed in Chapter Four, requests the percentage of the task responsibilities for each relevant stage in the purchasing process associated with each category of potential participants.

Second, the purchase specification questions as well as the decision matrix are administered to a small (10–15) pilot sample of target firms. Special care is taken so that several participants answer each of the two questions independently. Personal interviewing is generally used here. The information collected is analyzed to assess the convergent validity of the measurements obtained. If satisfactory, the questions are retained for the final survey. Otherwise the comments of those interviewed are incorporated and new prototype questions are developed and administered to another sample. The convergent validity of the measurements obtained within the pilot sample gives an estimate of the measurement error inherent in the procedure. This information can be used as additional input to the calibration of the feasibility model, in the implementation of the microsegmentation methodology and in assessing sample-size needs.

Sample Selection: Implementation of the final survey requires consideration of the potential market size for the product. If the number of target companies is small, say less than 100, gathering information from all of them might be considered. Often, the potential market for the product contains a large number of customers, and a representative sample has to be drawn.

Sample size determination is not an easy question. This is especially true when, as in our case, information is collected about more than one item. In such a situation, the sample size may vary substantially from one item to another for a given precision. The optimal sampling scheme may also vary across items.

A sound decision should be based on a systematic analysis of the loss incurred through a decision made on the basis of an erroneous estimate of market share for the product, say 1(e), where e denotes the error of estimate. Although the actual value of e cannot be predicted in advance, sampling theory (Cochran, 1963) enables us to find the frequency $f(e/n)$ for a given sampling method. Hence, the expected loss for a given sample size is

$$L(n) = \int 1(e) f(e/n)\, de$$

If $C(n)$ is the cost of a sample of size n where $C(n) = F + Vn$ (F = fixed cost; V = variable cost of sampling), a reasonable procedure is to choose n to minimize $C(n) + L(n)$, that is:

$$\text{Choose } n^* \text{ such that } n^* = \min_n\ [C(n) + L(n)]$$

Appendix 9.2 presents a procedure for sample size determination based on decision theory. Given sampling cost information and the industrial marketing manager's knowledge about the future success of the new product, the procedure identifies the sample size that maximizes the Expected Net Gain of Sampling.

In practice, the difficulty in specifying loss functions usually requires a more pragmatic method of sample size determination and selection (such as a two-stage sampling procedure*). Our experience suggests that samples of 130–170 companies provide stable estimates of most quantities of interest.

9.2.3 Decision Participant Measurements

At the individual decision participant level, product awareness, perceptions, and preferences for the major product alternatives available in the market are measured. Product awareness can be obtained through survey questions asking potential decision participants what product(s) or brand(s) of product they recall in the product class. Several other methods, commonly used in consumer goods marketing to measure brand awareness (Johnson, 1967) can also be used. In addition to brand awareness, media consumption patterns are measured. Both measurements are used to calibrate the awareness model.

The measurement of individual perceptions, evaluations and preferences for product alternatives requires more complex methods. In industrial markets it is often difficult to expose potential buyers to a physical product because of transportation and time. There is also a risk of prematurely alerting the competition to the development of the new product; this is more easily concealed in a concept statement.

For these reasons, the use of concept statements, describing each product in the class considered, is a reasonable alternative. Because of the technical orientation of most industrial buyers, the use of concept statements to measure individual percep-

---

*First identify a member of top management in each company in the sample using published sources of information. Second, ask him to specify those members of his organization who, in his judgement, would be most likely to participate in the purchase of a product in the class investigated. Only individuals identified at this second stage are interviewed. This increases the likelihood of reaching key decision participants.

tions and preferences seems to be as suitable in application to industrial markets as it has proven to be in consumer markets where the method has been used with considerable success (Hauser and Urban, 1977). Exhibit 9.5 presents the concept statement of a standard absorption industrial cooling system.

Individual product perceptions are recorded along a set of perceptual scales that

Exhibit 9.5. Concept statement for a conventional absorption air conditioning system (ABSAIR).

ABSAIR consists of an absorption chiller, a boiler, piping, pumps and control equipment.

To provide cooling, an absorption chiller utilizes a refrigerant (e.g. water) and an absorbant (e.g. lithium bromide) in conjunction with an evaporator, absorber, generator and condenser as diagrammed below. In the evaporator, the refrigerant, in a vacuum, is vaporized by a sprayer. As it evaporates, the refrigerant absorbs heat from the water used to cool the building. The refrigerant vapor is then absorbed by the solution in the absorber. The resulting solution is heated in the generator to drive off the refrigerant. At the condenser, the refrigerant vapor condenses and rejects heat to the environment. The refrigerant then returns to the evaporator to start the cycle again.

The boiler uses oil, natural gas, or electricity for power. The system can also be driven by commercially produced steam. The absorption chiller is then independent of the heating system unless both use a common boiler.

The absorption chiller may be located on the roof or in the building. Maintenance costs for ABSAIR are approximately 20% lower than those of compressor a/c systems. It is less efficient that compression a/c systems in that to cool a given load, ABSAIR requires between 15–20% more energy. The absorption chiller has a longer expected life than the other a/c systems. ABSAIR's economic life is around 25 years. In addition, since it has almost no moving parts, an absorption chiller is relatively quiet and vibration free.

The other elements of ABSAIR: fans, pumps, piping and control equipment are generally the same as those in compressor a/c systems.

The initial investment cost of ABSAIR may be significantly more than for compressor systems. This difference, however, tends to reduce as the installation size increases.

ABSAIR appeals to companies that need a large amount of a/c or use steam for other industrial processes and want to make additional use of that steam. ABSAIR has been typically used by hospitals and pharmaceutical plants where abundant steam exists. Currently, there are between 3000 and 5000 of those industrial a/c systems in use.

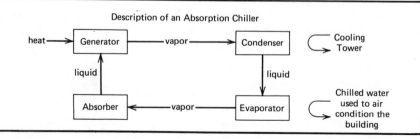

Description of an Absorption Chiller

include the relevant attributes used by individuals to assess products in the class investigated. Development of these scales follows a three step procedure:

1. A series of open-ended interviews is conducted with potential decision participants to identify all relevant product attributes.
2. Perceptual scales are developed, one for each attribute. We have used with success seven-point agree-disagree opinion statements. Exhibit 9.6 presents some of the perceptual items used in the industrial cooling study.
3. The items are administered to a small number of decision participants within pilot sample companies. Statistical analysis is then used to identify those items that exhibit significant discriminating power across product alternatives (see Choffray, 1977). Only these items are retained in the final survey instrument.

The measurement of individual preferences, in view of their instability, calls for several parallel methods. We have used both rank ordering of available alternatives and constant-sum paired comparisons. The latter method allows the development of ratio scaled preference measures that can then be used as metric input to individual preference formation models (see Torgerson, 1958).

The use of two methods of preference measurement allows identification of individuals whose preferences are inconsistent or unstable. By this, we mean that the rank ordering of the choice alternatives is different for a given individual,

Exhibit 9.6 Sample perceptual items used in the industrial cooling study

	(Circle one number for each item)		
	N/A	Strongly disagree	Strongly agree
1. The system provides reliable air conditioning.	☐	1 2 3	4 5 6 7
2. Adoption of the system protects against power failures.	☐	1 2 3	4 5 6 7
3. The effective life of the system is sensitive to climate conditions.	☐	1 2 3	4 5 6 7
4. The system is made up of field-proven components.	☐	1 2 3	4 5 6 7
5. The system conveys the image of a modern, innovative company.	☐	1 2 3	4 5 6 7
6. The system cost is acceptably low.	☐	1 2 3	4 5 6 7
7. The system protects against fuel rationing.	☐	1 2 3	4 5 6 7
8. The system allows us to do our part in reducing pollution.	☐	1 2 3	4 5 6 7

depending on which of the two measurements is used. These individuals are re-moved from the analysis before calibrating individual preference models.

Exhibit 9.7 summarizes the results of the analysis of reported preferences for industrial cooling systems. Inconsistency of preference was more frequent than we expected for a high technology product. Although they are not statistically signifi-cant, these results suggest that corporate people (both Top Managers and Corporate Engineers) are less consistent in their preference judgements than people working at the plant level (Plant Managers, Production Engineers).

9.2.4 Managerial Measurements

Development of group decision models requires assumptions about the type of interaction that takes place between decision participant categories.

The measurement methodology relies on the marketing manager's experience with the product class. The final input to the industrial response model consists of the manager's specification of those models of interaction that best reproduce his understanding of the purchasing decision process for the companies that fall in each microsegment. This procedure was discussed in Chapter Seven.

9.3 ADMINISTRATION

There are three common ways of gathering information from the sample of poten-tial customers: (1) mailed interviews, (b) personal interviews and (c) telephone interviews.

1. *Mailed Interviews* are the cheapest to administer. After a potential decision par-ticipant is identified, he is mailed a survey instrument and asked to respond. There are several important disadvantages:

   - *Low response rate:* mailed interviews returns greater than 30% are unusual. A large potential market is needed to allow this kind of low response and still have a sufficiently large sample. Nonresponse bias may be important here.
   - *Slow returns:* surveys will drift in 2, 3 and 4 months after they have been mailed. Follow-ups are usually needed and this takes even longer.

Exhibit 9.7   Individual preference stability in the industrial cooling study

	Production engineers	Plant managers	Corporate engineers	Top managers	Total
Consistent Preferences	29	19	21	30	99
Inconsistent Preferences	3	3	6	7	19
Total	32	22	27	37	118

$\chi^2 (3) = 2.14$

- *Incomplete returns:* Some questionnaires come back only partially completed.
- *Bad data:* misunderstandings and errors occur in self-administered questionnaires.

2. *Personal Interviews* correct most of the problems of mailed surveys. They can usually be done quickly, have almost a 100% response rate, and they minimize the effects of incomplete returns and bad data. The difficulties here are expense and logistics. Your potential customers may be spread all over creation and it may cost a fortune to get someone out to talk to a representative sample. Sometimes you get lucky; try arranging your personal interviewing at a trade show. With suitable incentives your potential customers may come to you to be interviewed.

3. *Telephone Interviews,* when properly designed, can give you the control of a personal interview at a cost only slightly more than a mailed survey. Contact the interview prospect by phone and elicit cooperation. Make an appointment for the (phone) interview. (Do it during business hours for more accurate information; evening interviews tend to be less serious and somewhat disorganized). Mail a copy of the survey form to the interviewee with careful instructions about what questions he should complete before the call and what data he should collect. Call him and transcribe the information by phone, answering his questions and clarifying any ambiguities as you go along. Ask him to mail back his completed form for verification. Reward him well: he has worked hard for you.

Used in this way, some very complex questions can be asked over the phone. In either the telephone interview or the personal interview case, it is essential that the interviewer be well trained. Technical questions about the product, the product class, other products, and the like will come up; the interviewer's credibility will be lost (along with the data) if he cannot handle the questions.

9.4 INDUSTRIAL MARKET RESEARCH SYSTEMS: WHERE ARE WE?

We can collect this kind of information for a new product that looks like a possible winner. But, the company may need that same information for all its product markets.

Many industrial companies currently face the problem of developing a market research information and control system. One crucial problem is the creation of a relevant data base. Two approaches are used for this purpose, depending on the type of information required.

9.4.1 Measuring Product-Market Information

The General Electric Company, in a forerunner of the PIMS program (see Abell and Hammond, 1979), has used a product-market questionnaire as a basis for developing a data base. What G.E. recognized is the need for technical support to guarantee a high level of reliability in collecting data. One important aspect of the support is to make sure that everybody in the company understands concepts like Gross Margin, ROI, and the like, and to be sure everyone answers the same questions.

Collection of accurate product-market information about industrial products has been one of the major objectives of the ADVISOR project, a joint A.N.A.-M.I.T. research program aimed at modeling industrial budgeting decisions in industrial markets (Lilien, 1979). The questionnaire developed for that study covers several hundred relevant pieces of information for industrial marketing decision making. Some of the companies in the ADVISOR study are using this data form to generate product-market data internally.

9.4.2 Collecting Behavioral Information

Behavioral information, such as the composition of buying centers and decision participants' product perceptions and preferences, requires that measurements be taken within customer organizations. Aside from the methods discussed in Section 9.2, there is increasing interest among industrial marketers for tracking attitudes and behavior over time. A customer panel can provide this data.

A panel consists of a set of potential customers that agree to provide behavioral and preference data over time. Panels usually last several months and provide a rich environment for both cross-sectional and time series data. Mortality, a major difficulty with panels, may now be controlled by the use of rolling-sample procedures similar to those discussed in Carmen (1974).

An industrial panel provides the ideal framework for studying changes in the dynamics of organizational buying, such as changes in buying center composition, changes in decision participants' preferences, and changes in organizations' need specification dimensions. It may also provide empirical support for selecting models of group choice in specific microsegments.

We feel that panels, as support for industrial marketing research, will see increasing use in the years to come.

9.5 SUMMARY AND CONCLUSION

This chapter reviewed the general structure of an individual market research support system. We discussed each of the components of such a system: optimization procedures, models, statistical methods, and data bases for use with the industrial market model proposed here.

The measurement procedures outlined here can and will be improved upon in the future. As we grow more sophisticated in our understanding of processes, both our models and associated measurements will continue to improve. In this respect, recent research, such as the ADVISOR project, provides new tools for product-market information gathering. Of great promise is the use of behavioral and purchasing panels in the industrial area.

CHAPTER TEN
Implementation and Use

The greatest homage to truth is to use it.

> R. W. Emerson

We lose much by fearing to attempt.

> S. N. Moffitt

The procedure outline here is a new product. Many readers will acknowledge that there are some interesting ideas but some, not being congenital innovators, will wait for others to try the procedures first. This is the way all new products diffuse; this chapter is designed to help make that diffusion a little easier.

10.1 THE PERSONAL NATURE OF IMPLEMENTATION

The first application in any organization is the hardest. The more an application changes the way new products are analyzed and developed in an organization, the more resistance there will be. This is natural. One way to overcome that resistance is to show personal benefits (to the associated managers) as well as organizational benefits.

As we stressed in Chapter Two, organizational decisions are personal decisions at the base. But consider the reward structure in most large companies. Exhibit 10.1 illustrates with an example.

There, the manager can choose to introduce a new product or stay with the existing line. In the first case he has a 50% chance of losing $500 thousand for the firm and getting himself fired. If he is lucky and the organization makes $1 million, he gets a promotion. In the second case, he is certain to make $100 thousand for the firm, and he will get his normal salary increase.

If the firm is large enough, the right alternative (from the firm's perspective) is to introduce the product that returns an expected $250 thousand versus $100 thousand for staying with the existing line. But the manager is putting his job on the line for a 50% chance of a promotion. Which brings longer hours, more headaches, higher tax brackets, and, probably, little measurable change in living standard. He quite reasonably chooses to stay with the current line of products.

The way to implement (sell) the modeling approach is to stress not only the expected return associated with risk reduction to the firm, but the personal return as well. This varies with the individual. If a manager is considering this approach in the first place, he has some characteristics of an innovator. Develop these. Encourage him to exploit the status associated with the use of a new procedure: show the

Exhibit 10.1   Organizational and personal rewards for risk

Choice alternative	Probability		Organizational consequences	Personal consequences
Introduce the New Product	Case 1	P = 0.5	+$1 MM	Promotion
		P = 0.5	–$500 M	Firing
Stay with the Old Offering	Case 2	P = 1.0	+$100 M	Normal Salary Increase

value of the information in allowing him to base his decisions on quantitative analysis, not guesswork. Consider professional pride — have him cooperate in writing up the application for a professional journal or industry meeting.

There are many strategies for successful implementation. Most include these five rules:

1. Involve the manager in the process from the beginning. There is an additional important benefit for using the manager as a resource early in the process — it greatly improves the likelihood of implementation.
2. Determine the expected organizational benefits from the application.
3. Determine the expected personal benefits and stress them.
4. Make certain the manager fully recognizes that the output of the research is but one input into the decision.
5. Follow-through counts. Make sure implementation is built into the research process.

Rule 4 above is especially important. Over-selling can have two consequences: if the model works poorly, no future applications are possible, regardless of whether the poor results came from screwy data, a poor questionnaire design, or any other explainable reason. If the model works well, the situation may be even worse. The manager may turn into a zealot, preaching the use of the procedure for all problems.

Care must be taken to avoid the single-tool syndrome, related in the parable that Russ Ackoff tells: A man received a screwdriver for Christmas. It was the very finest screwdriver in the whole world, and he had never had one before. He became very excited and in a short time had tightened all the screws in his house. Now there were no more screws to be tightened. The man had a file and he went around his house, filing notches in all the nails he could find. He then began tightening all the nails: new applications for his screwdriver, of course!

The output of quantitative analysis is only one input into the decision-making process. It is not a cure-all. When the analyses are properly performed and the results understood, the manager has important guidance for his decision process. But will he try it, and will he use it?

Lee Adler has noted that a good many marketing executives see marketing as an art form, and they do not want it to be any other way. This is part of the problem. And, strangely enough, this situation is especially acute in industrial markets.

Irwin Gross of Du Pont gave a speech at M.I.T. not long ago, and he spoke about this problem. Many industrial companies, he noted, promote marketing managers through the product-developer-champion approach. A scientist spends long years in school and longer years in the laboratory, slowly and carefully collecting data, performing experiments, improving his results. The scientific method of hypothesis → experiment → inference → rehypothesis and so forth is sacred.

His product succeeds. He is promoted; he is now a marketing man. What does he do? As though released from the bondage of his scientific past, he runs his business by the seat of his pants. This syndrome is so common, so widespread, notes Gross, that case-examples are superfluous.

Why is this? Our engineer-scientist (and most industrial marketing managers have technical training) has been brought up to view marketing as a qualitative discipline. ("Oh, your field is marketing? Well, in my family, my wife does the marketing! HarHarHar. . ." goes the stale cocktail-party line.) This feeling is reinforced by the sales force, those people-people who see each new client as a special case.

We view purchasing behavior as follows:

$$\text{Behavior} = \text{generality} + \text{specificity}.$$

When we try to analyze it, we can, at best, accurately assess the generality, that set of conditions that are common. The specificity — the unique elements associated with the behavior of any particular customer (random error in statistical analysis) — remains unexplained.

In the situations engineers are used to, the effect of specificity is insignificant; in marketing management systems, the effect can be quite large. The proper assessment does not compare generality to specificity in a particular situation but notes the magnitude of the generality itself. If the analysis yields important, new quantitative insight, then that should be sufficient to establish the value of the analysis.

In assessing the value of the procedures suggested here, we simply suggest that the optimist's life is the happier one: he sees the partially filled glass as half full. And half a glass can be a good deal better than none at all.

To tie together some of these thoughts we compare, in Exhibit 10.2, what the industrial marketing manager wants with what research usually gives him.

Exhibit 10.2   What the manager wants and what research gives him

The industrial marketing manager wants	Research gives him
1. Support for decisions he wants to make,	Possible support for opposite decisions,
2. In a black and white statement,	Uncertainty,
3. Immediately (if not sooner),	Research-performance delays,
4. In simple language, and	Complex statements and concepts, and
5. At no cost.	A possible budget headache.

10.2 VALUE/COST OF IMPLEMENTATION

Suppose you have produced a successful product in the laboratory — how much is market research worth? In Mansfield's and Wagner's (1975) terms, let us assume Technical Completion (see Section 1.2.4). The probability of failure at this stage

= Probability of failure in commercialization
+ Probability of economic failure and successful commercialization
= Probability of failure in commercialization given technical success (= 0.35)
+ Probability of economic failure given commercialization
x Probability of commercialization given technical success (= 0.26 × 0.66 = 0.17)
So probability of failure = 0.35 + 0.17 = 0.52.

The costs associated with these failures vary but Mansfield and Rapoport (1975) give some data from the Chemical Industry. These are displayed in Exhibit 10.3.

Precommercialization costs are roughly equal to Specification plus Prototype/ Pilot Plant = $1.36 million. Postcommercialization, which equals tooling and manufacturing plus start-up = $2.90 million. We can estimate expected losses here as

$$\begin{array}{l} \$1.36 \text{ MM} \times 0.35 = \$476{,}000 \\ \$2.90 \text{ MM} \times 0.17 = \underline{\$493{,}000} \\ \phantom{\$2.90 \text{ MM} \times 0.17 = } \$969{,}000 \end{array}$$

or roughly $1 million. The cost of applying the complete market assessment procedure, while varying from application to application is about 5% of the expected loss. Clearly only a small dent need be made in the expected losses noted above for a careful market assessment procedure to pay for itself!

These numbers have to be used with a bit of care, since investments vary considerably from industry to industry: Mansfield (1968a) found costs associated with pharmaceutical firms only about 20% of those above. The costs of early market assessment still match favorably, however: most funds are risked in the final testing and introduction stages, and it is important to eliminate unsuccessful new products before they lead to a major loss in investment.

As a way of cutting the cost of market research even further, consider Ex-

Exhibit 10.3 Cost of industrial product innovation in the chemical industry (adapted from Mansfield and Rapoport, 1975)

	($000's)	Percent
Applied Research	890	17.0
Specifications	680	13.0
Prototype/Pilot Plant	680	13.0
Total Development Cost	2,250	43.0
Tooling and Manufacturing Facilities Plus Start-Up	2,932	57.0
Total Development and Introduction Investment	$5,182	100.0%

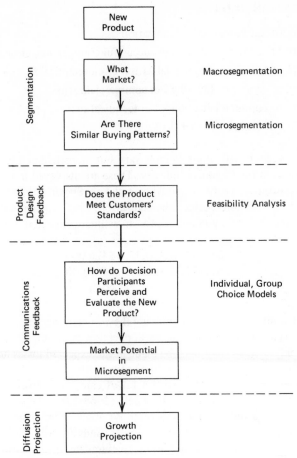

Exhibit 10.4. Conceptual separation of the procedure

Exhibit 10.5 Separation of the procedure

	Output
Microsegmentation	• Sets of organizations with similar purchasing patterns • Relative sizes of segments and segment characteristics
Feasibility	• Product design trade-offs • Guidance for product optimization
Choice Models	• Sensitivity of choices to change in positioning, communication • Suggestions for targeting personal and impersonal communication strategies
Diffusion Projection	• Projection of rate of penetration of the new product

hibit 10.4, a simplification of Exhibit 1.11. As we can see from that exhibit, the procedure developed here separates into four subprocedures. Each of them is problem-specific and cost significantly less to apply than the whole market assessment model. Exhibit 10.5 reviews the elements in that exhibit.

10.3 A CASE ILLUSTRATION: THE POTENTIAL MARKET FOR THIS BOOK

The methodology developed here has been used so far for a range of new industrial products including photovoltaic cells, computer terminals, satellite copiers, and more recently, for the book you are reading. For the purpose of illustration, we review this last application.

In a project completed in 1979 (see Smith and Rosenthal, 1979), the market for this book was assessed, using the methodology it proposes: the first step included a literature review, focus group interviews, and publisher interviews.

The book was found to have two markets — industrial marketing managers and libraries — plus a third — academics and students — that was less likely to be affected by price or repositioning. The academic-student market was therefore estimated at 300 volumes, independent of price and positioning.

A decision was made to develop a structured measurement instrument to assess response from the managerial and the library macrosegments separately.

A model of the decision process, paralleling Exhibit 1.11, was developed to aid in evaluating the results. Exhibit 10.6 gives an outline of this model. The product (this book) appeals to managers, libraries and academics and students. As we will indicate later, managers with technical and those with nontechnical orientations evaluate the book differently.

A two-step model was developed for each macrosegment: awareness, followed by choice given awareness. The intermediate models of feasibility and individual choice were combined for this (more simple) application.

Management controls include the price for the book (affecting feasibility and choice), communications level (affecting awareness) and positioning (nontechnical versus technical) which affects choice and feedback into the product offering itself.

Total market potential for this book, using multiple secondary sources, was estimated approximately as follows for each macrosegment:

100,000 — marketing managers

  1,000 — libraries

    300 — academics and students

A sample of marketing managers and libraries was selected. A total of 94 acceptable questionnaires were received from managers, 106 from libraries.

A choice model was calibrated, relating probability of respondent choice to price, book evaluation (following exposure to a concept statement) and personal variables. These choice models revealed the following:

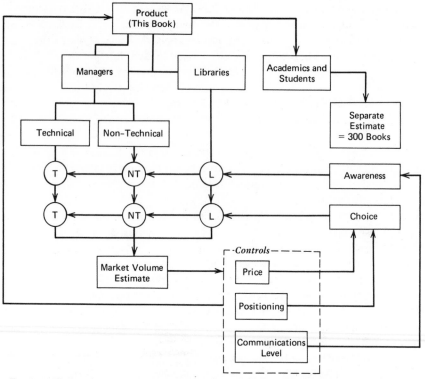

Exhibit 10.6. An operational model for assessing the market for this book.

1. Libraries value the publisher and the author (and his affiliation) most highly when making a book choice. The level of direct applicability and the technical nature is of less concern to them. Managers, on the other hand, find the technical/nontechnical nature of the book key and are less concerned with either the publisher or the author's affiliation.

2. The managers were found to be a heterogeneous group, comprising some who spend much time in R&D and Engineering and some who spend very little time there. The correlates of their probability of buying the book varied considerably.

   • The R&D group preferred a book with a technical orientation; the nontechnical group preferred a more managerial type.

   • Probability of book purchase was higher among the R&D group if:

     (a) they felt management was a qualitative field, and
     (b) their company was *not* marketing oriented.

   The reverse of each of these statements held for the nontechnical group.

3. All other things being equal, at all prices, the average likelihood of book purchase was higher for librarians than for managers.

   In addition, a key strategic alternative was considered: producing two books, one to appeal to the technical, R&D audience and another to a nontechnical audience. To evaluate this alternative (from the publisher's standpoint), a profit relationship was developed.

Cost for producing a book has a set-up component and a variable cost component. A cost equation was devised by regressing total cost against volume, estimated at several levels. Price was considered a decision variable, and the calculation of unit margin included costs for marketing, royalties, and retailer markup.

A total profit model was constructed, summing profit across market segments. A managerial input variable was the fraction of the potential population aware of the book. We use the constant k to refer to this quantity.

Consider assessing tradeoffs in a one-book versus a two-book strategy and in developing a best book price. Exhibit 10.7 gives demand estimates for the one and the two book strategy as a function of price and awareness. The two-book strategy always produces more volume. But is it more profitable?

Exhibit 10.8 gives some answers. Here we see that for $k = 0.05$, the one book strategy is more profitable; for $k = 0.35$, the two-book strategy dominates; for $k = 0.15$, however, the two-book strategy is better at some prices and the one-book at others. This exhibit also shows that, across a wide range of awareness levels and relatively independent of the selection of a one- or a two-book strategy, book price should be in the $16–$20 range.

Exhibit 10.9 compares the total profit from the book for different values of k, when book price is $17. Here we see that for $k > 0.14$, a two-book strategy is preferred, while for $k < 0.14$ a one-book strategy is better.

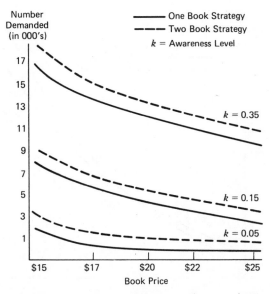

Exhibit 10.7. Number of books demanded in $15 to $25 price range under optimistic, best guess, and pessimistic awareness level assumptions (for one- and two-book strategies).

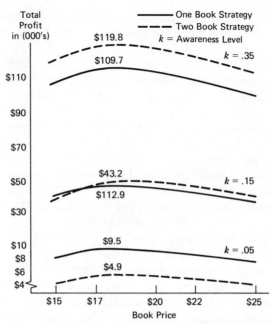

Exhibit 10.8. Total profits in $15 to $25 price range under optimistic, best guess, and pessimistic awareness level assumption (for one- and two-book strategies).

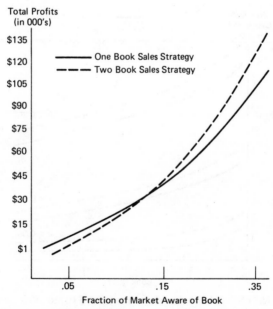

Exhibit 10.9. Total profits at different market awareness levels for one- and two-book sales strategies. Book price fixed at $17.

176

The results of this analysis have been passed on to the publisher; by the time you read this, you will know if they were implemented. The key recommendations are

- If market promotion can raise awareness to 15% or above, consider bringing out two books. Otherwise, a one-book strategy is safer.
- This book should be priced in the $16–$20 range.
- Promotional material aimed at libraries should stress the quality of the publisher and the prestige of the author.
- Promotion aimed at technical managers should stress completeness and thoroughness of treatment.
- Promotional material aimed at nontechnical managers should stress the ease of understanding and direct applicability of the material.
- Finally, a test on the title of the book suggested that "Market Planning for New Industrial Products" had the broadest appeal.

As a final exercise, the conditions under which it would be cost-effective to perform this level of research in studying the market for a new book were developed. This analysis appears to be cost-effective when projected book volume sales exceed about 15,000 copies. Thus, if a publisher is projecting sales greater than that amount, for a single volume or a series, quantitative market analysis of this type is cost-justified.

10.4 CONCLUSIONS AND UNFINISHED BUSINESS

The book has covered a lot of ground and has presented what, to some, might be challenging material. Our procedure has focused on the idiosyncratic nature of the industrial purchasing process. We have developed a procedure — called microsegmentation — to identify firms that have similar buying patterns.

We have stressed the issues of product awareness and feasibility and their relationship to market potential. The chapters on individual and group choice were directed at a careful evaluation of individual differences in industrial purchasing behavior. Finally, we addressed the problem of establishing time-varying forecasts of market potential.

As we have noted throughout, the analysis suggested here in no way replaces managerial judgment. Rather, the models and the output of the analysis, when properly used, will complement managerial effectiveness by providing more useful information on which to base decisions.

But more needs to be done. The models here are in their infancy. They need testing on a large number of cases. Competitive interactions need to be incorporated in the model structure. Group choice models need empirical testing. As we discussed in Chapter Nine, industrial buying panels may take an important step toward answering questions about group decision making. The decision matrix needs years of testing and refinement before it will be generally accepted as a valid operational tool.

There is much left to be done by the researcher and developer interested in industrial marketing problems. Much has been accomplished, however, in the development of tools to support industrial marketing planning decisions. As managers become accustomed to using these tools, they will be better able to integrate the methods of science with their intuition in making industrial marketing decisions.

APPENDIX 3.1.

Cumulative Forecasting Procedures

A3.1.1 SIMPLE MOVING AVERAGES

Let S_t = forecast for time t

X_t = actual value at time t

N = number of values included in the average.

Forecasting with moving averages can be represented as

$$S_{t+1} = \frac{1}{N} \sum_{i=t-N+1}^{t} X_i$$

$$= \frac{X_t - X_{t-N}}{N} + S_t$$

The latter expression makes it clear that the new forecast, S_{t+1}, is a function of the preceeding moving average forecast S_t. If X_t corresponds to a basic change (e.g. step change) in the basic pattern of variable X, it is clearly difficult for the method to account for that change. Note also that the larger N, the smaller $(X_t - X_{t-N})/N$ will be, so that the smoothing effect increases.

A3.1.2 EXPONENTIAL SMOOTHING

Here, using the notation above,

$$S_{t+1} = \alpha X_t + (1 - \alpha)S_t$$

where $0 \leqslant \alpha \leqslant 1$ is selected on an empirical basis by the analyst. By successive substitution, we get

$$S_{t+1} = \alpha X_t + \alpha(1 - \alpha) X_{t-1} + \alpha(1 - \alpha)^2 X_{t-2} + \alpha(1 - \alpha)^3 X_{t-3} + \ldots$$

Hence the term exponential, since the $(n + 1)$th term above is

$$\alpha(1 - \alpha)^n X_{t-n}$$

A high value of α gives past forecasts and past data (included in S_t) little weight. A low value of α weights the most recent period very little compared to all other past observations.

A3.1.3 HIGHER FORMS OF SMOOTHING

Moving averages and exponential smoothing are not very effective in the presence of complex data patterns such as trend, seasonal and cyclical patterns. Higher forms of smoothing address some of these issues.

A3.1.3.1 Double Moving Averages

This procedure starts by computing a set of single moving averages, and then computes another moving average based on the first moving average values.
  Let

$$S'_{t+1} = \text{single moving average forecast for time } t$$

$$S''_{t+1} = \text{double moving average forecast for time } t$$

$$S'_{t+1} = \frac{1}{N} \sum_{i=t-N+1}^{t} X_i$$

$$S''_{t+1} = \frac{1}{N} \sum_{i=t-N+2}^{t+1} S'_i$$

A3.1.3.2 Moving Averages with Trend Adjustments

With an increasing trend, a single or double moving average always lags the actual series. Also, the double moving average is always below the simple moving average. Thus it is possible to forecast by taking the difference between the single moving average and the double moving average and adding it back to the single moving average. This is essentially what is done when the technique of double moving averages is applied to forecasting. Specifically

$$S_{t+m} = \text{forecast } m \text{ periods in advance}$$

$$b = \text{adjustment to the forecast}$$

then

$$a = 2S'_{t+1} - S''_{t+1}$$

$$b = \frac{2}{N-1}(S'_{t+1} - S''_{t+1})$$

and

$$S_{t+m} = a + bm$$

A3.1.3.3 Double Exponential Smoothing

The method of double exponential smoothing is completely analogous to that of double moving averages. Thus

$$S'_{t+1} = \alpha X_t + (1 - \alpha)S'_t$$

$$S''_{t+1} = \alpha S'_{t+1} + (1 - \alpha)S''_t$$

$$a = 2S'_{t+1} - S''_{t+1}$$

$$b = \frac{\alpha}{1 - \alpha}(S'_{t+1} - S''_{t+1})$$

$$S_{t+m} = a + bm$$

where α is the exponential smoothing constant, and m = number of periods ahead we wish to forecast. Double exponential smoothing adapts rapidly to changes in patterns, such as step changes.

A3.1.4 ADAPTIVE FILTERING

The methods of forecasting reviewed above are based on the idea that a forecast can be made using a weighted sum of past observations. This can be written in general as:

$$S_{t+1} = \sum_{i=t-N+1}^{t} W_i X_i \text{ where}$$

S_{t+1} = forecast for period $t + 1$

    W_i = weight assigned to observation i

    X_i = observed value at i, as before

    N = number of observations used in computing S_{t+1} (and so, the number of weights required).

Adaptive filtering attempts to determine a best set of weights. The usual criterion used is that the weights should minimize the average mean squared forecasting error. The result of applying this procedure is a very simple updating rule:

$$W' = W + 2keX$$

where

$$W' = \text{the revised vector of weights}$$

W = the old set of weights

k = a scalar, learning constant

e = the forecasting error in the last period

X = the vector of observed values

The equation states that the revised weights should equal the old set of weights adjusted for the most recently observed error. The adjustment is based on the error for that forecast, the observed values and the learning constant k.

As an initial set of weights, $\dfrac{1}{N}$ will generally suffice, where N corresponds, for example, to the length of a complete cycle in the data pattern. Specification of k, the learning constant, requires more thought. Several rules of thumb are available to help in that choice (see Wheelright and Makridakis, 1978).

The procedures used to revise weights use nonlinear optimization methods and usually require computer support for implementation.

A3.1.5 BOX-JENKINS APPROACH

Box and Jenkins' approach to forecasting is based on an iterative procedure that derives a specific model from inspection of the estimated autocorrelation function and partial autocorrolation function.

Box and Jenkins propose three general classes of models for describing any type of stationary process (processes that remain in equilibrium about a constant mean level): (a) Auto Regressive (AR), (b) Moving Average (MA), and (c) mixed Auto Regressive and Moving Average (ARMA).

An AR model is of the form

$$Y_t = \phi_1 Y_{t-1} + \phi_2 Y_{t-2} \ldots + \phi_p Y_{t-p} + \epsilon_t$$

where the ϵ_t are independent, normally distributed random shocks with constant variance; ϵ_t is assumed to be independent and normally distributed with mean zero and constant variance σ^2. In more compact form:

$$\phi(B)Y_t = \epsilon_t$$

where $\phi(B) = 1 - \phi_1 B - \ldots - \phi_p B^p$ is termed the AR(p) operator and (B) is the Backshift operator: $BY_t = Y_{t-1}$

This model is called autoregressive because Y_t, the variable of interest is in some way regressed on its past values.

An MA model is of the form:

$$Y_t = \epsilon_t - \phi_1 \epsilon_{t-1} - \phi_2 \epsilon_{t-2} - \ldots - \phi_q \epsilon_{t-q}$$

where ϵ_t is the current error and $\epsilon_{t-1} \ldots \epsilon_{t-q}$ are the values of lagged errors.

In a more compact form:

$$Y_t = \theta(B)\epsilon_t$$

where $\theta(B) = 1 + \theta_1 B + \ldots + \theta_q B^q$ is the MA(q) operator.

This model implies that the variable of interest is a linear function of previous values of the error, rather than the variable itself.

An ARMA model is of the form

$$Y_t = \phi_1 Y_{t-1} + \ldots + \phi_p Y_{t-p} + \epsilon_t + \theta_1 \epsilon_{t-1} + \ldots + \theta_q \epsilon_{t-q}$$

This model represents the combination of an AR and a MA model. It expresses future values of a variable as a linear combination of both past values and forecasting errors.

In compact form, this model can be written

$$\theta(B)Y_t = \theta(B)\epsilon_t$$

with $\phi(B)$ and $\theta(B)$ polynomials in B, of degree p and q respectively.

Models of the ARMA class exhibit stationary behavior if the roots of $\phi(B) = 0$ are outside the unit circle and exhibit explosive, nonstationary behavior if the roots are inside the unit circle.

To handle homogeneous nonstationary time series, Box and Jenkins introduce the ARIMA — Autoregressive Integrated Moving Average — class of models. These models have the form

$$f(B)Y_t = \theta(B)\epsilon_t$$

where $f(B)$ is a nonstationary autoregressive operator, such that d of the roots of $f(B) = 0$ are unity and the remainder are outside the unit circle. Interested readers should refer to Box and Jenkins (1976) for additional information.

In a real life situation, choice of one of these models is made on the basis of the autocorrelation and partial autocorrelation functions of the residuals. Experience is then used to select the model that best fits the observed pattern. Some automatic procedures have also been developed to help the nonexpert in his search for the best model (Nelson, 1973). Proper model specification leads to selecting values of the parameters — the ϕ's, θ's and f's — that leave residuals randomly distributed about the model's predictions.

Completeness and versatility are undoubtedly the main advantages of the Box and Jenkins approach. In practice, however, the analytical complexity of the models and the expertise needed in selecting the most appropriate ones have limited its use to date.

A3.1.6 MULTIPLE REGRESSION

We might feel that the demand potential, Y, for a firm is related to the number of employees X_1 and the number of establishments X_2, in a linear fashion. Then we would have

$$Y_i = a_0 + a_1 X_{i1} + a_2 X_{i2} + \epsilon_i$$

where ϵ_i is a random disturbance, and $\{\epsilon_i\}$ are assumed to be independent and distributed as $N(0, \sigma^2)$. Regression analysis is concerned with estimating the parameters a_0, a_1, a_2, (call $\hat{a}_0, \hat{a}_1, \hat{a}_2$ these estimators) to minimize the sum of the squared errors of prediction. So the problem may be summarized:

Choose $\hat{a}_0, \hat{a}_1, \hat{a}_2$ so that

$$\sum_i (Y_i - \hat{Y}_i)^2 = \sum_i (Y_i - \hat{a}_0 - \hat{a}_1 X_{i1} - \hat{a}_2 X_{i2})^2$$

is minimized.

As currently used, most regression analyses are based on

- linear models (or models which can be so transformed).
- equal weighting of all data items.
- least squares criteria for parameter estimation.

Procedures exist, however, which allow (a) estimation of models nonlinear in the parameters, (b) unequal weighting of data points, and (c) bounded loss functions for parameter estimation — so called robust regression methods: see Hoerl and Kennard (1970) for some details.

The strength of regression analysis is that causal variables, including those variables of structural importance to understanding demand, can be included in a relationship. If the input data satisfy certain criteria, statistical inferences can be made and the accuracy of prediction precisely stated. The weakness of these models lies in the fact that a considerable amount of data is needed to produce significant results, and that the commonly used least squares fitting procedures are very sensitive to unusual or extreme points and weight all points equally. As with any widely used technique, regression is therefore frequently misused and misinterpreted. For those interested readers, an excellent treatment of regression analysis is found in Draper and Smith (1966).

A3.1.7 ECONOMETRIC ANALYSIS

Econometric analysis is concerned with the general interdependence of phenomena which lead to systems of simultaneous equations. These equations frequently have several variables in common.

In econometric form we might have

$$\text{Sales} = f(\text{GNP, Promotion, Business Climate Index})$$

$$\text{Promotion} = g(\text{Business Climate Index, Sales, Margin})$$

$$\text{Margin} = h(\text{Sales, Promotion, Cost})$$

As in regression analysis, the analyst must

- choose the functional form of each of the equations,
- estimate their parameters simultaneously, and
- test for the statistical significance of the results obtained.

A key advantage of econometric forecasting is that a response variable in one equation may be a predictor variable in another equation. This frees the user from having to estimate or forecast as many variables externally. The estimation of equation parameters is subtle and complex, however, compared to single equation regression models. Full information maximum likelihood and two and three stage least squares have been developed to solve such problems. Most multiple equation econometric applications are made at the corporate level for large corporations and for national economies, because of their complexity and expense. See Theil (1971); Fisher (1966), or Goldberger (1964) for more information about these methods.

APPENDIX 3.2.

More About Input-Output Analysis

Let X_i = sales of industry i

x_{ij} = sales of industry i to industry j

Y_i = final sales by industry i to consumers.

A set of input-output equations can be displayed as follows:

$$(X_1 - x_{11}) - x_{12} \ldots - x_{1n} = Y_1$$
$$-x_{21} + (X_2 - x_{22}) \ldots - x_{2n} = Y_2$$
$$\cdots \quad \cdots \quad \cdots$$
$$-x_{n1} - x_{n2} + (X_n - x_{nn}) = Y_n$$

If we define $a_{ij} = x_{ij}/X_j$ = input coefficient of product i into sector j, we get:

$$(1 - a_{11})X_1 - a_{12}X_2 \ldots - a_{1n}X_n = Y_1$$
$$\vdots \qquad\qquad\qquad \vdots$$
$$- a_{n1}X_1 - a_{n2}X_2 - \ldots + (1 - a_{nn})X_n = Y_n$$

If the set of final demands, $Y_1 \ldots Y_n$, are known, the system can be solved for the n total outputs, $X_1 \ldots X_n$. The general solution for the unknown X's can be represented as

$$X_1 = A_{11}Y_1 + A_{12}Y_2 + \ldots + A_{1n}Y_n$$
$$X_2 = A_{12}Y_1 + A_{22}Y_2 + \ldots + A_{2n}Y_n$$
$$\vdots$$
$$X_n = A_{n1}Y_1 + A_{n2}Y_2 + \ldots + A_{nn}Y_n$$

where A_{ij} indicates how much output X_i of the ith sector would be affected by a unit increase in the consumption of good j.

It can be clearly seen that, when it exists,

$$\begin{bmatrix} A_{11} \ldots\ldots A_{1n} \\ \vdots \\ A_{n1} \ldots\ldots A_n \end{bmatrix} = \begin{bmatrix} (1 - a_{11}) - a_{12} \ldots - a_{1n} \\ \vdots \\ -a_{n1} - a_{n2} \ldots (1 - a_{nn}) \end{bmatrix}^{-1}$$

Thus the matrix A_{ij} is the inverse of the matrix of input coefficients.

For there to be a set of outputs $X_1 \ldots X_n$ capable of satisfying any set of final deliveries $Y_1 \ldots Y_n$, it is necessary that all elements of A_{ij} be nonnegative. A sufficient condition for this is that in the original structural matrix:

$$\begin{bmatrix} a_{11} \cdots a_{1n} \\ \cdot \\ \cdot \\ \cdot \\ a_{n1} \qquad a_{nn} \end{bmatrix}$$

the sum of coefficients in each column (or row) $\sum_{j=1}^{n} a_{ij} \leqslant 1$ and at least one column

or row be smaller than one. If this is not satisfied, the economy will be unable to sustain itself (See Leontief, 1966).

Input-output theory can be made dynamic by considering intersectoral dependence involving lags or rates of change over time. This dependence is accounted for by looking at material stocks. The stock of goods produced by sector i which sector j must hold per unit of its full capacity output is called its capital coefficient of good i in sector j and is designated by b_{ij}. A column of capital coefficients describes the capital structure associated with a sector. The matrix

$$\begin{bmatrix} b_{11} \cdots \cdot b_{1n} \\ \cdot \\ \cdot \\ \cdot \\ b_{n1} \cdots \cdot b_{nn} \end{bmatrix}$$

describes the capital of the whole national economy. The usage of current inputs as well as capital stocks is the basis of dynamic input-output theory. A general way to describe these relationships is to use separate variables to designate the flows of inputs and of outputs absorbed or produced in different years. The balance between the output of the ith sector and utilization in year t can be described by the following differential equation:

$$X_i(t) - a_{i1}X_1(t) - a_{i2}X_2(t) \ldots - a_{in}X_n(t) - b_{i1}\frac{dX_1(t)}{dt}$$

$$- b_{i2}\frac{dX_2(t)}{dt} \ldots - b_{in}\frac{dX_n(t)}{dt} = Y_i(t)$$

If the time path of all $Y_i(t)$ are known (as well as initial values for $[X_i(t)]$), the system of n such linear differential equations can be solved for $X_i(t)$ for all i and t. In practice, discrete analogues to the equation above are usually substituted and solved. Other complexities, such as time and capacity-varying technical coefficients and accounting for idle stock (resulting from excess capacity), can be handled analytically at the expense of reduced simplicity of interpretation and solution. (See Leontief, 1966, for more details).

Development
of the Decision Matrix

A.4.1.1 THE PROBLEM

Little is known about how to measure the role played by different decision participants in industrial buying decisions. Studies typically involve the survey of a large
cross-section of firms. There, aggregate frequencies of purchasing process involvement, by industry, are computed for each of several organizational functions —
Scientific American (1969); Buckner (1967); Stevens and Grant (1975).

Some studies also measure the relative influence of different decision participants
(Weigland, 1968; McMillan, 1973; Grashof and Thomas, 1976; Silk and Kalwani,
1978). Most report the poor reliability of self-reported data about personal influence. Breaking influence into more specific areas improves the reliability of the
measurements — Patchen (1963); Corey (1971). Kelly's (1974) work tends to
support that hypothesis. He concludes that there is little disagreement between
decision participants about who in the organization had performed any of five
major functions.

Available research suggests that work aimed at measuring involvement in the
industrial purchasing process should

- Be limited to a single product at a time. This maximizes the chance of identifying
  interorganizational variation in the purchasing process without the risk of con-
  tamination from differences in product characteristics (Kelly, 1974).
- Break the decision process into managerially meaningful areas of influence. This
  improves the reliability of self-reported data (Patchen, 1963; Corey, 1971).
- Recognize that the measurement of the involvement or noninvolvement of participants in the purchasing process leads to more reliable results than the measurement of their relative influence. (Grashof and Thomas, 1976; Silk and Kalwani,
  1978).

A.4.1.2 THE DECISION MATRIX

We propose a set of criteria for a measurement instrument designed to assess
purchasing process involvement. The instrument should be:

- *Specific:* the instrument should be flexible enough to adapt to different products.
- *Simple:* the instrument should be understandable and unambiguous.
- *Robust:* the instrument should prevent nonsensical answers of the type "in our
  company all functions would be involved in all stages of the purchasing process
  for this product."
- *Economical:* the instrument should be administrable through standard marketing
  survey methods.
- *Internally valid:* independent measurements within the same firm should lead to
  similar results.

Here, we propose a "decision matrix" as such a measurement instrument. A decision matrix is a double-entry table whose rows list categories of individuals involved in the decision process in customers' organizations and whose columns list the stages in the decision process. The respondent indicates what percentage of the task-responsibilities for each stage in the process belongs to each category of decision participant in his organization. The request for constant-sum information forces respondents to specify only these decision participant categories that play a substantial role in each phase of the decision process or whose involvement in a specific phase is certain. A less constrained version of this method that did not request constant-sum information was used in several other studies. (See for instance Buckner, 1967, *Scientific American,* 1969).

Section 4.4 (and associated Exhibit 4.8) describes and illustrates the decision matrix used in the solar cooling study. As the development of the instrument showed, the decision matrix is entirely product-market dependent: the purchase of one industrial product may involve different categories of individuals and a different disaggregation of the decision process than another. These differences can be incorporated in the decision matrix.

Microsegment Formation by Cluster Analysis

The microsegmentation approach developed here uses agglomerative hierarchial clustering methods. These methods use as input a dissimilarity — or similarity — matrix in which each cell describes the degree of dissimilarity between any two entities in the sample. We first show how to develop similarity indices.

A.4.2.1 SIMILARITY MEASURES

Let x_{ijh} denote the entry in row j and column h of the decision matrix answered by company i. This value represents the percentage of the task-responsibilities associated with decision phase, h, $h = 1$ . . . H, associated with participant j, $j = 1$ . . . J, in the adoption process for company i, $i = 1$ . . . I. We have:

$$x_{ijh} \geqslant 0 \text{ for all } i, j, h$$

$$\sum_{j=1}^{J} x_{ijh} = 1 \text{ for all } i, h$$

A participant category, say j, is said to be involved in phase h of the purchasing process for company i whenever:

$$x_{ijh} > \epsilon$$

Now we face the problem of defining ϵ. Two possible choices are:

- We can set $\epsilon = 0$. This would be reasonable in view of the request in the decision matrix for constant sum estimates of involvement in each phase of the decision process. Respondents are actually forced to mention only those categories of participants whose involvement they are sure of. (Appendix 4.3 describes the convergent validity of this approach.)

- Alternatively, we can set $\epsilon = \theta$, where θ is a function of the reliability of the measurements obtained with the decision matrix. For example, θ could be set at the 95 percentile of the empirical distribution of observed discrepancies between decision process involvement estimates obtained from different individuals in the same firm. In this case $x_{ijh} > \epsilon$ is equivalent to being 95% certain of involvement by individual j in phase h in firm i.
  Let:

$$\delta_{ijh} = \begin{cases} 1 \text{ if } x_{ijh} > \epsilon \\ 0 \text{ if } x_{ijh} \leqslant \epsilon \end{cases}$$

The pattern of involvement of various groups of participants in the decision process for a given firm i can then be viewed as a $(J \times H)$ – dimensional vector Δ_i containing only 0's and 1's:

$$\Delta_i = \{\delta_{i11}, \ldots, \delta_{iJ1}, \delta_{i12}, \ldots, \delta_{iJ2}, \ldots, \delta_{i1H}, \ldots, \delta_{iJH}\}$$

One such vector characterizes each firm in the sample.

The choice of a similarity index is now equivalent to measuring the associations between two vectors of binary variables. Hence, we are mostly limited to matching coefficients, many of which have been used widely in numerical taxonomy — Sokal and Sneath (1963); Bijnen (1973).

Our analysis makes it preferable from the standpoint of interpretation to use dissimilarity measures rather than similarity measures. We therefore suggest the following dissimilarity coefficient between two firms, r and s, using the decision matrix data:

$$D^2{}_{rs} = \sum_{j,h} (\delta_{rjh} - \delta_{sjh})^2$$

This coefficient may be viewed as a member of a more general class of distance functions involving the relationships between sets of $(0,1)$ entities (Curry, 1976). As such, $D^2{}_{rs}$ satisfies the properties of nonnegativity, symmetry and the triangle inequality required of distances (Restle, 1959). It may therefore be used as metric input in any subsequent analysis.

A.4.2.2 MODIFICATION OF DECISION MATRIX DATA TO ACCOUNT FOR REPORTING BIAS

We assume above that the results in the decision matrix, $\{x_{ijh}\}$, are reported without bias, even if reported with error. In constructing the δ_{ijh} this is not a serious problem. However, if we wish to use the data in their original, metric form (for the multiperson choice model or if a different dissimilarity measure is to be constructed), we must eliminate respondent bias.

The main source of respondent bias is overstatement of the respondent's own role with the (consequent) understatement of the role of other decision participants. We need to use the following three assumptions to arrive at a simple solution to the problem.

Assumption 1: (Respondent Independence) On average, the importance of an individual (i.e., x_{ijh}) in the process, given that $x_{ijh} > 0$, should be the same independent of the category of the responding individual. This means that it should not matter who (what job category) in an organization completes the decision matrix — the importance of, say, the purchasing agent should be the same whether he completes the matrix himself or an engineer completes it.

Assumption 2: (Job-Bias Independence) The degree of personal bias associated with the reporting of importance is, on average, independent of job title. This assumption can be relaxed if the analyst can replace it with approximate estimates of individual bias (see below).

Assumption 3: (Company-Bias Independence) Similar to Assumption 2, here the degree of personal bias associated with the reporting of importance, is, on average, independent of specific company or organization. This assumption can be relaxed if multiple measures within the same organization can be developed.

Following these assumptions we proceed as follows. First, fix h, the column of the decision matrix; the procedure is applied to each column independently and sequentially. Let x_{ij} be job category j's involvement as specified by a respondent from company i.

Define the following:

$$(1) \qquad y_{kj} = \frac{\displaystyle\sum_{i \in \{k\}} x_{ij}}{\displaystyle\sum_{i \in \{k\}} \delta_{ij}} , j, k = 1, \ldots J$$

where

$\{k\}$ is the set of all respondents, $i = 1 \ldots I$

whose participant category is $k, k = 1 \ldots J$.

and

$$\delta_{ij} = \begin{cases} 1 \text{ if } x_{ij} > 0 \\ 0 \text{ otherwise} \end{cases}$$

Thus, we have a total of I respondents. Each belongs to one of J participant categories. We sum the levels of involvement and divide by the number of nonzero entries. y_{kj} can be interpreted, then, as the average involvement of decision participant category j as seen by members of decision participant category k. We now look for a transformation of $\{y_{kj}\}$, call it $\{a_{kj}\}$, to $\{y_{kj}*\}$. Our ideal, transformed $y_{kj}*$ has, by assumption, the following properties:

$$(2) \qquad y*_{kj} = y*_{wj} \text{ for all } k, w, j$$

and

$$\sum_{j} y*_{kj} = 1 \text{ for all } k$$

We apply our transformation in the following manner: Let

$$y^*_{kj} = a_{kj} y_{kj}$$

Then (2) yields:

(3a) $a_{kj} y_{kj} = a_{wj} y_{wj}$ for all k, w, j

(3b) $\sum_j a_{kj} y_{kj} = 1$ for all k

Equation (3a) represents $J^2 - J$ independent equations, and equation (3b) adds 1 independent equation. The $J - 1$ other equations are reduced to an equivalent equation by the application of (3a). Thus we have $J^2 - J + 1$ independent equations in J^2 unknowns. Assumption 2 adds the following $J - 1$ conditions.

(3c) $a_{11} = a_{22} = \ldots = a_{JJ}$

If we wish to drop assumption 2, we need to add a different set of $J - 1$ conditions. In general:

(3d) $a_{22} = k_2 a_{11}, a_{33} = k_3 a_{11}, \ldots, a_{JJ} = k_J a_{11}$

If the analyst wishes to assume that purchasing agents (Category 1) overstate their importance by 50% more than do engineers (Category 2), that is equivalent to $a_{22} = 1.5 a_{11}$ or $k_2 = 1.5$. Assumption 2 is a default condition with $k_i = 1$ for $i = 2, \ldots J$.

If we wish to drop assumption (3) through the use of multiple measures in the same organization, equation (1) is modified, redefining $\{k\}$ as:

> $\{k\}$ is the set of all respondents whose participant category is $k, k = 1, \ldots J$ and who are employed in organizations $m, m = 1, \ldots M$.

In this case, the analysis follows, with completely independent adjustments performed for each organization $m, m = 1, \ldots M$.

Now, this system will have an interpretable solution for realistic $\{y_{kj}\}$ as long as all $y_{kj} > 0$. Zero values for y_{kj} lead to unbounded solutions in the set of equations (3a). Eliminating rows and columns with zero entries (usually job categories of negligible importance in the decision process) will eliminate this problem.

Going back to our original matrix, we can now modify the x_{ij} as follows:

(4) $x_{ij}^* = \dfrac{x_{ij} a_{k(i),j}}{\sum_j x_{ij} a_{k(i),j}}$

where $k(i)$ refers to the job category that respondent i belongs to. The results of equation (4) are then a set of involvements, uncontaminated by respondent bias.

A.4.2.3 HIERARCHICAL CLUSTERING FOR MICROSEGMENT FORMATION

We now face the problem of grouping organizations, using whatever measure of interorganizational similarity we have chosen. For this purpose, we use cluster analysis.

The general problem addressed by cluster analysis is how to partition a heterogeneous set of entities — in our case, industrial firms — into mutually exclusive homogeneous subsets. To solve this problem, many cluster analytic models portray the entities as points in a metric space and search for regions in this space characterized by a high density of points. Clusters are formed from entities that are close to one another, but distant points become members of different clusters. An excellent review of cluster analysis is provided by Hartigan (1975).

The microsegmentation procedure developed here uses agglomerative hierarchical clustering methods. These methods form clusters by grouping most similar entities in the same clusters. They generate solutions that can be graphically presented as hierarchical trees or dedrograms.

Agglomerative hierarchical clustering methods have two advantages over other clustering methods. First, they do not require any information about the number or composition of clusters. Second, they provide a visual representation of intracluster formation that can help interpret the clusters.

At each stage in the clustering process agglomerative methods form new clusters that minimize some function of intercluster distances. The dissimilarity matrix is then recomputed to express the relationship between the new clusters and the remaining entities. The main difference among agglomerative clustering algorithms is found here: some define intercluster distances that assume only ordinal dissimilarity measures (see for instance Johnson, 1967); others assume an underlying metric and algebraically manipulate intercluster distances. (See for example Ward, 1963). Both classes of methods are used here.

The use of cluster analysis for industrial market microsegmentation requires that several problems be solved (Choffray, 1977). These include:

1. Tests on the sensitivity of cluster analysis results to extreme observations or outliers.
2. Tests on the nonrandomness of the structure observed in a dissimilarity matrix, and the determination of the number of clusters to be retained.
3. Determination of the nonuniqueness of the clustering solution retained.

The major steps of the microsegmentation procedure are as follows:

Step 1: Computation of the Dissimilarity Matrix
for the Macrosegment.

This step involves the computation of the dissimilarity matrix using the measure D^2_{rs} defined earlier. Each entry in this matrix expresses the difference between firm r and firm s in the composition of their buying centers.

Step 2: Identification of Outliers.

This step involves identification of outliers, organizations whose decision process bears little resemblance to that of other organizations. Inclusion of such organizations in any of the microsegments retained would reduce intrasegment homogeneity and make it harder:

- to get a good description of the pattern of involvement within the microsegment, and
- to determine the link between microsegment membership and other observable organizational characteristics.

Following Blashfield (1976), single linkage cluster analysis is used to identify outliers. This method defines the distance between a new cluster t — made up of firm n and v — and some other cluster w — as:

$$d_{tw} = \min (d_{nw}, d_{vw})$$

Hence, the quantity d_{tw} is the distance between the two *closest* members of cluster t and w.

A cluster identified by single linkage analysis is a group of entities such that every member of the cluster is more similar to at least one member of the same cluster than it is to any member of any other cluster. As a result, single linkage analysis has the tendency to form long clusters that are weakly connected. This property, called chaining, provides a powerful tool to identify firms that share little similarity with the rest of the sample. After examination of the decision process of these firms, they are removed from the analysis and their purchasing decision process is the object of a separate analysis.

For example, in the solar cooling case, 10 extreme companies were identified. They appear at the lower end of the hierarchical classification in Exhibit 4.14. Careful analysis of these 10 companies — clusters 5, 6 and 7 — eliminated them from further consideration.

Step 3: Nonrandomness of the Data Structure.

The next step concerns the nonrandomness of the data structure and the determination of the number of clusters.

This question is nontrivial. Cluster analysis methods, designed to form groups of similar entities in a data set, are very successful even when the entities are randomly generated.

As noted by Fleiss and Zubin (1960), a key defect in most clustering procedures is the absence of a statistical model. Some theoretical work has recently appeared in the literature and involves the application of graph theory to cluster analysis — Hubert (1974). Ling (1973) proposes a probability theory of cluster analysis. He recognizes, however, that no compelling argument justi-

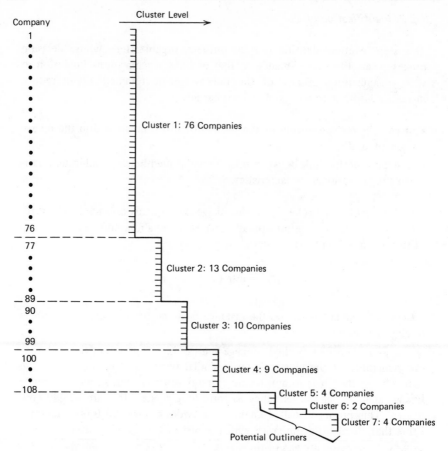

Exhibit 4.14. Single linkage cluster analysis for total sample.

fies his particular choice of model, and that in most real situations the conditions required by his model are not entirely satisfied.

In the absence of a satisfactory statistical model, simulation is recommended to investigate the nonrandomness of the structure observed in a dissimilarity matrix and to determine a statistically significant range of clustering solutions.

The idea behind the simulation approach is that a researcher is not interested in a pattern of cluster formation that does not substantially differ from that which would be obtained if the dissimilarities had been generated independently.

Fast cluster analysis programs (Dalziel, 1974) are generally available and relatively cheap to use. Moreover, it is our experience that cluster analytic solutions obtained from randomly generated dissimilarities are quite stable, so that a small number of simulations (5–10) is usually sufficient to get an estimate of the expected number of clusters and an estimate of the standard deviation of that number at various clustering levels.

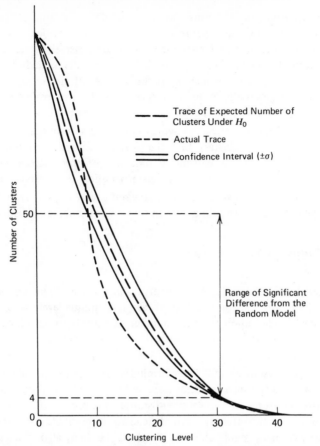

Exhibit 4.15. Results of the simulation study of the number of clusters: solar cooling study.

Exhibit 4.15 reproduces the results of the simulation analysis performed for the industrial air conditioning system microsegmentation.

This simulation involved cluster analyzing 10 dissimilarity matrices whose individual entries were generated randomly from the same empirical distribution of observed dissimilarities.

The number of clusters obtained from the observed dissimilarity matrix at various clustering levels departs significantly from the number that would be observed at these levels under the null hypothesis. Interestingly enough, the zero information trace intersects the observed trace, indicating that:

• The actual data are characterized by a larger number of small, closely connected clusters.

• As the clustering proceeds, the dissimilarity matrix for the 108 companies contains significantly fewer clusters than would be observed under the random model hypothesis.

Therefore, meaningful structure exists in our data. Decision process similarities between industrial organizations in our sample typically leads to a smaller number of microsegments than would be observed under a random model. Interpreted in another way, the simulation results indicate that within the range $(50 < n_\alpha < 4)$, where n_α is the number of clusters assumed, the data contain substantially more connected clusters — as evidenced by the smaller clustering level — than under the null hypothesis.

When we consider these results — which indicate that a four cluster solution represents the fewest clusters that significantly depart from the random model — together with the parsimony objective of the microsegmentation methodology, it appears that a four cluster solution is a reasonable choice.

In case no clustering level is found that significantly departs from the random model, the analysis should conclude that microsegmentation is infeasible.

Step 4: Cluster Invariance Analysis.

This step involves the cluster membership invariance. There are two main reasons why cluster analytic solutions are not unique even when the researcher has decided upon the final number of clusters to be retained in his analysis. The first one has to do with the way a clustering method handles tied dissimilarities.

The second reason for the indeterminacy of cluster analytic solutions occurs because clustering algorithms assume different scaling properties of the dissimilarity measures and compute distances between cluster entities differently. As a result, different methods lead to different cluster composition except for extremely stable clusters. Which of the many algorithms available should you use?

To date no answer has been provided. Each clustering technique has its advocates and its critics (see the discussion by Anderberg, 1973). Very few empirical studies compare relative performances. A recent analysis by Blashfield (1976), however, suggests that some of these methods might be more accurate than others in recovering clusters generated under a mixture model involving several different populations.

For our purposes, the question of indeterminacy of cluster solutions is of considerable importance. The nature of dissimilarity measures defined over a finite set of binary variables (typically $J \times H$ variables in the decision matrix) suggests that tied dissimilarities will occur in any data set of reasonable size. In addition, the microsegments must be very stable, if the remaining analysis is to make sense.

We suggest here using several clustering algorithms in parallel and analyzing the composition of the resulting clusters. If the set of clusters retained are indeed real, their composition will vary little across clustering methods. This criterion of composition invariance across clustering models has also been proposed by Everitt (1974).

For this purpose, we suggest three common agglomerative clustering models. Interested readers are referred to Hartigan (1975), Anderberg (1973), and Dalziel (1974) for more complete descriptions of these algorithms.

Complete Linkage Cluster Analysis: According to this method, a cluster is defined as a group of entities in which each member is more similar to all members of the same cluster than it is to members of any other cluster. At each clustering stage, after cluster u and v have been merged, the dissimilarity between the new cluster — say t — and some other cluster w is determined by:

$$d_{tw} = \max(d_{uw}, d_{vw})$$

An advantage of complete linkage analyses over most other clustering methods is that it requires only ordinal dissimilarity measures. The solution is therefore invariant under a monotonic transformation of the dissimilarity matrix.

A main criticism of complete linkage analysis, however, is that as an entity cannot join a cluster until it obtains a given similarity level with all members of this cluster, the probability of a cluster obtaining a new member becomes smaller as the size of the cluster increases. This property, known as space-diluting (Lance and Williams, 1967), means that the effective distance between a cluster and some nonmember increases as the size of the cluster increases.

Average Linkage Cluster Analysis: Average linkage analysis represents a compromise between single linkage analysis — which characterizes a cluster by the longest link needed to connect any of its members to some other one — and complete linkage analysis.

In average linkage analysis, a cluster, t, is characterized by the mean of the distances between all pairs of distinct items within the cluster:

$$\text{size of cluster }(t) = \frac{2}{n_t(n_t - 1)} \sum_{r \neq s \in t} d(r, s)$$

where n_t is the number of entities in t and the summation is over all pairs of points $r \neq s$ in t. A cluster is then defined as a group of entities in which each member has a greater mean similarity with all members of the same cluster than it does with all members of any other cluster.

Sneath and Sokal (1973) claim that average linkage cluster analysis is the best hierarchical method yet proposed. Evidence suggests, however, that this method is more likely than some other clustering methods to form nonconformist groups as the sizes of the clusters increase (Williams, Clifford and Lance, 1972).

Minimum Variance Cluster Analysis: Ward (1963) and Ward and Hook (1963) have described a general method of hierarchical clustering that, at each step, maximizes an objective function reflecting an investigator's particular purpose. Although the method is general and encompasses most other hierarchical methods, Ward illustrates it with an error sum of squares objective function that is better known than his general procedure.

The objective of this latter method is to find at each stage of the classification process the two clusters that minimize the increase in the total within cluster error sum of squares. A recent analysis of the relative performance of alternative cluster analytic methods by Blashfield (1976) suggests that this technique is consistently most accurate in recovering data generated under a mixture model involving several different populations.

Exhibit 4.16 gives a comparative analysis of the degree of convergence between four clustering methods used in the solar cooling study. A conservative analysis would now only consider those organizations that were classified consistently across clustering methods.

Step 5: Microsegment Characteristic Analysis.

The final step of the microsegmentation methodology concerns the identification of differences across microsegments in terms of:

- the general pattern of decision participants involvement, and
- the external characteristics of the firms they each comprise.

These questions can be addressed through the use of either univariate (Scheffe, 1959) or multivariate (Morrison, 1976) analysis of variance methods.

Of more interest is the use of the external characteristics of a firm to assess

Exhibit 4.16. Comparative analysis of the degree of convergence between four clustering methods

	Complete linkage	Average linkage	Minimum within variance	Minimum increase in within sum of squares
Complete Linkage	—	—	—	—
Average Linkage	62% (93.89)	—	—	—
Minimum Within Variance	61% (99.18)	87% (232.05)		
Minimum Increase in Within Sum of Squares	64% (127.99)	84% (213.60)	86% (213.60)	

Upper Number: Percentage of Consistent Classification
Lower Number: Chi-Square Estimate with 9 d.f.

the likelihood that it belongs to a given microsegment. For this purpose multivariate discriminant analysis can be used. The problem addressed by this statistical method is the prediction of which group an entity belongs to on the basis of a set of prediction variables. Let a firm's discriminant score Z_i be a linear function of some of its external characteristics ($x_j, j = 1 \ldots J$). Such characteristics might be its size, level of decentralization, and so forth.

We thus have:

$$Z_i = b_o + b_1 x_{i1} + b_2 x_{i2} + \ldots + b_J x_{iJ}$$
$$= b_o + \sum_j b_j x_{ij}$$

Determination of the discriminant coefficients ($b_o \ldots b_J$) is made in such a way as to maximize some function of the distance between groups in the discriminant space. Affifi and Azen (1972) and Lachenbruch (1975) provide excellent reviews of the statistical foundations of discriminant analysis.

In the solar cooling study, a four group multivariate discriminant analysis was performed to predict microsegment membership. (See Choffray, 1977) The model led to 47% correct classification. This is considerably more than would have been obtained by randomly assigning the companies to four segments of sizes equal to those retained in the analysis ($c_{pro} = 27\%$).

Validity of Decision Matrix Measurements

The analysis of purchase involvement and the study of interfirm differences requires assessment of the validity of the measurements obtained with the decision matrix.

A common denominator of most validity concepts is that of agreement or convergence between independent approaches. (Ayer, 1956; Campbell and Fiske, 1959). Suppose that several decision participants in the same organization filled out the decision matrix separately. The extent of the agreement between these individuals about the categories of individuals involved in the phases of the purchasing process is a measure of the convergent validity of the measurement procedure.

To investigate measurement validity, decision process involvement was measured twice, with different individuals, in several firms. Two products were studied in this validity analysis: the industrial cooling system (12 firms), and an intelligent computer terminal (13 firms).

We used two approaches to assess the convergent validity of the decision matrix measurements. The first, a simulation approach, considers if separate measurements in the same firm agree more than separate measurements in different organizations. The second method, investigating the ability of respondents to discriminate between decision phases, is developed in detail in Choffray (1977).

We use the following notation

$$V = (v_i, v_i'): i = 1, \ldots N_1$$

denotes the subsample of N_1 companies for which two measurements (v_i, v_i') were obtained with the decision matrix. We call this sample the validation sample.

$$C = v_j^* : j = 1, \ldots N_2$$

denotes the subsample of N_2 companies for which only one measurement was obtained with the decision matrix. We call it the main sample.

A.4.3.1 SIMULATION APPROACH TO VALIDATION

Here we use both the validation sample and the main sample. Our objective is to see if agreement between separate measurements of involvement in the same firm is significantly higher than measurements in different firms.

We are concerned here with measuring involvement of different categories of decision participants in the decision process and not with measuring the extent of their involvement. Hence, we use the similarity measure developed in Appendix 4.2.1.

Our analysis is as follows. First, we compute the similarity s_i between each pair (v_i, v_i') of measurements in the validation sample. The quantities v_i and v_i' are vectors of binary variables reflecting the involvement or noninvolvement of categories of participants in phases of the decision process in company i. Then, we compute an average similarity index:

$$S = \frac{1}{N_1} \sum_{i=1}^{N_1} s_i$$

Next, we generate the distribution of the statistic S under the hypothesis of mutually independent measurements. For this purpose, the main sample is augmented by adding one observation chosen randomly from each pair (v_i, v_i') in the validation sample. This augmented sample – called the Analysis Sample – includes $N = (N_2 + N_1/2)$ observations and represents independent measurements because each is from a different firm. The similarity coefficient among all different pairs of observations in the analysis sample is computed. There are $N(N-1)/2$ such similarities from which samples of size N_1 are drawn randomly, with replacement. Each of these samples leads to an estimate of S.

The results of the simulation analysis for the solar cooling data and the intelligent terminal data are reported in Exhibit 4.17. These results are based on 5000 samples of size N_1 drawn randomly under H_0. They indicate a substantially higher degree of agreement between separate measurements in the validation sample than in random samples of the same size generated under H_0. In view of the standard deviation of the distribution of the average similarity index under H_0, and the fact that none of the 5000 samples generated in both studies had an average similarity higher than that in the validation sample, H_0 is rejected at $\alpha < .001$. Hence, separate measurements obtained with the decision matrix in the same organization show a substantially higher degree of convergence than would be expected if these measurements had been obtained independently.

Exhibit 4.17   Results of the simulation approach to the validation of the measurements obtained with the decision matrix

	Industrial cooling system	Intelligent terminal
Average similarity index in the validation sample	$S = .825$ $(N_1 = 12)$	$S = .783$ $(N_1 = 13)$
Mean of the distribution of the average index of similarity under H_0	$E(S) = .641$	$E(S) = .652$
Standard deviation of the distribution of the average index of similarity under H_0	$\sigma(S) = .035$	$\sigma(S) = .037$

A.4.3.2 CONVERGENT AND DISCRIMINANT VALIDATION

An important question is whether respondents can discriminate between decision phases in terms of decision-participant involvement. The method used is a variant of the convergent and discriminant validation approach proposed by Campbell and Fiske (1959). It was developed to assess the validity of psychological tests, but the method is quite general and has been used in a variety of different research settings. The procedure requires an understanding of the Campbell and Fiske (1959) approach, beyond the scope of this work. Choffray (1977) develops the procedure in detail. Application of the procedure to the two data sets shows significant ability to discriminate between decision phases.

A.4.3.3 SUMMARY OF VALIDATION ANALYSIS

In sum, the results of our validation analysis indicate that:

- there is substantial agreement between separate measurements with a decision matrix completed by different individuals in the same company.
- the measurements obtained show evidence of discriminant validity across decision phases. This suggests that respondents discriminate between decision phases and the individuals involved.

The decision matrix is still a new measurement instrument. Its external validity needs to be assessed, through studies over time in organizations actually facing decision situations. At the same time, the ability of the decision matrix to assess the relative importance of individuals — in relationship to the decisions being made — should be studied. As Webster and Wind (1972a) note, "There are rich research opportunities in defining the influence of different members of the buying center at various stages of the process."

APPENDIX 5.1.
An Awareness
Response Model

A.5.1.1 AN AWARENESS RESPONSE MODEL

In this appendix we present a sample analytical function along with an illustration. The interested reader should consult Little (1979b) for other models and approaches that might be used for mapping advertising response.

Consider a given time period of unit length. The model assumes:

1. During that period, if there is no advertising, the fraction of the population evoking that product will decrease to a value W_0

2. No matter how much is spent, the fraction evoking the product in that period cannot exceed an amount W^*

3. There is some rate of advertising A that will maintain initial evoking share $W = W(A)$.

4. An estimate is available of evoking $W^1 = W(A^1)$ by the end of the period with a 50% increase in advertising ($A^1 = 1.5A$) over maintenance.

Exhibit 5.15 gives a representation of this information.

A smooth curve can then be put through the points. One is the function where

$$W = W_0 + (W^* - W_0)\frac{A^\delta}{\delta + A^\delta}$$

where the constants W_0, W^*, δ and γ are to be determined with the input data.

Exhibit 5.16 gives a pictorial representation of this curve. If $\gamma > 1$ the curve will be S-shaped. For $0 < \gamma \leqslant 1$ we obtain a concave function. The particular γ, of course will depend on the input data.

To take time delays into consideration, we further need to know:

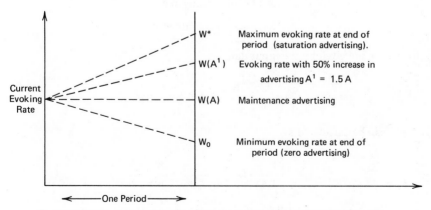

Exhibit 5.15. Input data for fitting an awareness response function.

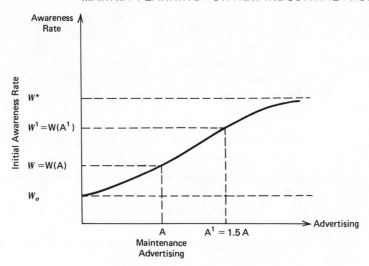

Exhibit 5.16. Awareness function.

- What value (Woo) awareness would decay to if there were no advertising for a long time?
- What fraction (ρ) of the current level awareness will decay to with zero advertising in a single period?

The model further assumes that the decay rate, ρ, is constant over time as is the affectable range ($W^* - W_o$).

This model can now be written as

$$W(t) = Woo + \rho\,(W(t-1) - Woo) + \Psi\,\frac{A(t)^\delta}{\delta + A(t)^\delta}$$

where

$$A(t) = \text{advertising at } t$$

$$W(t) = \text{evoking rate at } t$$

Woo, ρ, Ψ are given by the input data, as

$$\rho = \frac{Wo - Woo}{W - Woo}\; ; \Psi = W^* - Wo$$

and γ, δ can be calculated as

$$\gamma = \frac{1}{ln(1.5)}\; ln\left\{\frac{W^* - W}{W - Wo}\cdot\frac{W^1 - Wo}{W^* - W^1}\right\}$$

$$\delta = \left\{\frac{W^* - W}{W - Wo}\right\}$$

Little (1970) shows how advertising at t can be modified to reflect effective advertising (weighted by media and copy efficiency). In addition, nonadvertising effects on evoking (such as sales force effects) can be taken care of in a structure similar to the one in BRANDAID (Little (1975a, b)).

A.5.1.2 AN ILLUSTRATION

Suppose the marketing manager, in charge of solar cooling, provided the following information concerning air conditioning consultant awareness with respect to communication expenditures.

- current awareness level: $W = 0.41$
- short run awareness level in the absence of expenditures, $Wo = 0.39$
- short run awareness level if communication expenditures were pushed to saturation level, $W* = 0.51$
- long-run awareness level if communication expenditures were set to 0 for a long period of time, $Woo = 0.32$

Hence,

$$\rho = \frac{0.39 - 0.32}{0.41 - 0.32} = 0.778,$$

$$\Psi = .51 - .39 = .12,$$

and

$$\delta = \frac{0.51 - 0.41}{0.41 - 0.39} = 5.0$$

- Maintenance advertising expenditures, $A = \$0.68$ per target air conditioning engineer
- Awareness rate induced by a 50% increase in advertising expenditures $W^1 = W(1.5 \times \$0.68) = W(\$1.02) = 0.47$.

Hence,

$$\gamma = \frac{1}{1n(1.5)} \, 1n \left\{ \frac{0.51 - 0.41}{0.41 - 0.39} \cdot \frac{0.47 - 0.39}{0.51 - 0.47} \right\}$$

$$= 5.68, \text{ and}$$

thus, the response curve is S-shaped.

The awareness function for air conditioning is therefore given by:

$$W(t) = 0.32 + 0.778 \, (W(t - 1) - 0.32) + 0.12 \frac{(A(t))^{5.68}}{5.0 + (A(t))^{5.68}}$$

This function can then be used to assess changes in awareness level from the present rate as a function of communication spending strategy, $A(t)$.

APPENDIX 5.2.
Feasibility Model

Several approaches can be used to calibrate the market acceptance functions. They differ both in terms of the data they require and in the calibration procedure they use. Here we review two methods and discuss the approach we suggest for performing the analysis.

Development and calibration of the market acceptance function assumes:

1. There exists a number of need specification dimensions that companies use in screening new product alternatives. These are either continuous (cost must be less than X) or discrete (product must contain feature Y) variables. For a given company, only a subset of these dimensions may be relevant.
2. On relevant dimensions, organizations are capable of specifying (a) the minimum or maximum acceptable level of their requirements on a continuous specification, or (b) whether or not a discrete feature is required.

We introduce the following notation:

$$\bar{X} = \{X_j\} = X_1 \ldots XJ_d = \text{set of need specification dimensions, where}$$

$$j = 1 \ldots J_c \text{ are continuous dimensions}$$

$$j = J_{c+1} \ldots J_d \text{ are discrete dimensions.}$$

Note that the set of dimensions $j = 1, \ldots J_d$ are an *exhaustive* set of dimensions relevant for product choice in the class.
Thus:

$$X_{ij} = \text{maximum or minimum value of dimension j that is acceptable to}$$
$$\text{organization } i, j = 1 \ldots J_c \text{ or}$$

$$X_{ij} = \begin{cases} 1 \text{ if company } i \text{ requires discrete attribute } j; j = J_c + 1 \ldots J_d \\ 0 \text{ otherwise} \end{cases}$$

We assume a population of potential buying organizations, from which we sample I. Our problem is to determine

$$g(X^o) = \text{proportion of organizations that find product design } X^o \text{ acceptable.}$$

For a particular organization, a product is acceptable if it satisfies all of its requirements. Hence X^o is acceptable if and only if

$$X_1^o < X_{i1} \cap X_2^o < X_{i2} \cap \ldots \cap X_{J_c}^o < X_{iJ_c}$$

(We can assume that X_{ij} is a maximum value without loss of generality).
Note that for $j = J_c + 1, \ldots J_d$, an acceptable product design X^o is of the form
$$X_j^o = 1 \text{ if } X^o \text{ contains attribute } j.$$

and if $\displaystyle\sum_{j\epsilon\Delta^o} X_{ij} = 0$, where

Δ^0 = set of all discrete criteria which the product does
not possess.

(Note that if $\displaystyle\sum_{j\epsilon\Delta^o} X_{ij} > 0$, the company requires at least one attribute the product
does not possess.)

At the organizational level, acceptance of a product alternative follows a conjunctive decision rule. The purpose of the acceptance function is to approximate the process probabilistically for a segment of potential customer organizations.

Two methods of development and calibration of the market acceptance function can be used, depending upon the nature of the measurements collected.

Method 1: The Conjoint Measurement Approach: Conjoint methodology is based on a decompositional approach in which respondents react to a set of product profiles where characteristics are varied factorially. The method then attempts to find a set of utilities for the individual attributes that, given some composition rule (most often additive), are most consistent with the respondent's overall evaluation. Green and Wind (1973), and Green and Srinivasan (1978) provide overviews of this methodology. Wind, Grashof and Goldhar (1978) illustrate its use in providing guidelines for industrial product design.

Use of the conjoint measurement approach to develop and calibrate the acceptance response model assumes that we have identified relevant need specification dimensions along which discrete levels — corresponding to product designs — can be distinguished. The analysis then proceeds as follows:

Measurement Step: Decision participants in sampled target companies are presented product profiles whose design characteristics are varied factorially. The composition rule of additive, product profiles can be varied according to a latin square design from which only main effects of product characteristics on acceptance rate will be readable. If the composition rule allows for interaction effects among design features, product profiles will have to be presented according to a more complex fractional factorial scheme.

In each case, respondents are asked to sort profiles into those that are acceptable to their company and those that are not. To accomplish this task they are encouraged to use any source of information, including colleagues.

Calibration Step: A number of analytical methods can be used at this step. Among them, discriminant analysis (Lachenbruch, 1975) and probit analysis (Finney, 1952) are suitable, given the binary nature of the response variable. Given product profiles, these two methods permit assessment of the impact of design characteristics — expressed in the model as dummy variables — on the likelihood of market acceptance.

The conjoint measurement approach is useful when the number of need specification dimensions for the new product investigated is rather small ($\leqslant 5$) and when meaningful discrete design options can be distinguished. In such cases, the number of product profiles remains reasonable, so that reliable acceptance data can be obtained.

The method, however, has an important limitation in terms of the level of inter-action it allows among design characteristics. Most often, due to measurement constraints, a simple, additive composition model has to be assumed. Resulting design trade-off curves are then linear, a possible over-simplification. Estimation problems may also occur with this approach because of the presence of multi-collinearity among binary predictor variables.

Method 2: The Disjoint Measurement Approach: In many situations, the con-joint approach is not very useful due to the number of specification dimensions, their continuous nature and interactions. We present here an alternative approach which we call disjoint measurement.

Measurement Step: Along each relevant specification dimension, decision partici-pants are asked to specify the minimum or maximum value beyond which their organization would not consider the product. To perform this task, respondents use any available source of information.

Our experience with this method of measurement, which we discuss further in Chapter Nine, is that it provides more reliable estimates of companies' requirements. Decision participants find it easier to think in terms of rejection extremes than to assess composed product profiles.

Calibration Step: The calibration of the market acceptance function, based on the disjoint measurement approach is somewhat more complex. It requires the gen-eration of a large number of system designs, $\{X_r\}$, randomly, where randomly means in accordance with the joint empirical distribution of the critical acceptance levels. This forces our observations to be obtained in the areas of maximum sensitivity.

Let $x_{r\ell}$ be the level of dimension ℓ for design r, and $t_\ell(x_{r\ell})$ be the fraction of organizations finding $x_{r\ell}$ acceptable, independent of other dimensions. We then model market or segment response as

$$T(x_r) = \alpha \prod_{\ell=0}^{n} [t_\ell(x_{r\ell})]^{\alpha_\ell}$$

where α_ℓ, $\ell = 0, \ldots, n$, are parameters to be estimated.

This second approach allows development of complex market response models that are nonlinear in the design features as well as in the parameters. High-level interactions among design options may be tested and their impact on market accep-tance assessed. For more details see Choffray and Lilien (1979).

Clustering of Organizations: Independent of the approach used, organizations that share the same set of need specification dimensions must be analyzed together. This problem is not fundamentally different from that of microsegmentation, discussed in Chapter Four.

$$\text{Define } Q_{ij} = \begin{cases} 1 \text{ if organization } i \text{ considers specification} \\ \quad \text{dimension } j \text{ in its acceptance decision} \\ 0 \text{ otherwise} \end{cases}$$

Then two organizations, i, and i', share the same dimensions if, and only if, $Q_{ij} = Q_{i'j}$ for all j. In practice, we define a dissimilarity measure, and cluster analyze sampled companies using methods discussed in Chapter Four.

Clusters identified this way are not usually perfectly homogeneous, however. We make them homogeneous by estimating an acceptance level for the firm, for dimensions that are not binding equal to the mean or the median for the rest of the group. This procedure allows considerable flexibility in grouping the organizations without distorting the results of the logit regressions.

Adjustment of Calibration Procedures for Measurement Errors: The answers to the specification dimension questions may incorporate uncertainty and/or measurement errors.

Assume one specification dimension (the extension to n is straightforward). Let Y_{ki} = answer to the question by individual k in company i. Assume a simple error/ uncertainty model:

$$X_i = Y_{ki} + \epsilon_{ki}$$

where X_i is the *true* level of the acceptance criterion in company i and ϵ_{ki} is an error/uncertainty term.

Let

$$\delta_i = \begin{cases} 1 \text{ if } Y_{ki} < X^o \\ 0 \text{ otherwise} \end{cases}$$

where X^o is the level of the product-design dimension.

In the previous section, we would consider $f(X^o)$ = fraction of organizations that find X^o acceptable as

$$f(X^o) = \frac{1}{I} \sum_{i=1}^{I} \delta_i w_i$$

where w_i is a weighting factor, representing a method of relating the sample to the population.

Here we replace this form as follows: Let

δ_i = Prob $(X_i < X^o)$ where X_i is not observed.
If ϵ_{ki} is distributed normally as $N(0, \sigma^2)$ then:

$$\gamma_i = \text{Prob}\left\{\frac{X_i - Y_{ki}}{\sigma} < \frac{X^o - Y_{ki}}{\sigma}\right\}$$

$$= \phi\left(\frac{X^o - Y_{ki}}{\sigma}\right)$$

where ϕ is the cumulative standard normal distribution function.

We then calculate $f(X^0)$ as follows:

$$f(X^o) = \sum_{i=1}^{I} \gamma_i w_i$$

where $f(X^o)$ is now the expected proportion of firms that find X^o acceptable.

A simple way to estimate σ for any single dimension is to consider those firms in which multiple measurements exist. Call $K(i)$ the number of measurements in firm i.

We estimate $\hat{\sigma}$ as

$$\hat{\sigma}^2 = \frac{1}{\sum_{i \in I^*}(K(i) - 1)} \cdot \sum_{i \in I^*} \sum_{k=1}^{K(i)} (Y_{ki} - \bar{Y}_i)^2$$

where I^* is that subset of $\{I\}$ that has multiple measurements from the organization and

$$\bar{Y}_i = \frac{1}{K(i)} \sum_{k=1}^{K(i)} Y_{ki}$$

If the level of error varies across firms, σ_i can be estimated in an analogous way to that above.

The application of this procedure usually smooths out the evaluation of $f(X^o)$; in particular, it eliminates values of $f(X^o)$ of 0 or 1, problem areas for estimation.

Methodology to Assess Perceptual Differences Between Groups of Decision Participants

The investigation of perceptual differences between several groups of decision participants uses methods of multivariate analysis of variance.

Individual product perceptions represent observations on a K-dimensional vector. For a given product alternative, decision participant categories can be considered as experimental groups.

What is a perceptual difference, however? The issue of differences in participant groups' perception of a specific product alternative is not only a question of difference in location in the K-dimensional perceptual space. Rather, since the alternative presents the same characteristics to all individuals, it is mainly a question of interaction between group membership and perceptual responses.

The methodology proposed here uses Multivariate Profile Analysis (MPA) to investigate that question. A product profile is simply its vector of average ratings (centroid) on the original set of perceptual items computed for each category of decision participant.

As such, Multivariate Profile Analysis is a specific case of the general multivariate linear model, which allows investigation of response by group interaction when dependent variables are expressed in comparable units. An excellent presentation of the MPA technique is provided by Morrison (1976).

The model assumes that each k-observation is generated by the model:

$$x_{id} = \mu + \gamma_d + \epsilon_{id}$$

where the subscript $i = 1, \ldots I$, refers to a specific individual in participant category d with $d = 1, \ldots, D$.

In this model, μ is a general level vector parameter whose h^{th} component is common to all observations obtained on response variable h; γ_d is a vector whose components represent the effect of membership in participant category d on each response variable, and ϵ_{id} is a vector of disturbances. The MPA model assumes that the disturbance vector ϵ_{id} has a multinormal distribution with a zero mean vector and some unknown nonsingular covariance matrix Σ common to all experimental conditions.

The issue of perceptual differences across participant categories is investigated in two steps. First, a test for profile parallelism is performed. Then, a test for equality of levels is applied. Exhibit 6.11 in the body of the Chapter illustrates the concept of profile parallelism and profile level equality.

The hypothesis of profile parallelism, or no interaction between individual product perceptions and group membership, involves a simultaneous test on the slope of adjacent segments of the different groups' profiles. This hypothesis can be stated:

$$H_{01} : \begin{Bmatrix} \gamma_{11} - \gamma_{12} \\ \gamma_{1,K-1} - \gamma_{1K} \end{Bmatrix} = \ldots = \begin{Bmatrix} \gamma_{D1} - \gamma_{D2} \\ \gamma_{D,K-1} - \gamma_{D,K} \end{Bmatrix}$$

Hypothesis H_{01} can be tested by the largest characteristic root criterion using the Heck statistic (See Morrison, 1976). Rejection of this hypothesis indicates the existence of significant perceptual differences across categories of decision participants for the product investigated.

Assuming that the hypothesis of parallel profiles is not rejected, a test is performed to investigate the equality of profile levels. The test involves a one-way univariate analysis of variance on the sum of the K responses of each individual across all D groups. In terms of the previous notation this hypothesis becomes:

$$H_{02} : \sum_{k=1}^{K} \gamma_{1k} = \ldots = \sum_{k=1}^{K} \gamma_{Dk}$$

Rejection of H_{02} indicates a systematic perceptual difference among participant categories. This perceptual difference has the nature of an additive constant, suggesting that some participant categories give consistently more extreme perceptual ratings than other participant categories to the alternative investigated.

Rejection of the hypothesis of no perceptual differences across groups of decision participants calls for separate univariate analyses of variance on each of the response variables to assess the nature of these perceptual differences.

Methodology to Assess Differences In Evaluation Criteria Between Groups of Decision Participants

The methodology proposed here assumes that individuals who belong to a given group, — say design engineers, purchasing officers, and the like — share the same set of evaluation criteria. The methodology then addresses two questions.

- First, is the dimensionality of the evaluation space the same for different categories of decision participants? That is, do different groups of decision participants use the same *number* of evaluation criteria in their assessment of product alternatives?
- Second, assuming that the dimensionality of the evaluation space is the same for different groups of participants, are their *evaluation criteria* essentially similar?

A.6.2.1 MACRO STRUCTURE OF THE METHODOLOGY

Exhibit 6.16 outlines the methodology. The input to the analysis are the attribute ratings obtained for each of several product alternatives from each decision participant surveyed. Variance-covariance matrices of the ratings obtained on all attribute scales are computed for each group. These covariance matrices are computed across product alternatives assuming that the evaluation criteria derived for each group of decision participants are the same for all products in the class. This approach has been suggested and implemented by Urban (1975) in the consumer goods area; it increases the number of degrees of freedom for estimation of the evaluation criteria for each group.

The methodology proceeds as follows. First, a test for equality of all decision groups' covariance matrices is performed. This allows for an early detection of differences in the way individuals in each of these groups structure relevant product attributes into higher-order evaluation criteria (C). If the hypothesis of equal covariance matrices is accepted, the correlation matrix between perceptual ratings is computed across all individuals and factor analyzed (D). The dimensionality of the evaluation space is determined (E), and the composition of the evaluation criteria common to all categories of decision participants is appraised (F). In this case, the analysis concludes with no substantial differences across categories of decision participants in the evaluation criteria.

Rejection of the hypothesis of equal covariance matrices across decision groups suggests differences in evaluation spaces. Separate factor analyses are then performed (G). The dimensionality of the evaluation space is determined for each group (H). Inequality of dimensionality (I) indicates substantial differences (L).

On the other hand, when some groups have an evaluation space of the same dimensionality, additional tests for the equality of evaluation criteria are necessary (J). If all evaluation criteria are found to be identical, these groups have a common evaluation space and a factor analysis of their pooled correlation matrix is now required (D). If at least one of their evaluation criteria is different, the analysis con-

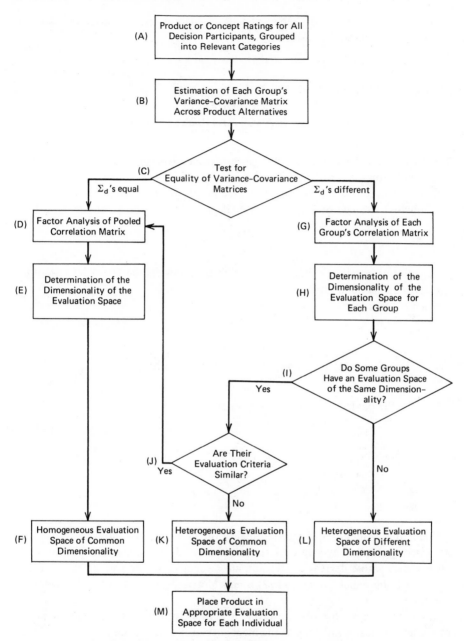

Exhibit 6.16. Outline of evaluation space methodology.

cludes at the existence of heterogeneous evaluation spaces across the decision groups with the given dimensionality.

A.6.2.2. MICRO STRUCTURE OF THE
METHODOLOGY: TEST FOR EQUALITY
OF VARIANCE COVARIANCE MATRICES

The hypothesis of equality of covariance matrices across groups of participants is tested with Box's criterion (1949).

Let Σ_d denote the population covariance matrix for decision group d and S_d be the unbiased estimate of Σ_d based on n_d degrees of freedom. Then, the hypothesis

$$H_O : \Sigma_1 = \ldots = \Sigma_D$$

of equality of covariance matrices across all D groups can be tested by a modified generalized likelihood-ratio statistic.

When H_O is true, the test statistic is

$$M = \sum_{d=1}^{D} n_d \ln|S| - \sum_{d=1}^{D} n_d \ln|S_d|$$

where S is the pooled estimate of the covariance matrix:

$$S = \sum_{d=1}^{D} n_d S_d \bigg/ \sum_{d=1}^{D} n_d$$

Under the assumption of multinormality of the perceptual ratings, the quantity M, when multiplied by appropriate scale factors, is approximately distributed as an F-variate whose degrees of freedom are a function of the parameters D, N, and n_d. (See Cooley and Lohnes, (1971), and Morrison (1976)), for a discussion of this test).

Box's test is very powerful, however. A Monte Carlo study found that the power of the test increases not only as the inequality of the covariance matrices increases, but also as the sample size or the number of variates increases (Greenstreet and Connor, 1974). Thus, rejection of the hypothesis of equality of groups' variance-covariance matrices by the Box criterion should be used only as an indicator of possible differences in evaluation spaces. Indeed, as common factor analysis does not make use of all information present in these matrices, it is possible that the evaluation spaces are similar even though the hypothesis of equality of covariance matrices is rejected.

Test for the Determination of the Number of Evaluation Criteria to be Retained for Each Participant Group: Our methodology uses common factor analysis to derive the evaluation space of the decision participant groups. But, how many factors should we retain? Rummel (1970) reviews a number of rules-of-thumb that have been developed to deal with this problem. These rules are very subjective, however, and are often subject to theoretical objections.

Here, we propose to use the parallel analysis technique (Humphreys and Ilgen, 1969) that provides an objective criterion for the determination of the dimensionality of evaluation spaces. The method involves factoring a second correlation matrix identical in the number of variables and observations to the original data matrix but obtained from randomly generated normal deviates. Montanelli and Humphreys (1976) provide a method of estimating the expected values of the latent roots of random data correlation matrices with squared multiple correlations on the diagonal. The following general equation predicts the size of these eigenvalues very accurately ($R^2 \approx .99$):

$$\log \lambda_i = a_i + b_i \log (N-1) + c_i \log \left\{ \frac{K(K-1)}{2} - (i-1) K \right\}$$

where i is the ordinal position of the eigenvalue, a_i, b_i and c_i are regression coefficients, N is the number of observations and K is the number of original variables.

The comparison between the actual and the zero-information eigenvalues provide a simple quantitative criterion for the determination of the dimensionality of the corresponding evaluation space. Exhibit 6.17 illustrates this approach for production engineers.

Test for the Similarity of Evaluation Criteria When Several Participant Groups Have an Evaluation Space of Same Dimensionality: When some groups have an evaluation space of the same dimensionality (Step I in the methodology), an additional test for the similarity of evaluation criteria is necessary. In terms of our factor analysis methodology, the problem is that of the relation between several factor solutions obtained in different samples from the same battery of variables. Although the problem is receiving increasing attention in the mathematical psychology literature (Joreskog, 1971; Please, 1973), no general solution has been found to date. As Harman, (1976) concludes in his recent review of the literature on the subject, "The empirical approach, employing indices of proportionality of factors . . . seems not inappropriate at this time for the identification of factors across different studies . . . (involving the same set of variables in different samples)."

Our approach to testing the equality of evaluation criteria is different from that typically used in the literature. Instead of attempting to assert the similarity between factor structure matrices, we concentrate on the similarity between predictive equations used to assess factor scores. Our test then compares pairs of factor measurement equations obtained from different samples (Choffray and Lilien, 1978).

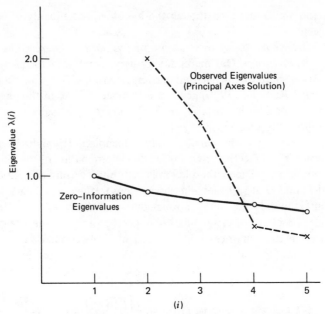

Exhibit 6.17. Determination of dimensionality of evaluation space for production engineers.

Consider two regression models.

(1) $$Y_1 = X_1\beta_1 + \epsilon_1$$

(2) $$Y_2 = X_2\beta_2 + \epsilon_2$$

where Y_i is $(n_i \times 1)$, X_i is $(n_i \times K)$, β_1 and β_2 are vectors of coefficients and ϵ_1, ϵ_2 are vectors of disturbances. The null hypothesis, $\beta_1 = \beta_2$, gives rise to the reduced model:

(3) $$Y = \begin{Bmatrix} X_1 \\ X_2 \end{Bmatrix} \beta + \epsilon$$

If we let e_1, e_2 and e be residual vectors associated with least squares estimation of (1), (2) and (3), respectively, then Chow (1960) shows that, under the null hypothesis,

(4) $$C = \left\{ \frac{e'e}{e_1'e_1 + e_2'e_2} - 1 \right\} \frac{N - 2K}{K}$$

is distributed as F with K, $(N-2K)$ d.f. (where $N = n_1 + n_2$).

Common factor analysis expresses each observed variable $\{x_k, k = 1, \ldots K\}$ as a linear combination of a small number of common factors $\{f_r, r = 1, \ldots R\ \}$ with $R \leqslant K$ plus a unique factor y_k

$$(5) \qquad x_{ki} = \sum_{r=1}^{R} a_{kr}f_{ri} + u_k y_{ki}$$

where a_{kr} and u_k are the factor pattern coefficients, and subscript i refers to a particular individual in the sample ($i = 1, \ldots N$).

The factors f_r, $r = 1, \ldots R$, however, are hypothetical *unobserved* constructs. In the case of most common factor analysis techniques, the factor scores have to be estimated indirectly. Linear regression on the original variables (x_k, $k = 1, \ldots K$) is often used for this purpose — Harman (1976). The model may be expressed as follows:

$$(6) \qquad f_{ri} = \sum_{k=1}^{K} \beta_{rk}x_{ki} + \epsilon_{ri}$$

where β_{rk} is the regression coefficient — or factor score coefficient — of factor f_r on variable x_k.

When the common factors are orthogonal, Harman (1976) shows that ρ_r^2 the coefficient of multiple correlation associated with the estimation of factor f_r can be calculated as

$$(7) \qquad \rho_r^2 = \sum_{k=1}^{K} b_{rk}a_{kr}$$

where the b_{rk}'s are least squares estimates of the β_{rk}'s and $\{a_{kr}\ k = 1, \ldots K;$ $r = 1 \ldots R\}$, are the correlations between the variable x_k's and the factor f_r's.

Under the usual assumptions of the common factor analysis model, it can be shown that:

$$(8) \qquad \sum_{i=1}^{N} (f_{ri} - \hat{f}_{ri})^2 = N(1 - \epsilon_r^2)$$

We can then use (8) in (4), as $\displaystyle\sum_{i=1}^{N} (f_{ri} - \hat{f}_{ri})^2$ is the sum of the squared residuals $e'_r e_r$ associated with the estimation of the factor scores f_r.

Hence, the statistic

(9)
$$C_r = \left\{ \frac{N(1 - \rho_r^2)}{n_1(1 - \rho_{r1}^2) + n_2(1 - \rho_{r2}^2)} - 1 \right\} \frac{N - 2K}{K}$$

can be used to test the equality of a specific factor obtained from the same set of variables in two different samples, where

ρ_{r1}^2, ρ_{r2}^2 are the squared multiple correlations associated with the estimation of factor r in sample 1 and 2 respectively,

ρ_r^2, is the squared multiple correlation associated with factor r in the pooled sample, and

N $= n_1 + n_2$

In terms of our methodology, Exhibit 6.18 outlines the steps involved in the computation of the test statistic, C_r, for assessing the similarity between evaluation criteria from different groups and an evaluation space of the same dimensionality. The exhibit involves only two groups, but the method is general and can be readily extended to any number of groups.

Assume that step 1 in the product evaluation space methodology led to the identification of R factors for groups 1 and 2. After rotation by the VARIMAX criterion, these factors provide the respective evaluation criteria. Call these evalua-

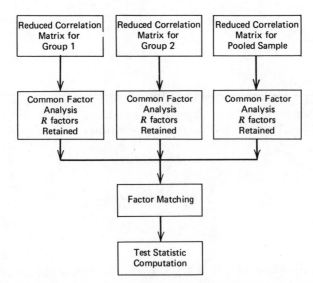

Exhibit 6.18. Outline of the procedure for assessing interdecision group differences in evaluation criteria.

Exhibit 6.19   Varimax rotated factor matrices for corporate engineers and plant managers

Item Number	Corporate engineer		Plant manager		Pooled sample	
	Factor 1	Factor 2	Factor 1	Factor 2	Factor 1	Factor 2
1	−0.726	−0.169	−0.037	−0.798	−0.783	−0.102
2	0.338	0.135	0.521	0.366	0.336	0.355
3	0.439	0.208	0.165	0.595	0.476	0.221
4	−0.776	−0.307	−0.287	−0.877	−0.810	−0.305
5	0.166	0.612	0.589	−0.026	0.087	0.616
6	−0.781	0.027	−0.208	−0.352	−0.603	−0.081
7	0.011	0.750	0.750	0.327	0.130	0.734
8	0.237	0.779	0.633	0.321	0.250	0.738
9	−0.388	0.202	0.127	−0.620	−0.483	0.148
10	0.571	0.408	0.420	0.407	0.496	0.418
11	0.830	0.407	0.227	0.727	0.780	0.344
12	0.320	0.692	0.788	0.284	0.293	0.729
13	0.253	0.350	0.703	−0.062	0.216	0.512
14	0.537	0.134	−0.227	0.445	0.490	0.011
15	0.082	0.471	0.772	−0.047	0.031	0.584
16	−0.180	0.458	0.604	0.057	−0.093	0.533
17	−0.486	0.079	−0.312	−0.487	−0.476	−0.090
Percent of Common Variance*	.59	.23	.57	.26	.59	.24
Coefficient of Determination	.902	.845	.897	.915	.879	.841

*The percentage of common variance is defined in terms of the principal axes solution.

Source: Choffray, 1977

Exhibit 6.20   Test for factor equality for plant managers and corporate engineers

	F-ratio	Degrees of freedom
A. Matched Factors: Plant Managers $f1$ Corporate Engineers $f2$	1.46	(17,119)
B. Matched Factors: Plant Managers $f2$ Corporate Engineers $f1$	2.14*	(17,119)

*Significant at .01 level.

Note: fi represents the ith factor in the original varimax solution for the corresponding decision group.

Source: Choffray, 1977

tion criteria $f_1^1, f_2^1 \ldots f_R^1$ and $f_1^2, f_2^2 \ldots f_R^2$, for group 1 and group 2 respectively and let $\rho_{11}^2, \rho_{12}^2 \ldots \rho_{1R}^2$ and $\rho_{21}^2, \rho_{22}^2 \ldots \rho_{2R}^2$ denote the coefficients of determination associated with the estimation of these factors.

To assess the similarity between pairs of potentially similar factors, we first compute the reduced correlation matrix between the K perceptual items in the pooled sample. The same number of common factors R are extracted and a VARIMAX rotation is performed to ensure both uniqueness and maximum interpretability. Let $f_1, f_2 \ldots f_R$ and $\rho_1^2 \, \rho_2^2 \ldots \rho_R^2$ denote the resulting evaluation criteria and their associated coefficients of determination in the pooled sample. Exhibit 6.19 gives the results of this procedure for corporate engineers and plant managers, where there are two factors.

Next, similar evaluation criteria are matched. Several methods can be used for this purpose. Usually, simple visual inspection of the three VARIMAX rotated factor structures and/or the use of simple matching coefficients will suffice to isolate potentially similar factors. Let f_ℓ^1, f_h^2 and f_g denote such a set of potentially similar factors for group 1, 2 and the pooled sample, respectively.

We can then compute the statistic C_r by Equation 9. When the value for C_r exceeds F: $(K, N - 2K; \alpha)$ where α denotes the level of significance of the test, the null hypothesis of equality of factor score coefficients, H_O: $\beta_\ell^1 = \beta_h^2$ is rejected. This leads to the conclusion that the two factors f_ℓ^1 and f_h^2 are different. Exhibit 6.20 gives the results of this test for our solar cooling sample.

APPENDIX 7.1.

Related Work on Multiperson Decision-Making

The purpose of this appendix is to put the developments of Chapter 7 into perspective by reviewing earlier work on models of multiperson choice. Research on models of multiperson decision making has involved a variety of academic disciplines. We distinguish three main schools of thought: (a) Economics; (b) Decision Analysis, and (c) Social Psychology. The assumptions that underlie the nature of individual and group choice behavior are different in these three schools and are summarized in Exhibit 7.3.

A.7.1.1. ECONOMICS

Economists have studied the preferences and choice behavior of economic "units" such as individuals, households and nations. Typically, they have been more concerned with individual preferences and choices than with groups.

Economists generally assume that an individual's preferences consist of a weak order relation defined over his choice set. Individuals are supposed to have complete information about all available alternatives. Their preferences are static over time and are uniquely determined by the observable and measurable characteristics of these alternatives. Moreover, it is assumed that individuals behave rationally; that is, they always choose the alternative they prefer most (see Newman (1965) for a comprehensive discussion of these assumptions).

For group preferences and choices, economists investigated the existence of social welfare functions. This problem can be stated as follows: given a set of individual preference orderings and a group preference ordering, does there exist a function that relates them and satisfies some reasonable assumptions about group functioning?

An important result in this area is Arrow's (1963) impossibility theorem. He shows that the only aggregation procedures to pass from individual preference structures to a group preference structure that satisfy five reasonable conditions are either imposed or dictatorial.

A related question is investigated by Fishburn (1969), who states conditions for a group ordinal preference structure to be written as the sum of monotone transformations of the ordinal individual preferences. More recently, Pattanaik (1973) studied the existence of a socially best alternative under various group decision rules when individual preference orderings are lexicographic.

The study of individual and group choice by economists is essentially axiomatic. For this reason it has been sometimes referred to as an algebraic theory of preference and choice behavior (Luce and Suppes, 1965). As Newman (1965) writes, "rational behavior is neither good nor bad, foolish nor wise, beautiful nor monstrous, it is simply behavior which obeys the axioms". Different axiom systems of rational behavior could be proposed and would inevitably lead to different preference structures for both individuals and groups. For this reason, economists' models of individual and group choice are of little help to describe the *actual* choice behavior of individuals and groups.

Exhibit 7.3 Comparison of the three approaches of analysis of multiperson decision making

	Individual level of knowledge for $a_J \epsilon \{A\}$	Nature of individual preference functions $u_i(a_j)$: Domain	Nature of individual preference functions $u_i(a_j)$: Characteristics	Nature of choice process	Choice criteria	Extension to group decision making
Economics	Perfect	Choice alternatives $\{A\}$	Deterministic Ordinal	Deterministic	$a^* = \max_{a_j \epsilon A} [u(a_j)]$	*Social Welfare Function* given $\{u_i(a_j); i = 1 \ldots I\}$ and $u_G(a_j)$ does f exist $\ni$ $u_G(a_j) = f\ \{u_i(a_j) \ldots\}$?
Decision Analysis	Probabilistic $a_j \sim \tilde{c}(a_j)$	Consequences of choice alternatives $\{C_A\}$	Deterministic Interval	Deterministic	$a^* \ni \max_{a_J \epsilon A} \{E[u(c_{a_j})]\}$	*Group Bayesians* (1) given $\{u_i(a_j); i = 1, \ldots I\}$ what is the nature of $u_G(a_j)$? (2) given $\{p_i[c(a_j)]; i = 1 \ldots I\}$ what is the nature of $p_G\ \{c(a_j)\}$?
Social Psychology	(1) Perfect	Choice Alternatives $\{A\}$	Deterministic Ratio	Probabilistic	$p(a^*, A) = f_j[u(a^*), \ldots u(a_J)]$[1]	*Social Decision Scheme* given $\{p_i(a_J): i = 1 \ldots I\}$ what is $p_G(a_J)$?
	(2) Imperfect	Choice Alternatives $\{A\}$	Probabilistic Ordinal	Deterministic[2]	$p(a^*, A) = p\{u(a^*) > u(a_j)\}\ \forall\ a_j \epsilon \{A - a^*\}$	

[1] f_j is strictly increasing in the first argument and strictly decreasing in the remaining $(J - 1)$ arguments.
[2] The individual chooses the alternatives that have the highest momentary utility.

A.7.1.2.DECISION ANALYSIS

Decision Analysis is concerned with the systematic analysis of decision-making under uncertainty. It provides decision makers with an analytical structure to make choices, when the consequences of the available alternatives are affected by uncertain events. The procedure consists in independently assessing the utility of each of the possible consequences and quantifying the decision maker's feelings about the likelihood that these uncertain events will occur. A rational decision maker then chooses that specific alternative that maximizes his expected utility.

Attempts have been made to extend this approach to problems involving several decision participants (Raiffa, 1968). The "group bayesians" consider that the behavioral assumptions implied by the decision analysis axioms of individual preferences and choice behavior are equally compelling when applied to a group acting as the decision-making unit. So, a decision group should develop its own utility function, combine the individual subjective probability estimates of its members into group probability estimates, and choose the alternative that maximizes its expected utility.

Neither of these two problems — aggregation of individual utility functions and aggregation of individual probability estimates — has been solved satisfactorily. Bacharach (1975) proves that under a reasonable set of axioms, the group ranking of the alternatives cannot be arrived at by any rules for separately combining the probabilities and the utilities. Studying the problem of aggregation of probability estimates in the case of panels of experts, Wrinkler (1968) suggests that several aggregation procedures should be used and their impact on the final decision be studied.

Keeney and Kirkwood (1975) address the problem of constructing a group cardinal utility function whose arguments are the individual utility functions of group members. They show that under two reasonable conditions about group functioning, the group utility function has a multiplicative form. The assessment of the function parameters, however, itself calls for a group decision whose solution is not evident.

The use of Decision Analysis to study group choice requires that a solution be found to these two important problems. The aggregation of individual utility functions is affected by interpersonal comparison of utilities. Although the axioms of modern utility theory, developed by von Neumann and Morgenstern (1944), do imply the existence of interval-scaled individual utility functions, these last do not possess a unique zero point and are expressed in terms of arbitrary units of measurement (Luce and Raiffa, 1957).

Moreover, the validity of some of the Decision Analysis axioms may be questioned when applied to group decision problems. This is especially true for the substitution principle, which assumes independence between the assessment of utilities and the quantification of judgments about uncertain events (see Raiffa, 1968).

In general, the interpretation of the Decision Analysis axioms raises problems even at the level of descriptive individual decision making. This leads Coombs, Dawes and Tversky (1970), to emphasize that the use of utility theory as a behavioral model "has to be supplemented by a psychological theory that accounts for situational variables that affect risky choices." In marketing, however, prescriptive utility theory has been used recently with some success to describe individual choice behavior (Hauser and Urban, 1977, 1979). From the previous discussion, it is not clear how this methodology could be extended to groups, however.

A.7.1.3. SOCIAL PSYCHOLOGY

The uncertainty with which individuals report preferences and the inconsistency that they exhibit when faced with choices involving complex alternatives have led psychologists to develop models of choice in which the traditional concept of preference is replaced by the notion of choice probability.

Probabilistic theories of preference and choice differ about the locus of the random element in the individual decision process (see Luce and Suppes, 1965, for a review). In random utility models, the utility values themselves undergo random fluctuations, and the choice mechanism is completely deterministic. An individual is assumed to choose the alternative that has the highest momentary utility.

Constant utility models, on the other hand, consider that the decision rule itself is subject to randomness, but individuals' subjective evaluations of the alternatives are constant over time. Selection probabilities are then defined as functions of the utility associated with the choice alternatives. Luce's (1959) model of individual choice is an example of this approach.

Social psychologists have also developed descriptive models of group choice behavior by making formal assumptions about the type of interaction that takes place among its members. The theory of social decision schemes (Davis, 1973) is concerned with the development and testing of such models. Its aim is to account for the distribution of group decisions when decision participants' choice probabilities are known. Up to now, it has centered mainly on task-oriented groups.

A social decision scheme may be viewed as an *approximation* of the actual interaction process which takes place within a group. It can be regarded as the way in which the group deals with all internal distributions of choices across its members.

The social decision scheme approach is concerned with modeling the group interaction as a combinatorial process. Assuming a set of mutually exclusive alternatives and letting the choice process of all decision participants be described by a probability mass function across these alternatives, one can compute the probability that the group members arrive at any particular internal distribution of choices. For any such internal distribution of choices the group decision scheme postulated is then used to yield the probability distribution of group choice.

As it stands now, the social decision scheme theory is not a general theory of group decision making. It makes no provisions for different types of tasks or stages in the decision process. Moreover, from a computational viewpoint, when the number of decision participants is larger than two, and they have different internal choice probabilities, it becomes difficult to compute group choice probabilities.

A.7.1.4. EVALUATION

Economists, decision analysts, and social psychologists have all faced the problem of modeling the group choice process. The approach used by economists leads to models that are neither measurable nor descriptive of behavior, and thus are of little use in the organizational buying context. Decision analysts have made considerable progress. Important questions are left unanswered, however, and their work tends to be more of a prescriptive nature. Some of the approaches of social psychologists, suitably refined, hold promise for modeling the interaction process that takes place in industrial purchasing. Their Social Decision Schemes have provided the basis on which we developed the classes of probabilistic models of group choice discussed in the next appendix.

Analytical Structure of Four Models of Group Choice

Four models of group choice are proposed here. Each model corresponds to a different conceptualization of the interaction process involved in industrial buying situations.

We make use of the following notation:

- d, $d = 1$ ... D, refers to the various categories of decision participants who are involved in the organizational choice process for the product under investigation.
- d_i refers to any individual belonging to category d.
- $A = \{a_j, j = 0, \ldots J\}$ stands for the feasible set of alternatives and defines the domain of individual and organizational preferences.
- An individual's preference structure is denoted μ_i. It assigns a ratio scaled preference score μ_{ij} to each feasible alternative $a_j \epsilon A$.
- $f_{\mu d}(\mu)$ is the multidimensional distribution of preference scores within decision participant category d.

We then define the probability that individual i, selected randomly from category d, actually chooses a_J from A, as

$$P_d(a_j) = \int_\mu p(a_j | \mu_i) f_{\mu_d}(\mu) d\mu$$

where $p(a_j | \mu_i)$ represents choice probabilities obtained from individual choice models. The uncertainty concerning $P_i(a_j)$ can then be assessed by

$$\text{Var}\ [P_d(a_j)] = \int_\mu [p(a_j | \mu_i) - P_d(a_j)]^2 f_{\mu d}(\mu) d\mu$$

A.7.2.1. WEIGHTED PROBABILITY MODEL

The Weighted Probability Model assumes that the group, as a whole, is likely to adopt a given alternative, say $a_0 \epsilon A$, proportionally to the relative importance of those members who choose it.

To keep the notation simple, let

$P_G(a_j)$ = probability that the group chooses a_j

w_d = relative importance, on the average, of decision participant d, $d = 1, \ldots D$, in the choice process for the microsegment investigated. So,

$$\sum_{d=1}^{D} w_d = 1$$

Then the weighted probability model postulates that

$$P_G(a_O) = \sum_{d=1}^{D} w_d P_d(a_0)$$

and the variance of that quantity is

$$\text{Var}[P_G(a_0)] = \sum_{d=1}^{D} w_d^2 \, \text{Var}[P_d(a_0)]$$

This model can be interpreted as a two-step sampling process where, in step one, the organization samples a single decision maker from the set of decision participants in proportion to each participant's relative importance in the choice process. In step two, the retained decision maker selects an alternative according to his own choice probabilities, $P_d(a_j)$.

There are two interesting special cases of the weighted probability model:

1. *Autocracy:* If $w_L = 1$, then all other $w_{i \neq L} = 0$, and a single decision participant, L, is the only one responsible for the group choice.
2. *Equiprobability:* If $w_d = 1/D$ for all d, then every decision participant has an equal chance of making the final decision. This is an appealing model, because it is a zero-information or naive model. The industrial marketing manager need only identify the decision participants and does not have to measure or provide subjective estimates of the importance coefficients.

The equiprobability form of the weighted probability model has received some empirical support in dyadic decision making (Davis, Cohen, Hornik and Rissman, 1973). Moreover, the model was found to accurately describe group risk shifts (Davis, 1973).

One must be careful, however, in interpreting these results. Indeed, although the cumulative frequencies of actual group decisions were reproduced accurately by the equiprobability model, these experiments mainly involved *ad-hoc* groups whose members had little experience in working together. The equiprobability model might then be a reasonable approximation to organizational choice behavior in situations that involve decision participants from different departments who are not accustomed to working together.

As an example, consider an organization with three decision participants: $1, 2, 3$ and three alternatives $A = \{a_0, a_1, a_2\}$ as in Exhibit 7.4.

Then $P_G(a_0) = .2w_1 + .3w_2 + .7w_3$. An equiprobability model with $w_i = 1/3$ $i = 1, 2, 3$ will yield $P_G(a_0) = .4$. An autocratic model with $w_1 = 1$ will yield $P_G(a_0) = .2$; with $w_3 = 1$ will yield $P_G(a_0) = .7$. These are upper and lower bounds on $P_G(a_0)$ for the weighted probability model. In terms of our example: $.7 \geqslant P_G(a_0) \geqslant 2$.

Exhibit 7.4   Individual choice probabilities $P_d(a_j)$

a_j	$P_1(a_j)$	$P_2(a_j)$	$P_3(a_j)$
a_0	.2	.3	.7
a_1	.5	.2	.2
a_2	.3	.5	.1

A.7.2.2 THE VOTING MODEL

The Voting Model attributes the same weight to all individuals involved in the group decision process. It states, however, that the probability $P_G(a_0)$ that the group will choose alternative a, is the likelihood that it is the choice of more decision participants than any other alternative.

$$\text{Let } x_{ij} = \begin{cases} 1 \text{ if } i\epsilon d \text{ chooses } a_j. \\ 0 \text{ otherwise} \end{cases}$$

$$\text{So, } \Pr(x_{ij} = 1) = P_d(a_j)$$

The number of decision participants who choose a_j is then given by:

$$z_j = \sum_{i=1}^{D} x_{ij}$$

and $P_G(a_0) = \text{Probability } [z_0 = \max_j (z_j)].$

If ties occur, in which case several alternatives are supported by the same number of decision participants, then

$$z_\ell = z_k = \max (z_j), \text{ for some } \ell \neq k$$

and we assume that these alternatives are equally likely to be the group choice.

A special case occurs when z_0 must be greater than z_{majority}, i.e., when $z_0 \geqslant (D/2 + 1)$ or $z_0 \geqslant (D + 1)/2$ according to whether the number of decision participants D in the microsegment is even or odd respectively. In this case, let $\Pr(z_j \geqslant z_{\text{majority}})$ represent that the *majority* of decision participants choose a_0.

As an example of the Voting Model, consider the choice probabilities in Exhibit 7.5. For the Voting Model, in which the probability of group choice is equal to the probability of choice by the largest number of participants, we get

Exhibit 7.5

Internal distribution of choices Ψ.			Probability of Occurrence Pr $(\Psi.)$	Number of decision participants supporting a_j		
$d = 1$	$d = 2$	$d = 3$		a_0	a_1	a_2
a_0	a_0	a_0	.042	3	0	0
a_0	a_0	a_1	.012	2	1	0
a_0	a_0	a_2	.006	2	0	1
a_0	a_1	a_0	.028	2	1	0
a_0	a_1	a_1	.008	1	2	0
a_0	a_1	a_2	.004	1	1	1
a_0	a_2	a_0	.070	2	0	1
a_0	a_2	a_1	.020	1	1	1
a_0	a_2	a_2	.010	1	0	2
a_1	a_0	a_0	.105	2	1	0
a_1	a_0	a_1	.030	1	2	0
a_1	a_0	a_2	.015	1	1	1
a_1	a_1	a_0	.070	1	2	0
a_1	a_1	a_1	.020	0	3	0
a_1	a_1	a_2	.010	0	2	1
a_1	a_2	a_0	.175	1	1	1
a_1	a_2	a_1	.050	0	2	1
a_1	a_2	a_2	.025	0	1	2
a_2	a_0	a_0	.063	2	0	1
a_2	a_0	a_1	.018	1	1	1
a_2	a_0	a_2	.009	1	0	2
a_2	a_1	a_0	.042	1	1	1
a_2	a_1	a_1	.012	0	2	1
a_2	a_1	a_2	.006	0	1	2
a_2	a_2	a_0	.105	1	0	2
a_2	a_2	a_1	.030	0	1	2
a_2	a_2	a_2	.015	0	0	3

(Note: For the Voting Model,
$P_G(a_0) = (.042 + .012 + .006 + .028 + .070 + .105 + .063) + \frac{1}{3}(.004 + .020 + .015$
$+ .175 + .018 + .042)$
$= .327 + (\frac{1}{3} \times .274) = .417)$

$$P_G(a_0) = .326 + (1/3 \times .274) = .417$$

$$P_G(a_1) = .200 + (1/3 \times .274) = .291$$

$$P_G(a_2) = .200 + (1/3 \times .274) = .291$$

In the same way, the majority model leads to:

$$\Pr(z_0 \geqslant 2) = .326$$

$$\Pr(z_1 \geqslant 2) = .200$$

$$\Pr(z_2 \geqslant 2) = .200$$

The Voting Model has received empirical support in conditions similar to those used to test the equiprobability model (Davis, 1973).

A.7.2.3 MINIMUM ENDORSEMENT MODEL

This model assumes that to be accepted by the group, an alternative, say a_0, has to be the actual choice of a prespecified number of decision participants involved in the choice process. Thus a group might, in theory, vote over and over again until the quota is reached.

An interesting special case of this model is the unanimity model. Empirical studies of the industrial purchasing process indicate that this latter model captures some of the essence of the multiperson choice involved in this process. (Buckner, 1967). It also reflects the so called management by concensus, reportedly practiced by Japanese businessmen.

Formally, the unanimity model implies that

$$P_G(a_0) = \frac{\displaystyle\prod_{d=1}^{D} P_d(a_0)}{\displaystyle\sum_{j=0}^{J} \prod_{d=1}^{D} P_d(a_j)}$$

assuming that individual preference distributions are mutually independent. This is the *conditional* probability that the product a_0 is selected, *given* that the group reached unanimity.

The unanimity model has a desirable property: The addition of an independent decision participant to the group does not affect the conditional probability $P_G(a_0)$ that the group will choose alternative a_0.

Assume that the new decision participant is the $(D + 1)$st. We get

$$P_G'(a_0) = \frac{\displaystyle\prod_{d=1}^{D+1} P_d(a_0)}{\displaystyle\sum_{j=0}^{J}\prod_{d=1}^{D+1} P_d(a_j)},$$

where G' is the original group plus the $D + 1_{st}$ participant.

As $P_{D+1}(a_j) = \dfrac{1}{J+1}$ for all $a_j \epsilon A$, by assumption, we get

$$P_G'(a_0) = \frac{\dfrac{1}{(J+1)}\displaystyle\prod_{d=1}^{D} P_i(a_0)}{\dfrac{1}{(J+1)}\displaystyle\sum_{j=0}^{J}\prod_{d=1}^{D} P_i(a_j)}$$

$$= P_G(a_0; A)$$

As an example, consider again the probabilities in Exhibit 7.4. Here, we get:

$$P_G(a_0) = \frac{.042}{.042 + .020 + .015} = .545$$

In the same way:

$$P_G(a_1) = .259$$
$$P_G(a_2) = .195.$$

The conditional nature of the Minimum Endorsement Model allows dynamic changes of decision participants' choice probabilities. Indeed, if the quota is not reached at the first vote, group members may update their choice probabilities. Various schemes can be devised to update such probabilities on the basis of past individual or group behavior. Implementation of the model here, however, assumed stationary individual choice probabilities.

A.7.2.4 THE PREFERENCE PERTURBATION MODEL

This model assumes that if a group does not reach unanimous agreement, it is most likely to choose the alternative that "perturbs" individual preference structures least. This may be referred to as "management by exception." Suppose the following pattern of individual preferences holds in a group of two:

Decision Participant	Preference Pattern	Probability of getting Pattern μ_k
$d = 1$	$\mu_{1\ell} : a_0 \geqslant a_1 \geqslant a_2$	$P_1(\mu_{1\ell}/A)$
$d = 2$	$\mu_{2h} : a_2 \geqslant a_0 \geqslant a_1$	$P_2(\mu_{2h}/A)$

where μ_{dk} means that individual ied exhibits an ordinal preference structure μ_k. Given the pattern of preference structures $\gamma_{\ell h} = \{\mu_{1\ell}, \mu_{2h}\}$, we define the perturbation $Q(a_j|\gamma_{\ell h})$ associated with the choice of alternative a_j as the total number of preference shifts necessary for a_j to be everyone's first choice. In the above example, we get:

$$Q(a_0|\gamma_{\ell h}) = 1$$
$$Q(a_1|\gamma_{\ell h}) = 3$$
$$Q(a_2|\gamma_{\ell h}) = 2$$

Assuming that all preference shifts are strictly comparable, we have:

$$P_G(a_0|\gamma_{\ell h}) = 3 P_G(a_1|\gamma_{\ell h})$$
$$P_G(a_0|\gamma_{\ell h}) = 2 P_G(a_2|\gamma_{\ell h})$$

and since

$$\sum_{j=0}^{J} P_G(a_j|\gamma_{\ell h}) = 1, \text{ we get}$$

$$P_G(a_0|\gamma_{\ell h}) = 6/11$$
$$P_G(a_1|\gamma_{\ell h}) = 2/11$$
$$P_G(a_2|\gamma_{\ell h}) = 3/11$$

Formally, given the multidimensional preference distribution for each decision participant category, we can compute the probability that a specific pattern of preference structures γ_w will occur across individuals. Here w represents a particular vector of preferences as follows:

$$\Pr[\gamma_w] = \Pr[\mu_{1k}, \mu_{2k}, \ldots \mu_{Dk}]$$

$$= \prod_{d=1}^{D} \Pr[\mu_{dk}]$$

where

$$w = 1, \ldots k^D$$

and

$$k = 1, \ldots (J + 1)!$$

assuming that individual (preference) distributions are mutually independent.

Letting $Q(a_j|\gamma_w)$ be the perturbation associated with alternative a_j in the pattern γ_w, we postulate that

$$\frac{P_G(a_j|\gamma_w)}{P_G(a_\varrho|\gamma_w)} = \frac{Q(a_\varrho|\gamma_w)}{Q(a_j|\gamma_w)}$$

If $Q(a_\varrho|\gamma_w) = 0$, then

$$P_G(a_\varrho|\gamma_w) = 1 \text{ and }$$

$$P_G(a_j|\gamma_w) = 0 \text{ for } j \neq \varrho.$$

Since the total number of possible preference shifts is fixed, these conditional probabilities are uniquely determined. Hence, the unconditional probabilities of group choice are given by:

$$P_G(a_j) = \sum_w P_G(a_j|\gamma_w) \cdot \Pr[\gamma_w]$$

Although it is conceptually simple, the Preference Perturbation Model entails combinatorial difficulties. Its justification follows from the observation that many groups seem to choose everybody's second choice, or more precisely, the alternative that perturbs individual preferences least.

As a numerical example, consider the data in Exhibit 7.6. In order to reduce computation, we have assumed that the group is composed only of two decision participants, 1 and 2. Assuming three alternatives $A = (a_0, a_1, a_2)$, there are $(3!)^2$ possible patterns of preference structures. Exhibit 7.7 enumerates these patterns, gives their probability of occurrence, and the perturbation associated with each alternative respectively. Exhibit 7.8 gives the probabilities of group choice conditional to the occurrence of each pattern γ_w.

We then get the unconditional probabilities of group choice:

$$P_G(a_0) = .271$$
$$P_G(a_1) = .334$$
$$P_G(a_2) = .394$$

This model has the desirable property that it can be used with ordinal preference data, while the other models require specification of interval or ratio-scaled preferences.

Exhibit 7.6 Hypothetical Data for Preference Perturbation Model

Pattern of individual preference structure			$Pr(\gamma_w)$	$Q(a_0|\gamma_w)$	$Q(a_1|\gamma_w)$	$Q(a_2|\gamma_w)$
γ_w	d_1	d_2				
γ_1	μ_1	μ_1	.0078	0	–	–
γ_2	μ_1	μ_2	.0312	0	–	–
γ_3	μ_1	μ_3	.0169	1	1	4
γ_4	μ_1	μ_4	.0091	2	1	3
γ_5	μ_1	μ_5	.0247	1	3	2
γ_6	μ_1	μ_6	.0403	2	2	2
γ_7	μ_2	μ_1	.0042	0	–	–
γ_8	μ_2	μ_2	.0168	0	–	–
γ_9	μ_2	μ_3	.0091	1	2	3
γ_{10}	μ_2	μ_4	.0049	2	2	2
γ_{11}	μ_2	μ_5	.0133	1	4	1
γ_{12}	μ_2	μ_6	.0217	2	3	1
γ_{13}	μ_3	μ_1	.0132	1	1	4
γ_{14}	μ_3	μ_2	.0528	1	2	3
γ_{15}	μ_3	μ_3	.0286	–	0	–
γ_{16}	μ_3	μ_4	.0154	–	0	–
γ_{17}	μ_3	μ_5	.0418	2	2	2
γ_{18}	μ_3	μ_6	.0682	3	1	2
γ_{19}	μ_4	μ_1	.0168	2	1	3
γ_{20}	μ_4	μ_2	.0672	2	2	2
γ_{21}	μ_4	μ_3	.0364	–	0	–
γ_{22}	μ_4	μ_4	.0196	–	0	–
γ_{23}	μ_4	μ_5	.0532	3	2	1
γ_{24}	μ_4	μ_6	.0868	4	1	1
γ_{25}	μ_5	μ_1	.0108	1	3	2
γ_{26}	μ_5	μ_2	.0432	1	4	1
γ_{27}	μ_5	μ_3	.0234	2	2	2
γ_{28}	μ_5	μ_4	.0126	3	2	1
γ_{29}	μ_5	μ_5	.0342	–	–	0
γ_{30}	μ_5	μ_6	.0558	–	–	0
γ_{31}	μ_6	μ_1	.0072	2	2	2
γ_{32}	μ_6	μ_2	.0288	2	3	1

Exhibit 7.6 (Continued)

Pattern of individual preference structure			$Pr(\gamma_w)$	$Q(a_0|\gamma_w)$	$Q(a_1|\gamma_w)$	$Q(a_2|\gamma_w)$
γ_{33}	μ_6	μ_3	.0156	3	1	2
γ_{34}	μ_6	μ_4	.0084	4	1	1
γ_{35}	μ_6	μ_5	.0228	–	–	0
γ_{36}	μ_6	μ_6	.0372	–	–	0

Exhibit 7.7 Hypothetical distribution of ordinal preference structures

Preference structure μ_k	$Pr[\mu_{1k}]$	$Pr[\mu_{2k}]$
$\mu_1 = a_0 \geqslant a_1 \geqslant a_2$	.13	.06
$\mu_2 = a_0 \geqslant a_2 \geqslant a_1$	.07	.24
$\mu_3 = a_1 \geqslant a_0 \geqslant a_2$	.22	.13
$\mu_4 = a_1 \geqslant a_2 \geqslant a_0$	.28	.07
$\mu_5 = a_2 \geqslant a_0 \geqslant a_1$	.18	.19
$\mu_6 = a_2 \geqslant a_1 \geqslant a_0$	.12	.31

Exhibit 7.8 Derived Group Choice Probabilities: Preference Perturbation Model

Pattern of individual preference structure	$P_G(a_0|\gamma_w)$	$P_G(a_1|\gamma_w)$	$P_G(a_2|\gamma_w)$
γ_1	1	0	0
γ_2	1	0	0
γ_3	.444	.444	.111
γ_4	.272	.545	.181
γ_5	.545	.181	.272
γ_6	.333	.333	.333
γ_7	1	0	0
γ_8	1	0	0
γ_9	.545	.272	.181
γ_{10}	.333	.333	.333

(continued)

Exhibit 7.8 (Continued)

Pattern of individual preference structure	$P_G(a_0\|\gamma_w)$	$P_G(a_1\|\gamma_w)$	$P_G(a_2\|\gamma_w)$
γ_{11}	.444	.111	.444
γ_{12}	.272	.181	.545
γ_{13}	.444	.444	.111
γ_{14}	.545	.272	.181
γ_{15}	0	1	0
γ_{16}	0	1	0
γ_{17}	.333	.333	.333
γ_{18}	.181	.545	.272
γ_{19}	.272	.545	.181
γ_{20}	.333	.333	.333
γ_{21}	0	1	0
γ_{22}	0	1	0
γ_{23}	.181	.272	.545
γ_{24}	.111	.444	.444
γ_{25}	.545	.181	.272
γ_{26}	.444	.111	.444
γ_{27}	.333	.333	.333
γ_{28}	.181	.272	.545
γ_{29}	0	0	1
γ_{30}	0	0	1
γ_{31}	.333	.333	.333
γ_{32}	.272	.181	.545
γ_{33}	.181	.545	.272
γ_{34}	.111	.444	.444
γ_{35}	0	0	1
γ_{36}	0	0	1

APPENDIX 8.1.

The PV Diffusion Model

This appendix gives the technical details of the PV diffusion model. The model considers the following controlling influences:

1. Cost per unit of energy produced.
2. Relative cost of other energy sources.
3. The perception of risk in adopting the innovation.
4. External factors such as government policy.
5. Noneconomic factors such as aesthetics and energy savings.

The model follows the increase in PV installations and unit cost decreases over time. All variables related to number of installations are split into private sector and government parts. The variables that we want to follow are:

X_{it} = number of government PV installations in sector i at time t.

Y_{it} = number of private PV installations in sector i at time t.

Z_i = average installation size (in kilowatts) in sector i.

C_t = cost per kilowatt of PV at time t.

Hence,

$$N_{it} = \sum_{s=0}^{t-1} (X_{is} + Y_{is})Z_i$$

is cumulative kilowatts installed in sector i before t, and

$$N_t = \sum_i N_{it}$$

is cumulative kilowatts across sectors.

Cost is modeled as an exponentially decreasing function of the cumulative number of installed kilowatts. A standard form for a cost decline is constant doubling, where cost is discounted by a fraction λ when cumulative production doubles, or

$$C_t = C_o \lambda^{\log_2(N_t/N_o)}, \quad 0 < \lambda \leq 1$$

where C_o is initial cost.

The question is, at the next time step how many additional square feet will be bought as a function of this cost? Our assumptions imply that the fraction of consumers who will buy are those who find the cost low enough and the number of earlier successful installations high enough (subject to their perception of PV). Data from earlier work suggest that the cost and number of successful installation components of the decision are approximately independent and so can be described as independent probability distributions, say $f_{C_i}(c)$ for cost and $f_{S_i}(s)$ for successes in sector i. Note that the model we develop below in no way requires independence. However, it does make our notation a bit clearer to assume independence at this point. If we let

$$S_{it} = \sum_{k=1}^{t} X_{ik} + Y_{ik}$$

denote the total number of PV installations in sector i at time t, we get

$$\int_{C_t}^{\infty} f_{C_i}(c)dc = 1 - F_{C_i}(C_t)$$
$$= \text{the probability that } C_t \text{ is accept-}$$
able, and

$$\int_{-\infty}^{S_{it}} f_{S_i}(s)ds = F_{S_i}(S_{it})$$
$$= \text{the probability that } S_{it} \text{ successes}$$
are acceptable in sector i.

To model the potential market at time t in sector i, we distinguish between old and new installations so as to discriminate between retrofit and original equipment installations with a simple functional form. Let P_{it} denote market potential represented by retrofit installations, and Q_{it} denote potential for new installations. Total market potential in t is thus given by

$$M_{it} = P_{io} + \sum_{k=1}^{t} Q_{ik}.$$

Before time t, $S_i(t-1)$ installations have already been made. Hence, the number of private installations in t is given by

$$Y_{it} = (M_{it} - S_i(t-1) - X_{it}) \, (1 - F_{C_i}(C_t)) \cdot (F_{S_i}(S_i(t-1)) \cdot G$$

where G denotes the product-perception-choice probability part of our market assessment procedure, (i.e., the fraction who buy, given acceptability).

We can now use this model to formulate a simple decision problem for the government. The government's problem is to decide how much to spend and how to allocate demonstration project resources. This becomes find X_{it} to maximize

$$\sum_i \sum_t Y_{it}$$

subject to

$$\sum_i X_{it} C_t Z_i < B_t \text{ for all } t$$

where

$$B_t = \text{annual government budget constraint.}$$

This model has been implemented as a system of computer programs written in PL/1 on the Multics System at M.I.T. See Lilien (1978) for documentation details.

Analysis of the Timing of Demonstration Programs: As developed here, the PV model is a simulation model that allows us to evaluate the effect of various policy options on diffusion. A look at some simple models will give us insight into the structure of sensible policies.

A basic diffusion model (see Appendix 8.2 for fuller development) is one by Bass (1969). We introduce the following notation:

Let

$S(t)$ = number of firms having adopted an innovation by time t ($S(0) = 0$).

S^* = total number of firms considered eligible to adopt the innovation.

p = coefficient of innovation; this equals the rate of product adoption when there have been no previous purchases.

q = coefficient of imitation; the effect of previous purchases on the rate of adoption.

In essence, Bass' model is as follows:

(1)
$$\frac{dS(t)}{dt} = \left(p + q\frac{S(t)}{S^*}\right)(S^* - S(t)).$$

As formulated here, this model has no controllable variables. Let us consider the problem that the government (or a private sector marketer) faces when deciding how to accelerate or control this process. We take the point of view of the government, where the government can develop demonstration programs.

Let

> $A(t)$ = number of government-sponsored demonstration programs installed by time t. In private sector terms these marketer-placed units are called "reference-installations."

Note that the class of demonstration programs that is most appropriate for analysis here are of the "cooperative" or "government-support" types. Here an agency of the government requests a builder/developer and a buyer to submit a proposal for a project. The government shares the cost and, from time to time, will inspect and monitor the performance of the system. Most such projects show little external sign of being government-sponsored. By design they are supposed to be similar to private sector-purchased systems.

Thus, it is not unreasonable to assume that imitators in equation (1) are equally impressed by any successful project, whether it be government sponsored or privately owned. We also assume that the demonstration programs affect neither the coefficient of innovation, p, nor the coefficient of imitation, q. (See Kalish and Lilien (1979) for some suggestions on how to relax these assumptions). Following these assumptions, we get:

(2)
$$\frac{dS(t)}{dt} = (p + q^1 T(t))(S^* - S(t))$$

where

$$T(t) = S(t) + A(t)$$

and

$$q^1 = q/S^*.$$

Suppose that $A(\infty) = C$ (the government will ultimately set up a total of C demonstration programs). Our first question is how, given this model, these installations should be timed to hasten the diffusion of the new product.

This is analyzed as follows:

The form of equation (2) allows separation of $dS(t)/dt$ into two components.

$$\frac{dS(t)}{dt} = \frac{dS_1(t)}{dt} + \frac{dS_2(t)}{dt}$$

where

$$\frac{dS_1(t)}{dt} = p[S^* - S(t)] + \frac{q}{S^*} S(t)[S^* - S(t)]$$

and

$$\frac{dS_2(t)}{dt} = \frac{q}{S^*} A(t)[S^* - S(T)].$$

Since, at any time, t, $dS_2(t)/dt$ is greater when $A(t)$ is greater, $dS_2(t)/dt$, (and, hence, $dS(t)/dt$) will be maximal when all demonstration program resources are allocated as early as possible.

According to this model, then, it cannot pay to delay allocation of demonstration resources. In considering allocation of effort across sectors of the economy or across regions, we need only be concerned with the *initial* level of support since any delay can be improved, as above, by acceleration in time.

Optimal Macrosegment or Regional Allocation of Resources: Here we postulate a simple response problem which leads to some general results about regional development policies. The purpose of the marketing program is to accelerate total market diffusion.

We assume that q, the imitation rate, is a function of the level of marketers' sampling support, that is

$$q = f(A)$$

Model (1) therefore becomes

(3) $$\frac{dS_i(t)}{dt} = [S_i^* - S_i(t)] \ [p_i + f_i(A_i(t))S_i(t)]$$

where subscript i refers to market segment i.

The previous result has indicated that, according to the diffusion model, it cannot pay for us to delay allocation. Thus, we need only consider the level of sampling support in the *first* period if we wish to allocate sampling effort across markets. It can be shown that the optimal solution depends on the shape of the imitation functions $q_i = f_i(A_i)$. In particular,

- If all $f_i(A_i)$ are concave, the optimal policy is to allocate sampling effort over markets according to incremental innovator returns.
- If all $f_i(A_i)$ are convex, the optimal policy is to allocate resources to only one region.
- If all $f_i(A_i)$ are S-shaped, showing a convex and then a concave region, the optimal solution leads to a policy of allocating resources to markets one at a time, in order of decreasing response rate, until the strictly concave region is reached.

The results here are quite powerful. The photovoltaic work described in Chapter 8 has demonstrated that the insight we gain from the analysis is valuable for industrial marketing planning. In particular, we have shown that:

- Delaying market development resources is unlikely to be effective. This assumes no customer feedback will be used to modify the product.

- Concave imitation response implies a spread-out strategy. Suppose the effect of each installation on market acceptance were less than the effect of the previous one. Then, market resources should be spread as widely as possible.

- Convex imitator response implies a concentrated strategy. Suppose the second application had more effect on potential buyers than the first, the third more than the second, and so on. In this case, all resources should be concentrated in a single area.

- S-shaped response implies concentrate in one area at a time then spread out. S-shaped response combines the early effects of convex response with the later effects of concave response. This (most realistic) case suggests building up an area to a point where it is self-sustaining and then going on.

The economics of purchase and varying market potentials have not been considered here. However, the results, though not meant to be definitive, do suggest conditions under which certain policies — over regions, macrosegments and time — are preferable to others.

Diffusion and Substitution Models: The State of the Art

The area of diffusion and substitution has its roots in the theory of contagious diseases, or the spread of epidemics (Bailey, 1975). Contagion models assume that the population is of constant size $(N + 1)$ or growing at a known pace throughout the time of the study. For our purposes we can think of the population being divided as

Susceptible — those individuals who are uninfected and susceptible to infection (Potential Buyers).

Infectious — those individuals who are infected and are contagious (Purchasers).

Initially, we assume there is only one infectious individual and N susceptible people. The rate of growth of the infectious population is assumed to be proportional to the number of contacts between those who are susceptible and those who are infectious.

We introduce the following notation. Let

$S(t)$ = number infectious at time t.

$M(t) = [S^* - S(t)]$ = number susceptible at time t.

S^* = initial number of susceptibles, assumed constant here.

q = probability that contact between one infectious and one susceptible will cause the susceptible individual to become infectious.

Mathematically the rate of growth of the epidemic is given by:

(1) $$dS(t)/dt = qS(t)M(t)$$

Using the assumption that the population size is fixed at S^*, that $M(0) = S^* - 1$ and $S(0) = 1$, the solution to equation (1) is given by:

(2) $$M(t) = \frac{S^* \, [S^* - S(t)] \, e^{-qS^*t}}{1 + [S^* - S(t)] \, e^{-qS^*t}}$$

Now $S(t)$ can be obtained by using the result that $S(t) = S^* - M(t)$.

Also of interest is the graph of the rate of growth of the epidemic as a function of time. A mathematical expression for $dS(t)/dt$ is as follows:

(3) $$\frac{dS(t)}{dt} = \frac{S^* e^{-qS^*t}}{1 + [S^* - S(t)] \, e^{-qS^*t}}$$

In applying the contagion model to the innovation process we think of $M(t)$ as those individuals who have not yet adopted the innovation and $S(t)$ as those who have adopted the innovation (cumulative sales) and have an effect on adoption behavior. A contagion model can be developed to include the case where there is a third group — those who have adopted, but too recently to have any effect on the behavior of others. In such a case, the exposed group is included in the contagion model.

Let us now review some of the more popular diffusion models. Mansfield's (1968b) model is based on the assumption that the probability that a firm will introduce a new technique is (a) an increasing function of the proportion of firms already using it, (b) an increasing function of the profitability of doing so, and (e) a decreasing function of the size of the investment required. It is assumed that all firms in the market will eventually adopt the innovation. It is also assumed that the profitability of installing the innovation relative to that of alternative investments is appreciably greater than unity.

Let us introduce the following notation:

$S(t)$ = number of firms having introduced the innovation at time t.

S^* = total number of firms considered eligible to adopt the innovation

k = integration constant

Following a series of arguments (similar to those for the contagion models) Mansfield obtains that

$$S(t) = \frac{S^*}{1 + e^{-(k+qt)}}$$

Mansfield's assumptions lead to estimating q, the imitation or contagion coefficient as a linear function of the relative profitability of installing the innovation and the size of the investment required.

Following this basic work have been a series of model modifications. Fisher and Pry (1971) apply Mansfield's logistic model to 17 product areas, described in Section 8.1. Blackman (1974) develops a model that does not assume 100% penetration will be reached. The form of that model is

$$\frac{d\,S(t)/S^*}{dt} = p\frac{S(t)}{S^*}\left(F - \frac{S(t)}{S^*}\right)$$

where F = fraction of the market penetrated.

Floyd (1968) adds a linear patch to the Blackman and Fisher-Pry models which tend to over-predict near the end of the forecast period. His model under-predicts.

Sharif and Kabir (1976) modify the Floyd patch. Stapleton (1976) suggests the use of a cumulative normal curve — the so-called Pearl (1925) curve — to model the S-shaped phenomenon. Nelson, Peck and Calacheck (1967) postulate that the S-shape follows from a gradual movement from one form of equilibrium to another when a new product enters the market. A simple mathematical statement of this phenomenon assumes that the percent adjustment in any one period is proportional to the percent difference between the actual level of adoption of the innovation and the level corresponding to the new equilibrium. Thus, we obtain:

$$\log S(t) - \log S(t-1) = p[\log k - \log S(t)]$$

where $S(t)$ is the level of adoption and k, the new equilibrium. If we replace $\log S(t) - \log S(t-1)$ by $\dfrac{d \log S(t)}{dt}$ and $p = -\log \beta$, we get

$$\frac{d \log S(t)}{dt} = \log \beta \, [\log k - \log S(t)] ,$$

the differential equation associated with the Gompertz function.

A key extension of these types of models was proposed by Bass (1969):

$$\frac{dS(t)}{dt} = \left[p + q \, \frac{S(t)}{S^*} \right] [S^* - S(t)]$$

This model adds an innovation term to the Mansfield model and seems to describe the adoption of consumer durables well.

A number of recent extensions have been made to these models, addressing the issues of relating three key quantities — innovation, imitation, and ultimate potential — to marketing variables.

Robinson and Lakhani (1975) relate the imitation rate to product price, incorporating a price elasticity into the diffusion equation. Horsky and Simon (1978) incorporate the effect of advertising on the rate of innovation. Hernes (1976) allows for time-dependent variations in both the innovation and imitation rates, following from the changing characteristics of the population. Bass (1978) updates his model, incorporating a production-cost learning effect. His model assumes that the coefficient of innovation and imitation are functions of demand elasticity and of the learning parameter in an experience curve of production cost. Mahajan and Peterson (1978) relate the imitation effect to the competitive structure of the market being entered. Dodson and Muller (1978) suggest that the ultimate purchasing population size varies according to awareness, which is affected by advertising and by word-of-mouth. Hauser (1978) couples Bass' model with perception-preference-choice models in forecasting adoption and growth. The interested reader should refer to Mahajan and Peterson (1979) and Hurter and Rubenstein (1978) for more thorough reviews of these efforts.

On the plus side, almost all of these models report good descriptive results. They fit historical data well. However, as Mahajan and Peterson note, "a unified theory to incorporate relevant marketing variables into the basic growth models is not apparent."

APPENDIX 9.1.

Some Available Computer Codes

Chapter 9 was devoted to a presentation of an industrial market research system that provides relevant data. The interface between methodology and data is usually provided by a computer. It is therefore logical that we devote some time in this appendix to a brief review of available computer codes that might be used to perform part of the analysis.

There are many computer programs, packages, and interactive systems that can be used to perform single tasks (e.g. decision participant evaluation space analysis) in the market assessment procedure. The choice among them should be based on criteria such as cost, immediate availability, prior experience, and such technical features as accuracy, modularity, file management systems, and so forth.

It is not our goal to provide an exhaustive list of codes usable for implementing our methodology. Rather, we suggest some that we have found useful; you may prefer others.

We summarize in Exhibit 9.1 the major tasks that require computer support. For some of the tasks, commercial computer codes are not directly available. This is the case for the simulation analysis in Chapter Five, Chapter Seven, and Chapter Eight.

SPSS, the Statistical Package for the Social Sciences (University of Chicago: National Opinion Research Center) Nie, et al (1975), is a powerful, user-oriented statistical package. It provides a wide range of univariate and multivariate statistical codes. In implementing the methodology, SPSS might be useful for performing Multiple Regression and Factor Analysis (Chapter Six) as well as Discriminant Analysis (Chapter Four). The package is well documented and our experience with it suggests that a few hours of practice is sufficient for a computer novice to become comfortable with it. SPSS also provides a versatile file management system

Exhibit 9.1 Major tasks in the methodology requiring computer help

Chapter	Task	Method needed
Chapter Three:	Evaluating Market Potential	Forecasting Procedures Econometric Modeling
Chapter Four:	Industrial Market Segmentation	Cluster Analysis Discriminant Analysis
Chapter Five:	Awareness and Feasibility	Simulation/Mathematical Programming/Optimization
Chapter Six:	Individual Preference and Choice	Multivariate Analysis of Variance Factor Analysis Multiple Regression
Chapter Seven:	Group Choice Behavior	Simulation
Chapter Eight:	Diffusion, Share Projection Analysis	Simulation Mathematical Programming

particularly useful in generating intermediate results between phases of the methodology.

BMDP, the Biomedical Computer Programs, P-Series, is a powerful package which can be used for many of the same tasks as SPSS. In addition, it can be used for Cluster Analysis (Chapter Four) and Multivariate Analysis of Variance (Chapter Six). Our experience with this package, however, indicates that it requires a bit more computer sophistication from the user than SPSS.

IMSL, the International Mathematical and Statistical Library (IMSL, Houston), is a powerful set of tools for general use. It is made up of a large set of FORTRAN computer programs that are input-output free subroutines. These are called upon by the user in a main program to produce desired results. The library can be used for econometric modeling and forecasting (Chapter Three), Discriminant Analysis (Chapter Four), Mathematical Programming/Optimization (Chapter Six), Multivariate Analysis of Variance, Factor Analysis and Multiple Regression (Chapter Seven). IMSL routines are well documented and provide references to the original material. Our experience is that the library is one of the most complete and powerful currently available. However, programming experience is needed to use the package.

A very powerful set of programs for cluster analysis (Chapter Four) is provided by Anderberg (1973). The programs are quite efficient and provide some features not offered in other libraries (e.g. aids to interpreting clustering results). The book in which the programs appear is well balanced and provides a comprehensive treatment of classification problems. We have used these programs for microsegmentation analysis. However, the potential user of these programs needs some (not much) programming skill in FORTRAN. Another useful source of computer programs for cluster analysis is Hartigan (1975).

Some interactive computer systems deserve mention, too. The PLATO System (New York: OR/MS Dialogue, Inc.) is a powerful, user-oriented interactive computer program that covers a wide range of forecasting techniques and univariate and multivariate statistical methods. Its file management system is quite versatile. Many users like working at a console with an intelligent interactive system that raises questions and prompts the user.

TROLL (available through the National Bureau of Economic Research, Cambridge, Massachusetts), is a very powerful interactive computer system that allows sophisticated econometric and statistical analysis. As with PLATO, it can be used to perform most of the forecasting and statistical tasks needed for implementing the market assessment methodology. TROLL, however, requires more user expertise, although it offers many more experimental programs and options.

This short discussion about computer codes illustrates the choice to be made by the user between

- an interactive system (PLATO, TROLL)
- a package (SPSS, BMDP)
- a library of routines (IMSL, Anderberg's programs).

A tradeoff has to be made between cost and potential for sophisticated analysis on one side and the user's computer experience and technical proficiency on the other. We have used all codes discussed here. Others, probably as useful, are available too. Check those routines and systems that you know how to use and are comfortable with, add those noted above to cover gaps, and you should be in a good position for implementation.

A Model for Sample Size Determination

Decision Theory (Raïffa, 1968) provides a framework for sample size determination. The approach combines the marketing manager's uncertainty about the market share for the new product, the expected value of sample information, and the cost of getting it. This appendix illustrates how the decision analysis approach could be used for determining sample size in a typical implementation of our methodology.

The decision problem our marketing manager is faced with is the introduction or rejection of the new industrial product. Implementation of our methodology, by producing an estimate of the future share for the product, reduces his uncertainty. This problem can then be cast in the following Bayesian framework.

Define

$f_s'(s)$ the prior density function of market share for the new product.

$f_s''(s)$ the density function of market share for the new product posterior to market assessment through our methodology.

a_1, a_2 the decision choice (a_1: introduce the product; a_2: reject the product).

$v(a_i, s)$ the value (or utility) associated with decision i if actual market share happens to be s. We may assume without loss of generality that $v(a_i, s) = K_i + k_i s$. Our example later will clarify the meaning of parameters $K_i\, k_i$.

Our manager's problem can then be pictured as follows

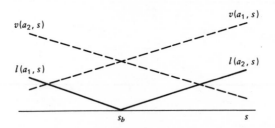

where $1(a_i, s)$ denotes the opportunity loss of having taken decision a_i if actual market share is s. Hence

$$1(a_1, s) = (k_1 - k_2)(s_b - s)$$
$$1(a_2, s) = (k_1 - k_2)(s - s_b)$$

In the absence of any other information, the optimal decision a_0 is that which maximizes prior expected return. So we have:

$$a_0 = \begin{cases} a_1 \text{ if } \bar{s}' > s_b \\ a_2 \text{ if } \bar{s}' < s_b \end{cases}$$

Where

$$s_b = \left\{ \frac{K_1 - K_2}{k_2 - k_1} \right\}, \text{ and}$$

$$\bar{s}' = \int_0^1 s f_{s'}(s) \, ds = \text{mean of prior distribution}$$

The Expected Value of Perfect Information (EVPI) is the expected opportunity loss (EOL) associated with the optimal decision on the basis of managements prior uncertainty. It provides an upper bound on the amount that management might pay for market research.

$$\text{EVPI} = \text{EOL}(a_o, s)$$

$$\text{EPVI} = \begin{cases} \int_{s_b}^1 (k_2 - k_1)(s - s_b) f_s'(s) \, ds \text{ if } \bar{s}' < s_b \text{ i.e. } a_o = a_2 \\ \int_o^{s_b} (k_2 - k_1)(s_b - s) f_s'(s) \, ds \text{ if } \bar{s}' > s_b \text{ i.e. } a_o = a_1 \end{cases}$$

If the cost of running a market assessment procedure were more than EVPI in the particular product market investigated, it should not be implemented.

If this is not the case, what is the expected gain? Estimation of future market share for the product provides the manager with additional information with which to review his prior distribution of market share. Let $f_s''(s)$ denote the posterior distribution of s conditional on a market share prediction z.

The optimal decision *a posteriori, a*∗, is that which maximizes posterior expected return.

So we have:

$$a_* = \begin{cases} a_1 \text{ if } \bar{s}'' > s_b \\ a_2 \text{ if } \bar{s}'' < s_b \end{cases}$$

where $\bar{s}'' = \int_0^1 s f_s''(s) \, ds = \text{mean of posterior distribution}$.

The conditional expected losses are then given by

$$\text{EOL}(a_*, s) = \begin{cases} \int_{s_b}^1 (k_2 - k_1)(s - s_b) f_s''(s) \, ds \text{ if } \bar{s}'' < s_b \text{ i.e. } a_* = a_2 \\ \int_o^{s_b} (k_2 - k_1)(s_b - s) f_s''(s) \, ds \text{ if } \bar{s}'' > s_b \text{ i.e. } a_* = a_1 \end{cases}$$

Given a market share prediction, z, obtained through the use of some assessment procedure, we can assess its value for decision making. This value, called Value of Sample Information, VSI, is developed as follows:

if $a_o = a_1$ that is, $s_b < \bar{s}'$

$$\text{VSI} = \begin{cases} 0 \text{ if } s_b < \bar{s}'' \text{ as we do not change the decision, and} \\ \int_0^1 v(a_2,s)f_s''(s)\,ds - \int_0^1 v(a_1,s)f_s''(s)\,ds \text{ if } s_b > \bar{s}'' \\ \text{since from } a_1, \text{ which was the optimal act } a\ priori, \text{ we} \\ \text{switch to } a_2 \text{ after market assessment.} \end{cases}$$

$$= \begin{cases} 0 \text{ if } s_b < \bar{s}''; \\ K_2 + k_2\bar{s}'' - (K_1 + k_1\bar{s}'') = (K_2 - K_1) + (k_2 - k_1)\bar{s}'' \\ \qquad\qquad = (k_2 - k_1)(\bar{s}'' - s_b) \text{ if } s_b > \bar{s}'' \end{cases}$$

if $a_o = a_2$, that is $s_b > \bar{s}'$

$$\text{VSI} = \begin{cases} 0 \text{ if } s_b > \bar{s}'' \\ (k_2 - k_1)(s_b - \bar{s}'') \text{ if } s_b < \bar{s}'' \end{cases}$$

Taking the expectation with respect to the outcome of the market assessment procedure, we get the Expected Value of Sample Information, EVSI. This can be compared with the cost of getting the estimate (fixed cost of methodology implementation F, plus variable cost of sampling V) to infer the optimal sample size.

Then the Expected Net Gain, ENG, of market assessment is

$$\text{ENG}(n) = \text{EVSI} - F - Vn,$$

where n is the sample size. The optimal size n_o should then be chosen such that:

$$\text{ENG}(n_o) = \max_n (\text{ENG})$$

Use of this approach to assess optimal sample size in a typical implementation of our methodology assumes we consider market share as the probability of adoption for any firm in the target market. Furthermore, the estimate provided by the assessment procedure is viewed as the result of a sequence of Bernoulli trials.

Assume sample observations are normally distributed with known dispersion and the prior distribution of the process mean is normal. Empirical evidence indicates that such approximations usually lead to sample size estimates quite close to the true-optimum — Raiffa and Schlaifer (1961).

Consider the following example: a decision involving the introduction of a new piece of machinery. The necessary investment for production and tooling was estimated at $0.25 million. From past experience and industry estimates, a share point in the market is worth \$6000. In addition, if the product were introduced, \$200,000 would accrue from royalties on process patents. Hence we have the following value functions:

$$v(a_1, s) = 0.2 + 0.6\, s \text{ in \$ million}$$

$$v(a_2, s) = 0.25 - 0.6\, s$$

and $s_b = 0.0417$

Further assume that management's prior uncertainty can be approximated by a normal distribution with

- expected value $\bar{s}' = 0.0500$
- standard deviation $\sigma_s' = 0.0475$
  (precision $h^{-1} = 0.0475$ and pseudo size $n' = 21$)

To estimate optimal sample size under the normal approximation, following Raiffa and Schlaifer (1961), we compute quantities:

$$D = \frac{|s_b - \bar{s}'|}{\sigma_s'} = 0.1747$$

$$Z = \sigma_s'\, h^{1/2} \left\{ |k_2 - k_1| \frac{h^{-1/2}}{k_s} \right\}^{1/3} = 6.470$$

based on a variable cost of sampling $k_s = \$10$.

From the table of optimal sample size with normal sampling (Chart I in Raiffa and Schlaifer (1961)) we get:

$$\frac{n_o}{\left\{ |k_2 - k_1| \dfrac{h^{-1/2}}{k_s} \right\}^{2/3}} = 0.157$$

Hence $n_o \simeq 139$.

With this sample size, the Expected Net Gain (ENG) from implementation of the market assessment procedure may be obtained from the Net Gain of an optimal sample with normal sampling (Chart II, Raiffa and Schlaifer, 1961).

$$\frac{\text{ENG}}{\left\{ |k_2 - k_1|^2\, h^{-1}\, k_s \right\}^{1/3}} \simeq 1.8$$

hence ENG $\simeq \$15,857$

Note that this expected net gain accrues only from our knowledge of market share based on optimal sample size. It does not consider any of the other benefits (decision process characterization, product design and positioning improvements) of the market assessment procedure developed here.

Thus Bayesian analysis provides an operational structure for a more quantitative assessment of optimum sample size. The expected net gain from market share information obtained on that basis, should be added to the managerial value of the behavioral, and product positioning and design information provided by our market assessment procedure.

References

Abell, Derek and John S. Hammond. *Strategic Market Planning: Problems and Analytical Approaches.* Englewood Cliffs, N.J.: Prentice-Hall, 1979.

Achenbaum, Alvin A. "Market Testing: Using the Marketplace as a Laboratory," pp. 4–31 to 4–54 in Ferber, R., ed., *Handbook of Marketing Research.* New York: McGraw-Hill, 1974.

Affifi, A. and S. Azen. *Statistical Analysis: A Computer Oriented Approach.* New York: Academic Press, 1972.

Allaire, Yvan. "The Measurement of Heterogeneous Semantic, Perceptual and Preference Structures," unpublished Ph.D. Thesis, Massachusetts Institute of Technology, Cambridge, MA, 1973.

Allaire, Yvan, A. J. Silk and Wing Hing Tsang. "A Fortran IV (IBM 360) Program for Multivariate Profile Analysis," *Journal of Marketing Research,* 10 (February 1973), pp. 81–82.

American Iron and Steel Institute. *Annual Statistical Report 1973.* Washington, D.C., 1974.

Anderberg, Michael R. *Cluster Analysis for Applications.* New York: Academic Press, 1973.

Andress, Frank J. "The Learning Curve as a Production Tool," *Harvard Business Review,* (January-February 1954), pp. 87–97.

Arrow, Kenneth J. *Social Choice and Individual Values.* Second edition, Yale University Press, 1963.

Ayer, A. J. *The Problem of Knowledge.* New York: St. Martin's Press, 1956.

Bacharach, Michael. "Group Decisions in the Face of Differences of Opinion," *Management Science.* Vol. 22, No. 2 (October 1975), pp. 182–191.

Baker, Michael J. *Marketing New Industrial Products.* London: Macmillan, 1975.

Bailey, N. T. J. *The Mathematical Theory of Infectious Diseases and Its Applications.* 2nd edition. New York: Homer Press, 1975.

Baldridge, Victor and Robert Burnham. "Organizational Innovation: Individual, Organizational and Environmental Impacts," *Administrative Science Quarterly,* 20 (June 1975), pp. 165–176.

Balthasar, Hans, Roberto Boschi and Michael Merke. "Calling the Shots for Research and Development," *Harvard Business Review* (May–June 1978), pp. 151–161.

Bass, F. M. "A New Product Growth Model for Consumer Durables," *Management Science.* Vol. 15, No. 5 (January 1969), pp. 215–227.

Bass, F. M. "An Integration of the New Product Growth Model with the Experience Cost Function and Optimal Pricing," Presented at the TIMS/ORSA National Meeting, New York City, May 1978.

Bereny, Justin A. *A Survey of the Emerging Solar Industry.* Solar Energy Information Services, Palo Alto, Calif., 1977.

Berger, A. "Factors Influencing the Locus of Innovation Activity Leading to Scientific Instrument and Plastics Innovations." unpublished Masters Thesis, Massachusetts Institute of Technology, Sloan School of Management, June 1975.

Bijnen, E. J. *Cluster Analysis.* The Netherlands: Tilburg University Press, 1973.

Blackman, A. W. "The Market Dynamics of Technological Substitution," *Technological Forecasting and Social Change.* 6 (1974).

Blashfield, Roger K. "Mixture Model Tests of Cluster Analysis: Accuracy of Four Agglomerative Hierarchical Methods," *Psychological Bulletin.* 83 (1976), pp. 377–388.

Bonoma, T. V., G. Zaltman and W. Johnson. *Industrial Buying Behavior.* Marketing Science Institute Report 77-117, December, 1977.

Booz, Allen and Hamilton. *Management of New Products,* 1965.

Boston Consulting Group. *Perspectives on Experience.* Boston, Mass.: Boston Consulting Group, Inc., 1970.

Box, George E. P. "A General Distribution Theory for a Class of Likelihood Criteria," *Biometrika,* 36 (1949), pp. 317–346.

Box, George E. P. and Gwilym M. Jenkins. *Time Series Analysis: Forecasting and Control.* Second edition. San Francisco, Calif.: Holden Day, 1976.

Boyden, J. "A Study of the Innovation Process in the Plastics Additives Industry," unpublished Masters Thesis, Massachusetts Institute of Technology, Sloan School of Management, January 1976.

Brand, Gordon T. *The Industrial Buying Decision.* New York: Wiley, 1972.

Briscoe, Geoffrey. "Some Observations on New Industrial Product Failures," *Industrial Marketing Management,* 2 (February 1973), pp. 151–162.

Bunker, Earl. "Intelligent Terminal Research Report," Boston, 1977.

Buckner, Hugh. *How British Industry Buys.* London: Hutchinson & Co, 1967.

Burriss, William. "Solar Powered Rankine Cycle Cooling Systems," in Francis de Winter, ed., *Solar Cooling for Buildings.* Washington, D.C.: U.S. Government Printing Office, 1974.

Calantone, Roger J. and Robert G. Cooper, "A Typology of Industrial New Product Failures," in Greenberg and Bellenger, eds., *1977 Educator's Conference Proceedings.* Chicago: American Marketing Association, 1977, pp. 492–497.

Campbell, Donald T. and Donald W. Fiske. "Convergent and Discriminant Validation by the Multitrait Multimethod Matrix," *Psychological Bulletin,* 52 (March 1959) pp. 81–105.

Cardozo, Richard N. "Segmenting the Industrial Market," in King, R. L., ed., *Marketing and the New Science of Planning.* Chicago: American Marketing Association, 1968.

Cardozo, Richard N. and James W. Cagley. "An Experimental Study of Industrial Buyer Behavior," *Journal of Marketing Research.* 8 (August 1971), pp. 329–334.

Carmen, James M. "Consumer Panels," in R. Ferber, ed., *Handbook of Marketing Research.* New York: McGraw-Hill, 1974, pp. 200–216.

Cattell, Raymond B. "The Meaning and Strategic Use of Factor Analysis," in Raymond B. Cattell, ed., *Handbook of Multivariate Experimental Psychology.* Chicago: Rand McNally, 1966.

Cheston, Richard and Philip Doucet. "Marketing Strategy Determination through Analysis of Purchasing Decision Structure in the HVAC Industry," unpublished Masters Thesis, Massachusetts Institute of Technology, Cambridge, MA, 1976.

Choffray, J-M. "A Methodology for Investigating the Structure of the Industrial Adoption Process and the Differences in Perceptions and Evaluation Criteria Among Potential Decision Participants," unpublished Ph.D. dissertation, Massachusetts Institute of Technology, Cambridge, MA., April, 1977.

Choffray, J-M. and G. L. Lilien. "Models of the Multiperson Choice Process with Application to the Adoption of Industrial Products," M.I.T. Sloan School of Management Working Paper No. 861-76, June, 1976.

Choffray, J-M. and G. L. Lilien. "Industrial Adoption of Solar Air Conditioning: Measurement Problems, Solutions and Marketing Implications," M.I.T. Sloan School of Management Working Paper No. 894-76, December, 1976.

Choffray, J-M. and G. L. Lilien. "Methodology for Investigating Differences in Evaluation Criteria Among Industrial Buying Influences," M.I.T. Sloan School of Management Working Paper No. 975-78, February, 1978.

Choffray, J-M. and G. L. Lilien. "A New Approach to Industrial Market Segmentation," *Sloan Management Review.* Vol. 19, No. 3 (Spring 1978), pp. 17–30.

Choffray, J-M., and G. L. Lilien, "DESIGNOR: Decision Support for Industrial Product Design." MIT Sloan School Working Paper, November 1979.

Chow, Gregory C. "Test of Equality Between Subsets of Coefficients in Two Linear Regressions," *Econometrica,* 38 (1960), pp. 591–605.

Christ, C. F. "Judging the Performance of Econometric Models of the U.S. Economy," *International Economic Review.* Vol. 16, No. 1 (1975), pp. 57–81.

Cochran, W. G. *Sampling Techniques.* second edition, New York: Wiley, 1963.

Cohen, Arnold D. "Solar Heating and Cooling of Buildings Phase O Feasibility and Planning Study: A Report by General Electric Company," in F. A. Iachetta, ed., *Solar Heating and Cooling of Buildings*. American Society of Heating, Refrigerating and Air Conditioning Engineers, 1975.

Cooley, William W. and Paul R. Lohnes. *Multivariate Data Analysis*. New York: Wiley, 1971.

Coombs, Clyde H., Robyn M. Dawes, Amos Tversky. *Mathematical Psychology: An Elementary Introduction*. Englewood Cliffs, N.J.: Prentice-Hall, 1970.

Cooper, Robert G. "Why New Industrial Products Fail," *Industrial Marketing Management*. 4 (December 1975), pp. 315–326.

Corey, E. R. *Industrial Marketing: Cases and Concepts*. second edition, Englewood Cliffs, N.J.: Prentice Hall, 1976.

Corey, Lawrence G. "People who Claim to be Opinion Leaders: Identifying their Characteristics by Self-Report," *Journal of Marketing*, 35 (October, 1971), pp. 48–53.

Cox, William E. Jr. *Industrial Marketing Research*. New York: Wiley, 1979.

Cox, William E. Jr. and George N. Havens, "Determination of Sales Potentials and Performance for an Industrial Goods Manufacturer," *Journal of Marketing Research*, Vol. 14, No. 4 (November, 1977), pp. 574–578.

Curry, David J. "Some Statistical Considerations in Clustering with Binary Data," *Multivariate Behavioral Research* (April, 1976), pp. 175–189.

Cyert, Richard M. et al. "Observation of a Business Decision," *Journal of Business*, 29 (October, 1956), pp. 237–248.

Czepiel, John. "Decision Group and Firm Characteristics in an Industrial Adoption Decision," in K. L. Bernhardt, ed., *Marketing: 1776-1976 and Beyond*, 29. Chicago: American Marketing Association, 1976.

Dalziel, Murray M. "Using AGCLUS: A Program to Do Hierarchical Clustering Analysis," Center for the Behavioral Sciences Computing Facility, Harvard University, January, 1974.

Davis, E. J. *Experimental Marketing*. London: New Company, 1970.

Davis, James H. "Group Decision and Social Interaction: A Theory of Social Decision Schemes," *Psychological Review*, Vol. 80, No. 2 (March, 1973), pp. 97–125.

Davis, J. H., J. L. Cohen, J. Hornik and K. Rissman. "Dyadic Decision as a Function of the Frequency Distributions Describing the Preferences of Members' Constituencies," *Journal of Personality and Social Psychology*. Vol. 26, No. 2 (1973), pp. 178–195.

Day, G. S. and R. M. Heeler. "Using Cluster Analysis to Improve Marketing Experiments," *Journal of Marketing Research*, 8 (August, 1971), pp. 340–347.

deSimone, Daniel V. *Technological Innovation: Its Environment and Management*. Washington, D.C.: U.S. Department of Commerce, 1967.

deWinter, Francis. *Solar Cooling for Buildings*. Washington, D.C.: U.S. Government Printing Office, 1974.

Dodge, H. Robert. *Industrial Marketing*. New York: McGraw-Hill, 1970.

Dodson, J. A. and E. Muller. "Models of New Product Diffusion through Advertising and Word-Of-Mouth," *Management Science*. Vol. 15, No. 4 (November 1978), pp. 1568–1579.

Draper, Norman and Harry Smith. *Applied Regression Analysis*. New York: Wiley, 1966.

Drucker, Peter F. *Management: Tasks – Responsibilities – Practices*. New York: Harper & Row, 1974.

Everitt, B. S. *Cluster Analysis*. London: Halsted Press, 1974.

Faris, Charles W. "Market Segmentation and Industrial Buying Behavior," *Proceedings*. Chicago: American Marketing Association, 1967.

Finney, D. J. *Probit Analysis*. Cambridge, England: Cambridge University Press, 1952.

Fishburn, Peter C. "Preferences, Summation, and Social Welfare Functions," *Management Science*. Vol. 16, No. 3 (November, 1969), pp. 179–186.

Fisher, F. M. *The Identification Problem in Econometrics.* New York: McGraw-Hill, 1966.

Fisher, F. M. "Tests of Equality Between Sets of Coefficients in Two Linear Regressions: An Expository Note," *Econometrica,* 38 (March, 1970), pp. 361–366.

Fisher, J. C. and R. H. Pry. "A Simple Substitution Model of Technological Change," *Technological Forecasting and Social Change,* Vol. 3 (1971), pp. 75–88.

Fleiss, J. L. and J. Zubin. "On the Methods and Theory of Clustering," *Multivariate Behavioral Research.* 4 (1969), pp. 235–250.

Fleming, William S. "Who are the Customers and What Might be the Potential Market," in F. de Winter, ed., *Solar Cooling of Buildings.* Washington, D.C.: U.S. Government Printing Office, 1974.

Floyd, A. "Trend Forecasting: A Methodology for Figure of Merit," *Proceedings of the First Annual Technology and Management Conference,* J. Bright, ed., Englewood Cliffs, N.J.: Prentice Hall, 1968.

Ford, Gary. "A Multivariate Investigation of Market Research," in R. Purham, ed., *1974 Combined American Marketing Association Proceedings.* Chicago: American Marketing Association, 1975.

Frank, Ronald E. William F. Massy and Yoram Wind. *Market Segmentation.* Englewood Cliffs, N.J.: Prentice Hall, 1972.

Gibson, R. L. Neidell and R. Teach. "Performance Space Analysis for an Industrial Product," *Operations Research Quarterly,* Vol. No. 2 (May, 1972).

Gold, Bela et al. "Diffusion of Major Technological Innovations in U.S. Iron and Steel Manufacturing," *The Journal of Industrial Economics,* 18 (July, 1970), pp. 218–239.

Goldberger, A. S. *Econometric Theory.* New York: Wiley, 1964.

Grashof, John F. and Gloria P. Thomas. "Industrial Buying Center Responsibilities: Self Versus Other Member Evaluations of Importance," in Kenneth L. Bernhardt, *Marketing: 1776–1976 and Beyond,* 39. Chicago: American Marketing Association, 1976.

Green, Bert F. "On the Factor Score Controversy," *Psychometrika,* 41 (June, 1976), pp. 263–266.

Green, Paul E. and Vithala R. Rao. *Applied Multidimensional Scaling.* Hindsale: The Dryden Press, 1972.

Green, Paul E. and Vithala R. Rao. "Rating Scales and Information Recovery – How Many Scales and Response Categories to Use?," *Journal of Marketing Research,* 7 (July, 1970), pp. 33–39.

Green, Paul and V. Srinivasan. "Conjoint Analysis in Consumer Research: Issues and Outlook," *Journal of Consumer Research.* Vol. 15 (September, 1978), pp. 103–123.

Green, Paul E. and Donald S. Tull. *Research for Marketing Decisions,* third edition, Englewood Cliffs, N.J.: Prentice Hall, 1975.

Green, Paul E. and Yoram Wind. *Multiattribute Decisions in Marketing: A Measurement Approach.* Hinesdale, Ill.: The Dryden Press, 1973.

Greenstreet, Richard L. and Robert J. Connor. "Power of Tests for Equality of Covariance Matrices," *Technometrics,* 16 (February, 1974), pp. 27–30.

Guiltman, J. and A. Sawyer. "Managerial Considerations for Market Segmentation Research," *American Marketing Association Combined Proceedings.* Chicago: American Marketing Association, 1974.

Haas, Robert. *Industrial Marketing Management.* New York: Petrocelli-Charter, 1976.

Hakansson, Hakan and Bjorn Wootz. "Supplier Selection in an Industrial Environment – An Experimental Study," *Journal of Marketing Research,* 12 (February, 1975), pp. 46–51.

Harding, Murray. "Who Really Makes the Purchasing Decision," *Industrial Marketing,* 51 (September, 1966), pp. 76–81.

Harman, Harry H. *Modern Factor Analysis.* Chicago: The University of Chicago Press, 1976.

Hartigan, John A. *Clustering Algorithms.* New York: Wiley, 1975.

Hartman, Raymond S. "A Generalized Logit Formulation of Individual Choice," M.I.T. Energy Laboratory Working Paper, 1978.

Hauser, John R. "A Normative Methodology for Predicting Consumer Response to Design Decisions: Issues, Models, Theory and Use," unpublished Ph.D. Thesis, Massachusetts Institute of Technology, 1975.

Hauser, John R. "Forecasting and Influencing the Adoption of Technological Innovations," Working Paper, Transportation Center, Northwestern University, September, 1978.

Hauser, John R. and F. S. Koppelman. "The Relative Accuracy and Usefulness of Alternative Perceptual Mapping Techniques," *Journal of Marketing Research,* Vol. 14, No. 3 (Nov. 1979), pp. 495–507.

Hauser, John R. and Glen L. Urban. "A Normative Methodology for Modeling Consumer Response to Innovation," *Operations Research,* Vol. 25, No. 4 (July–August 1977), pp. 579–619.

Hauser, John R. and Glen L. Urban. "Direct Assessment of Consumer Utility Functions: von Neumann-Morgenstern Utility Theory Applied to Marketing," *Journal of Consumer Research,* Vol. 5 (March 1979), pp. 251–262.

Hernes, G. "Diffusion and Growth – The Non-Homogeneous Case," *Scandinavian Journal of Economics,* 78 (1976), pp. 427–436.

Hillier, T. J. "Decision Making in the Corporate Industrial Buying Process," *Industrial Marketing Management* 4 (1975), pp. 99–106.

Hoel, Paul et al. *Introduction to Statistical Theory.* Boston: Houghton Mifflin, 1971.

Hoerl, Arthur E. and Robert W. Kennard. "Ridge Regression: Applications to Non-Orthogonal Problems," *Technometrics,* Vol. 12, No. 1 (February, 1970), pp. 69–81.

Hopkins, David S. "New-Product Winners and Losers," Report No. 773, *The Conference Board,* 1979.

Hopkins, David S. and Earl L. Bailey. "New-Product Pressures," *The Conference Board Record,* Vol. 7, No. 6 (June 1971).

Horsky, D. and L. S. Simon, "Advertising in a Model of New Product Diffusion," presented at the TIMS/ORSA National Meeting, New York City, May, 1978.

How the Electric Industry Buys. New York: Hayden, 1963.

Howard, John A. and J. N. Sheth. *The Theory of Buyer Behavior.* New York: Wiley, 1969.

Huber, Peter J. "Robust Statistics: A Review," *The Annals of Mathematical Statistics,* 43 (1972), pp. 1046–1057.

Hubert, Lawrence J. "Some Applications of Graph Theory to Clustering," *Psychometrika,* 39 (September, 1974), pp. 283–309.

Hummel, Thomas J. and Joseph R. Sligo. "Empirical Comparison of Univariate and Multivariate Analysis of Variance Procedures," *Psychological Bulletin,* 76 (1971), pg. 49–57.

Humphreys, L. G. and D. R. Ilgen. "Note on a Criterion for the Number of Common Factors," *Educational and Psychological Measurement,* 29 (1969), pp. 571–578.

Hurter, A. P. and A. H. Rubenstein, "Market Penetration by New Innovations: The Technological Literature," *Technological Forecasting and Social Change.* 11 (1978), pp. 197–221.

Isenson, R. "Project Hindsight: An Empirical Study of the Sources of Ideas Utilized in Operational Weapon Systems," in W. Gruber and D. Marquis, eds., *Factors in the Transfer of Technology,* Cambridge, MA: MIT Press, 1969.

Johnson, Stephen C. "Hierarchical Clustering Schemes," *Psychometrika,* 32 (September 1967) pp. 241–254.

Jones, Yan R. "Environmental, Social and Political Aspects of Solar Heating and Cooling of Buildings: A Report by TRW-Systems," in F. A. Iachetta, ed., *Solar Heating and Cooling of Buildings.* American Society of Heating, Refrigerating and Air-Conditioning Engineers, 1975.

Joreskog, K. G. "Simultaneous Factor Analysis in Several Populations," *Psychometrika,* 36 (1971), pp. 409–426.

Kaiser, H. F. "The Varimax Criterion for Analytic Rotation in Factor Analysis," *Psychometrika,* 23 (1958), pp. 187–200.

Kalish, S. and G. L. Lilien, "New Product Diffusion Models: Current Status and Research Agenda," MIT Energy Laboratory Working Paper, 1979.

Kanal, L. N. "Interactive Pattern Analysis and Classification Systems: A Survey and Commentary," *Proceedings of the I.E.E.E.,* 60 (1972), pp. 1200–1215.

Keeney, Ralph L. and Craig W. Kirkwood. "Group Decision Making Using Cardinal Social Welfare Functions," *Management Science.* Vol. 22, No. 4 (December, 1975), pp. 430–437.

Kelly, Patrick J. "Functions Performed in Industrial Purchasing Decisions with Implications for Marketing Strategy," *Journal of Business Research,* 2 (October, 1974), pp. 421–434.

Kennedy, C. and A. Thirlwall. "Surveys in Applied Economics: Technical Progress," *Economic Journal.* 82 (March, 1972), pp. 11–72.

Kotler, Philip. *Marketing Management, Analysis, Planning, and Control,* fourth edition, Englewood Cliffs, N.J.: Prentice Hall, 1980.

Krapfel, R. "A Decision Process Approach to Modeling Organizational Buying Behavior," in S. Jain, Ed., *Research Frontiers in Marketing: Dialogue and Directions.* Chicago, American Marketing Associates, 1978.

Lachenbruch, P. *Discriminant Analysis.* New York: Hesner Press, 1975.

Lance, G. N. and W. T. Williams. "A General Theory of Classificatory Sorting Strategies in Hierarchical Systems," *The Computer Journal.* 9 (1967), pp. 273–280.

Lavidge, Robert J. and Gary A. Steiner. "A Model for Predictive Measurements of Advertising Effectiveness." *Journal of Marketing* (October, 1961).

Lavin, Milton L. "A Comparison of Descriptive Choice Models," unpublished Ph.D. Thesis, Massachusetts Institute of Technology, 1969.

Lawley, D. N. and A. E. Maxwell. *Factor Analysis as a Statistical Method.* London: Butterworth, 1963.

Lehmann, Donald R. and James Hubert. "Are Three-Point Scales Always Good Enough?" *Journal of Marketing Research,* 9 (November, 1972), pp. 444–446.

Lehmann, Donald R. and John O'Shaughnessy. "Differences in Attribute Importance for Different Industrial Products," *Journal of Marketing,* 38 (April, 1974), pp. 36- 42.

Leontief, W. W. *The Structure of the American Economy, 1919–1939,* 2nd edition. New York: Oxford University Press, 1951.

Leontief, W. W. *Input-Output Economics.* New York: Oxford University Press, 1966.

Lessig, V. P. and J. O. Tollefson. "Market Segmentation Through Numerical Taxonomy," *Journal of Marketing Research,* 8 (November, 1971), pp. 480–487.

Levitt, Theodore. "Marketing Myopia," *Harvard Business Review,* 38 (July–August 1960), pp. 45–56.

Lilien, G. L. "Model Relativism: A Situational Approach to Model Building," *Interfaces.* Vol. 5, No. 3 (May, 1975), pp. 11–18.

Lilien, Gary L. "A Socio-Economic and Marketing Study for a Standard Fomento Factory in Puerto Rico – Year 1 Report," Dialogue, Inc. Report (September, 1976).

Lilien, Gary L. "The Diffusion of Photovoltaics: Background, Modeling, Calibration and Implications for Government Policy," M.I.T. Energy Laboratory Report No. 78–019, May, 1978.

Lilien, Gary L. "ADVISOR 2: Modeling the Marketing Mix Decision for Industrial Products," *Management Science,* Vol. 25, No. 2 (February, 1979). pp. 191–204.

Lilien, Gary L., Alvin J. Silk, Jean-Marie Choffray and Murlidhar Rao, "Industrial Advertising Effects and Budgeting Practices," *Journal of Marketing,* Vol. 40, No. 1 (January, 1976), pp. 16–24.

Ling, Robert F. "A Probability Theory of Cluster Analysis," *Journal of the American Statistical Association*, 68 (March, 1973), pp. 159–164.

Little, Arthur D. Inc. *Solar Heating and Cooling Constraints and Incentives: A Review of the Literature*, March, 1976.

Little, Blair and Robert Cooper. "Determinants of Marketing Research Expenditures for New Industrial Products," *Industrial Marketing Management*, Vol. 6, No. 2 (1977).

Little, John D. C. "Models and Managers: The Concept of a Decision Calculus," *Management Science*, Vol. 16, No. 8 (April, 1970), pp. B466–485.

Little, John D. C. "BRANDAID': A Marketing Mix Model, Part 1: Structure," *Operations Research*. Vol. 23, No. 4 (July–August 1975), pp. 628–655.

Little, John D. C. "BRANDAID: A Marketing Mix Model, Part 2: Implementation, Calibration and Case Study," *Operations Research*, Vol. 23, No. 4 (July–August 1975), pp. 656–673.

Little, John D. C. "Decision Support for Marketing Management," *Journal of Marketing*, Vol. 43, No. 3 (Summer 1979) pp. 9–27.

Little, John D. C. "Aggregate Advertising Response Models: The State of the Art," *Operations Research*, Vol. 27, No. 4 (July–August 1979), pp. 629–667.

Luce, L. Duncan. *Individual Choice Behavior: A Theoretical Analysis*. New York: Wiley, 1959.

Luce, R. D. and H. Raiffa. *Games and Decisions*. New York: Wiley, 1957.

Luce, L. D. and P. Suppes. "Preference, Utility and Subjective Probability," in Luce, Bush and Galanter (eds.), *Handbook of Mathematical Psychology III*. New York: Wiley, 1965.

McCarthy, E. J. *Basic Marketing: A Managerial Approach,* fifth edition, Homewood, IL: Richard D. Irwin, 1975.

McDonald, Philip R. and Joseph O. Eastlack, Jr. "Top Management Involvement With New Products," *Business Horizons*. Vol. 14, No. 6 (December, 1971), pp. 23–31.

McFadden, D. "Quantal Choice Analysis: A Survey," *Annals of Economic and Social Measurement*. (May, 1976), pp. 363–369.

McFadden, D. "Econometric Models for Probabilistic Choice Among Products," Paper Presented at the Conference on the Interfaces between Marketing and Economics, University of Rochester, April, 1978.

McGuire, Patrick E. and Earl L. Bailey. *Sources of Corporate Growth*. No. 24. New York: The Conference Board, 1970.

McKelvey, Bill. "Guidelines for the Empirical Classification of Organizations," *Administrative Science Quarterly*, 20 (December, 1975), pp. 509–525.

McMillan, James R. "Role Differentiation in Industrial Buying Decisions," in Thomas V. Greer, *Increasing Marketing Productivity*. Chicago: American Marketing Association, 1973.

McQuitty, L. L. "A Mutual Development of Some Topological Theories and Pattern-Analytic Methods," *Educational and Psychological Measurement*, 17 (L967), pp. 21–46.

Mahajan, V. and R. A. Peterson. "Innovation Diffusion in a Dynamic Potential Adopter Population," *Management Science*. Vol. 15, No. 4 (November, 1978), pp. 1589–1598.

Mahajan, V. and R. A. Peterson. "Innovation Diffusion and New Product Growth Models: An Assessment," *Journal of Marketing*, forthcoming.

Makridakis, Spyros and Steven C. Wheelwright. "Forecasting: Issues and Challenge for Marketing Management," *Journal of Marketing*. Vol. 41, No. 4 (October, 1977), pp. 24–38.

Makridakis, Spyros and Steven C. Wheelwright. *Forecasting: Methods and Applications*. New York: John Wiley, 1978.

Mansfield, Edwin. *The Economics of Technological Change*. New York: Norton, 1968.

Mansfield, Edwin. *Industrial Research and Technological Innovation* New York: Norton, 1968.

Mansfield, Edwin and John Rapoport. "Costs of Industrial Product Innovations," *Management Science*. 21 (August, 1975), pp. 1380–1386.

Mansfield, Edwin and Samuel Wagner. "Organizational and Strategic Factors Associated with Probabilities of Success in Industrial R&D," The *Journal of Business*. 48 (April, 1975), pp. 179–198.

March, James C. and Herbert A. Simon. *Organizations*. New York: Wiley, 1958.

Massy, W. F., D. B. Montgomery and D. G. Morrison. *Stochastic Models of Buyer Behavior*. Cambridge, Mass.: M.I.T. Press, 1970.

Materials Advisory Board, Division of Engineering, National Research Council, "Report of the Ad Hoc Committee on Principles of Research-Engineering Interaction." Publication MAB-22-M. Washington, D.C.: National Academy of Sciences – National Research Council, July 1966.

Meadows, D. "Data Appendix: Accuracy of Technical Estimates in Industrial Research Planning," MIT Sloan School of Management Working Paper No. 301-67, 1967.

Meadows, D. "Estimate Accuracy and Project Selection Models in Industrial Research," *Industrial Management Review* (Spring 1969).

Miller, G. A. "The Magical Number Seven, Plus or Minus Two: Some Limits on our Capacity for Processing Information," *Psychological Review*. 63 (1956), pp. 81–97.

Montanelli, Richard G., Jr., and Lloyd G. Humphreys. "Latent Roots of Random Data Correlation Matrices with Squared Multiple Correlations on the Diagonal: A Monte Carlo Study," *Psychometrica*. 41 (September, 1976), pp. 341–348.

Montgomery, D. B. and A. J. Silk. "Clusters of Consumer Interests and Opinion Leaders' Sphere of Influence," *Journal of Marketing Research*. 8 (August, 1971), pp. 317–321.

Montgomery, David B. and Glen L. Urban. *Management Science in Marketing*. Englewood Cliffs, N.J.: Prentice Hall, 1968.

Morrill, John E. "Industrial Advertising Pays Off," *Harvard Business Review*. Vol. 48 (March–April 1970), pp. 4–14.

Morrison, Donald F. *Multivariate Statistical Methods*, second edition, New York: McGraw-Hill, 1976.

Morrison, Donald G. "On the Interpretation of Discriminant Analysis," *Journal of Marketing Research*. 6 (May, 1969), pp. 156–163.

Mulaik, S. A. "Comments on the Measurement of Factorial Indeterminacy," *Psychometrika*. 41 (1976), pp. 249–262.

Murray, Thomas J. "The Hot New Computer Companies," *DUNS Review*. (January, 1979).

Muth, John F. "Rational Expectations and the Theory of Price Movements," *Econometrica*. Vol. 29, No. 3 (July, 1961), pp. 315–335.

Myers, J. G. and F. M. Nicosia. "On the Study of Consumer Typologies," *Journal of Marketing Research*. 5 (May, 1968), pp. 182–193.

Nau, H. R. *Technology Transfer and U.S. Foreign Policy*. New York: Praeger, 1976.

Naylor, T. H., T. G. Seaks, D. W. Wicherin, "Box Jenkins Methods: An Alternative to Econometric Forecasting," *International Statistical Review*. Vol. 40, No. 2 (1972), pp. 123–237.

Nelson, Charles R. "The Prediction Performance of the FRB-MIT-PENN Model of the U.S. Economy," *The American Economic Review*. Vol. 62 (December, 1972), pp. 902–917.

Nelson, Charles R. *Applied Time Series Analysis for Managerial Forecasting*. San Francisco: Holden Day, 1973.

Nelson, R. R., M. J. Peck and E. D. Kalacheck. *Technology, Economic Growth and Public Policy*. Washington, D.C. The Brookings Institution, 1967.

Newman, Peter. *The Theory of Exchange*. Englewood Cliffs, N.J.: Prentice Hall, 1965.

Nie, N. H. et al. *Statistical Package for the Social Sciences*. New York: McGraw-Hill, 1975.

Office of Economic and Cultural Development: Third Ministerial Meeting on Science. *Gaps in Technology: Scientific Instruments*. Paris, 1968.

O'Neal, Charles et al. "Adoption of Innovations by Industrial Organizations," *Industrial Marketing Management,* 2 (1973), pp. 235–250.

O'Rourke, Mary, James M. Shea and William Sulley. "Survey Shows Need for Increased Sales Calls, Advertising and Updated Mailing Lists to Reach Buying Influences," *Industrial Marketing,* 58 (April, 1973).

Ozanne, Urban B. and Gilbert A. Churchill. "Five Dimensions of the Industrial Adoption Process," *Journal of Marketing Research,* 8 (August, 1971), pp. 322–328.

Parket, Robert. "The Effects of Product Perception on Industrial Buyer Behavior," *Industrial Marketing Management,* 3 (April, 1972), pp. 339–346.

Parket, Robert. "The Challenge from Industrial Buyer Perception of Product Non Differentiation," *Industrial Marketing Management,* 2 (June, 1973), pp. 281–288.

Patchen, Martin. "Alternative Questionnaire Approaches to Measurement of Influence in Organizations," *The American Journal of Sociology,* 69 (July 1963), pp. 41–52.

Pattanaik, Prasanta K. "Group Choice with Lexicographic Individual Orderings," *Behavioral Science.* Vol. 18 (1973), pp. 118–123.

Pearl, R. *The Biology of Population Growth.* New York: Alfred A. Knopf, 1925.

Pegram, Roger M. and Earl L. Bailey. *The Marketing Executive Looks Ahead.* The Conference Board, 1967, No. 13.

Pessemier, Edgar A., Philip Burger, Richard Teach and Douglas Tigert. "Using Laboratory Brand Preference Scales to Predict Consumer Brand Purchases," *Management Science,* 17 (February, 1971), pp. B371–385.

Peplow, M. E. "Design Acceptance," in S. A. Gregory, ed., *The Design Method.* London: Butterworth, 1960.

Peters, Michael P. and M. Vankatesan. "Exploration of Variables Inherent in Adopting an Industrial Product," *Journal of Marketing Research,* 10 (August 1973), pp. 312–315.

Please, N. W. "Comparison of Factor Loadings in Different Populations," *British Journal of Mathematical and Statistical Psychology,* 26 (1973), pp. 61–89.

Purchasing Magazine, March 29, 1978, pp. 85–87.

"Purchasing Magazine Readers Have Something to Tell You About Chemicals," Report No. 10–A. New York: *Purchasing Magazine,* 1965.

Raiffa, Howard. *Decision Analysis.* Reading, Mass.: Addison Wesley, 1968.

Raiffa, Howard and Robert Schlaifer. *Applied Statistical Decision Theory.* Boston: Harvard University Division of Research, 1961.

Ranard, Elliot D. "Use of Input/Output Concepts in Sales Forecasting," *Journal of Marketing Research* (February, 1972).

Rao, Vithala R. and James E. Cox, Jr. *Sales Forecasting Methods: A Survey of Recent Developments.* Marketing Science Institute Report No. 78–119, December, 1978.

Rawnsley, Allan (ed.) *Manual of Industrial Marketing Research.* Chichester: John Wiley, 1978.

Restle, F. "A Metric and an Ordering on Sets," *Psychometrika,* 24 (1959), pp. 207–220.

Rippe, Richard D. and Maurice Wilkinson. "Forecasting Accuracy of the McGraw-Hill Anticipations Data," *Journal of the American Statistical Association,* Vol. 69, No. 348 (December, 1974), pp. 849–858.

Rippe, Richard, Maurice Wilkinson and Donald Morrison. "Industrial Market Forecasting with Anticipations Data," *Management Science.* Vol. 22, No. 6 (February, 1976), pp. 639–651.

Robinson, B. and C. Lakhani. "Dynamic Price Models for New Product Planning," *Management Science.* Vol. 21, No. 10 (June, 1975), pp. 1113–1122.

Robinson, Patrick J. and Charles W. Faris. *Industrial Buying and Creative Marketing.* Boston: Allyn and Bacon, 1967.

Rogers, Everett M. *Diffusion of Innovations.* New York: The Free Press, 1962.

Rogers, Everett M. "New Product Adoption and Diffusion," *Journal of Consumer Research,* 2 (March, 1976), pp. 290–301.

Rogers, Everett M. and Floyd F. Shoemaker. *Communication of Innovations: A Cross-Cultural Approach.* New York: The Free Press, 1971.

Rothwell, R., C. Freeman, A. Horsley, V. T. P. Jervis, A. B. Robertson and J. Townsend. "SAPPHO Updated – Project SAPPHO Phase II," *Research Policy,* 3 (1974), pp. 258–291.

Rummel, R. J. *Applied Factor Analysis.* Evanston, IL: Northwestern University Press, 1970.

Ryser, Herbert J. *Combinatorial Mathematics.* The Mathematical Association of America, Buffalo, 1963.

Sahal, D. "The Multidimensional Diffusion of Technology," in *Technological Substitution: Forecasting Technologies and Applications.* Linstone and Sahal, eds. New York: American Elsevier, 1976.

Scheffe, Henry. *The Analysis of Variance.* New York: Wiley, 1959.

Schewe, Charles and William Dillon. "Marketing Information System Utilization – An Application of Self-Concept Theory," *Journal of Business Research.* Vol. 6 (January 1978), pp. 67–79.

Scientific American. *How Industry Buys/1970.* New York: 1969.

Scott, Jerome E. "Product Acceptance and Market Demand of the Consumer," in F. de Winter, ed., *Solar Cooling of Buildings.* Washington, D.C.: U.S. Government Printing Office, 1974.

Scott, Jerome E. and Peter D. Bennett. "Cognitive Models of Attitude Structure: "Value Importance" is Important," in Fred C. Allvine, ed., *Relevance in Marketing: Problems, Research, Action,* 33 Chicago: American Marketing Association, 1971.

Scott, Jerome E. and Peter Wright. "Modeling an Organizational Buyer's Product Evaluation Strategy: Validity and Procedural Considerations," *Journal of Marketing Research,* 13 (August 1976), pp. 211–224.

Scott, Richard W. "Field Methods in the Study of Organizations," in James G. March, ed., *Handbook of Organizations.* Chicago: Rand McNally, 1965.

Servan-Schreiber, J-J. *The American Challenge.* New York: Avon Books, 1969.

Shapiro, Arlene K. *Input-Output Analysis as a Predictive Tool.* Washington, D.C.: Bureau of Economic Analysis, 1972.

Sharif, M. N. and C. Kabir. "A Generalized Model for Forecasting Technological Substitutions," *Technological Forecasting and Social Change.* Vol. 8, No. 4 (1976).

Sheth, Jagdish N. "A Model of Industrial Buyer Behavior," *Journal of Marketing,* 37 (October, 1973), pp. 50–56.

Sheth, Jagdish N. "Recent Developments in Organizational Buying Behavior," University of Illinois, College of Commerce and Business Administration Working Paper No. 317, August, 1976.

Silk, Alvin J. and Manohar U. Kalwani. "Intra-Organizational Differences in Ratings of Industrial Purchasing Involvement," MIT Sloan School of Management Working Paper, June 1978.

Silk, Alvin J. and Glen L. Urban. "Pre-Test Market Evaluation of New Packaged Goods: A Model and Measurement Methodology," *Journal of Marketing Research.* Vol. 15, No. 2 (May, 1978), pp. 171–191.

Smith, Patricia and Leslie Rosenthal. "Market Analysis for Professional Management Books: Model Development and Application." unpublished MS Thesis, M.I.T. Sloan School of Management, June, 1979.

Sneath, P. H. A. and R. R. Sokal. *Numerical Taxonomy.* San Francisco: Freeman, 1973.

Snedecor, George W. and William G. Cochran. *Statistical Methods.* 6th edition, Ames: The Iowa State University Press, 1967.

Sokal, R. R. and C. D. Michener, "A Statistical Method for Evaluating Systematic Relationships," University of Kansas Sci. Bull., 38 (1958), pp. 1409–1438.

Sokal, Robert R. and Peter H. Sneath. *Principles of Numerical Taxonomy.* San Francisco: Freeman, 1963.

Spekman, Robert. "A Macro-Sociological Examination of the Industrial Buying Center: Promise or Problems?," in S. Jain (ed.), *Research Frontiers in Marketing: Dialogue and Directions.* Chicago: American Marketing Association, 1978.

Stapleton, E. "The Normal Distribution as a Model of Technological Substitution," *Technological Forecasting and Social Change.* Vol. 8, No. 3 (1976).

Stevens, John and John Grant. *The Purchasing/Marketing Interface.* New York: Wiley, 1975.

Strong, E. K. *The Psychology of Selling,* first edition, New York: McGraw-Hill, 1925.

Sweeney, Timothy W. et al. "An Analysis of Industrial Buyers' Risk Reducing Behavior: Some Personality Correlates," in Thomas V. Greer, ed., *Increasing Marketing Productivity,* 35. Chicago. American Marketing Association, 1973.

Terleckyj, N. E. and H. Halper. *Research and Development: Its Growth and Composition.* New York: National Industrial Conference Board, 1963.

Thiel, Henri. *Principles of Econometrics.* New York: Wiley, 1971.

Thurstone, L. L. *Multiple Factor Analysis.* Chicago: University of Chicago Press, 1947.

Tiebout, Charles M. "Input-Output and the Firm: A Technique for Using National and Regional Tables," *The Review of Economics and Statistics.* Vol. 49, No. 2 (May, 1967), pp. 260–262.

Torgerson, Warren N. *Theory and Methods of Scaling.* New York: Wiley, 1958.

Toyoda, T. "Use of the Chow Test under Heteroscedasticity," *Econometrica,* 42 (May, 1974), pp. 601–608.

Udy, Stanley H. "The Comparative Analysis Of Organizations," in James G. March, ed., *Handbook of Organizations.* Chicago: Rand McNally, 1965.

United Nations Commission for Europe. *Factors of Growth and Investment Policies: An International Approach.* London Pergamon Press, 1978.

Urban, G. L. "Building Models for Decision Makers," *Interfaces.* Vol. 4, No. 3 (May, 1974), pp. 1–11.

Urban, Glen L. "PERCEPTOR: A Model for Product Positioning," *Management Science,* 21 (April, 1975), pp. 858–871.

Urban, Glen L. and John R. Hauser. *Design and Marketing of New Products.* Englewood Cliffs, N.J.: Prentice Hall, 1980.

Urban, Glen L. and Scott A. Neslin. "The Design and Marketing of New Educational Programs," M.I.T. Sloan School of Management Working Paper, No. 873-76, February, 1977.

Utterback, J. "The Process of Innovation: A Study of the Origin and Development of Ideas for New Scientific Instruments," *IEEE Transactions on Engineering Management,* November 1971.

Von Hippel, Eric A. "Has a Customer Already Developed your Next Product?," *Sloan Management Review,* 18 (Winter, 1977), pp. 63–74.

Von Hippel, Eric. "Transferring Process Equipment Innovations from User-Innovators to Equipment Manufacturing Firms," *R&D Management* (October, 1977).

Von Hippel, Eric A. "Successful Industrial Products from Customer Ideas," *Journal of Marketing.* Vol. 42, No. 1 (January, 1978), pp. 39–49.

von Neumann, J. and O. Morgenstern. *Theory of Games and Economic Behavior.* Princeton, N.J.: Princeton University Press, 1944.

Ward, J. H. "Hierarchical Grouping to Optimize an Objective Function," *Journal of the American Statistical Association,* 58 (1963), pp. 236–244.

Ward, J. H. and M. E. Hook. "Application of a Hierarchical Grouping Procedure to a Problem of Grouping Profiles," *Educational and Psychological Measurement,* 23 (1963), pp. 69–82.

Webster, Frederick E., Jr. "Modeling the Industrial Buying Process," *Journal of Marketing Research,* 2 (November, 1965), pp. 370–376.

Webster, Frederick E., Jr. "New Product Adoption in Industrial Markets: A Framework for Analysis," *Journal of Marketing,* 33 (July, 1969), pp. 35–39.

Webster, Frederick E. Jr. *Industrial Marketing Strategy.* New York: Wiley, 1979.

Webster, Frederick E., Jr. and Yoram Wind. "A General Model for Understanding Organizational Buying Behavior," *Journal of Marketing,* 36 (April, 1972), pp. 12–19.

Webster, Frederick E., Jr. and Yoram Wind. *Organizational Buying Behavior.* New York: Prentice Hall, 1972.

Weigland, Robert E. "Why Studying the Purchasing Agent is not Enough," *Journal of Marketing,* 32 (January 1968), pp. 41–45.

Weinstein, Albert. "Technological and Economic Considerations for Solar Heating and Cooling of Buildings: A Report by Westinghouse Electric Corporation," in F. A. Iachetta, ed., *Solar Heating and Cooling of Buildings.* American Society of Heating, Refrigerating and Air-Conditioning Engineers, 1975.

Wells, William D. "Group Interviewing," in R. Ferber, ed., *Handbook of Marketing Research.* New York: McGraw-Hill, 1974, pp. 2–133–146.

Westinghouse Electric Corporation. *Solar Heating and Cooling of Buildings: Phase O.* (May, 1974).

Wheelwright, Steven C. and Spyros Makridakis. *Forecasting Methods for Management,* second edition, New York: Wiley, 1977.

Wildt, Albert R. and Albert V. Bruno. "The Prediction of Preference for Capital Equipment Using Linear Attitude Models," *Journal of Marketing Research,* 11 (May, 1974), pp. 203–205.

Williams, Richard J. *Solar Energy: Technology and Applications.* Ann Arbor: Ann Arbor Science Publishers, 1974.

Williams, W. T. et al. "Group Size Dependence: A Rational Choice Between Numerical Classifications," *The Computer Journal,* 14 (1972), pp. 157–161.

Wilson, David T. "Industrial Buyers' Decision-Making Styles," *Journal of Marketing Research,* 8 (November, 1971), pp. 433–436.

Wilson, D. T. et al. "Industrial Buyer Segmentation: A Psychographic Approach," in Fred C. Allvine, ed., *Marketing in Motion.* Chicago: American Marketing Association, 1971.

Wind, Yoram. "Industrial Source Loyalty," *Journal of Marketing Research,* 7 (November, 1970), pp. 450–457.

Wind, Yoram. "Issues and Advances in Segmentation Research," *Journal of Marketing Research.* Vol. 15, No. 3 (August, 1978), pp. 318–337.

Wind, Yoram and Richard Cardozo. "Industrial Market Segmentation," *Industrial Marketing Management,* 3 (1974), pp. 153–166.

Wind, Yoram, John F. Grashot and Joel D. Goldhar. "Market Based Guidelines for Design of Industrial Products," *Journal of Marketing.* Vol. 42, No. 3 (July, 1978), pp. 27–37.

Wrinkler, Robert L. "The Consensus of Subjective Probability Distributions," *Management Science.* Vol. 15, No. 2 (October, 1968), pp. B61–B75.

Zaltman, Gerald, et al. *Innovations and Organizations.* New York: Wiley, 1973.

Author Index

287

Subject Index